Socialist Feminism

T0287934

"I do not know of any other book that so effectively explains socialist feminism and brings it into conversation with global social movements. There is a twenty-first-century timeliness and urgency to Afary's cogent and expansive case. Attendant to structures of capitalist accumulation and alienation, she considers how they are playing out in a global pandemic, planetary climate crisis, the oppression of Black lives, and the appropriation of reproductive labour. At a time when feminism is under fire, Afary has given us a powerful teaching tool!"

—Rosemary Hennessy, author of *Materialist Feminism and the Politics of Discourse* and *In the Company of Radical Women Writers*

"Frieda Afary is brilliant in this powerfully relevant critique of authoritarianism, capitalism, sexism, racism, and other forms of tranny. She methodically unpacks the historically complicated plethora of gender, race, and class theories to show us the way toward a contemporary approach to socialist feminism that is revolutionary. Afary presents a radical vision that challenges us all to think more critically toward reimagining and recentering the world of womyn and a world without prisons. Her analysis centers racial justice that is anti-heteropatriarchy, anti-oppressive, anti-sexist, and transformative."

—Romarilyn Ralston, Black feminist abolitionist and Executive Director of Project Rebound, California State University, Fullerton

"I highly recommend this very readable yet highly rigorous retelling and refiguring of socialist feminism. Afary's claim that humanism is far more flexible than the version that was dismissed in the 1980s is provocative and compelling. The book engages poststructural theory, as well as race and sexuality, and will be useful for scholar-activists in thinking through some of the most vexing questions posed by socialist feminism."

—Judith Grant, Emerita Professor, Ohio University and co-editor of *New Political Science: A Journal of Politics and Culture*

"When many of us are feeling discouraged with the state of our countries and of the world, Frieda Afary's timely book shows the way to understanding, consciousness, and activism. This book can help prepare young people to improve societies. As the grandmother of two African-American females, I am profoundly grateful for this amazing volume."

—Mary Elaine Hegland, Professor of Anthropology, Santa Clara University

"Frieda Afary has dared to challenge the world of intellectuals to define a new action paradigm. How do women protect themselves? Afary debunks the distortions in the 'self to other' relationships, and critically analyses the conditions leading us toward peril and destruction. Whether you read this book all at once or in small settings with friends, you will be better prepared to live within the 21st century."

—Wonda Powell, Emerita Professor of History, Los Angeles Southwest College

Socialist Feminism

A New Approach

Frieda Afary

First published 2022 by Pluto Press
New Wing, Somerset House, Strand, London WC2R 1LA
and Pluto Press Inc.
1930 Village Center Circle, Ste. 3-384, Las Vegas, NV 89134

www.plutobooks.com

British Library Cataloguing in Publication Data
A catalogue record for this book is available from the British Library

ISBN 978 0 7453 4775 2   Hardback
ISBN 978 0 7453 4773 8   Paperback
ISBN 978 0 7453 4777 6   PDF
ISBN 978 0 7453 4776 9   EPUB

This book is printed on paper suitable for recycling and made from fully
managed and sustained forest sources. Logging, pulping and manufacturing processes are expected to conform to the environmental standards of the
country of origin.

Typeset by Stanford DTP Services, Northampton, England

Simultaneously printed in the United Kingdom and United States of America

This book is dedicated to the memory of
Audre Lorde

Contents

Acknowledgments

First and foremost, I would like to thank my mother, Anvar Pirnazar Afary, for her love, guidance, support, and for encouraging me to pursue my passion for philosophy.

My experience as a student of Raya Dunayevskaya, founder of Marxist-Humanism in the United States, was a rewarding, life-changing and formative one which planted the seeds of many questions and ideas developed in this book.

Seminars on Aristotle, Kant, Hegel, Marx, Critical Theory, Simone de Beauvoir, with David Ozar, Victoria Wike, James Blachowicz, Ardis Collins, David Schweickart, David Ingram, Thomas Sheehan, and conversations with Judith Wittner, Hollace Graff, Julie Ward, Olufemi Taiwo and students at the Philosophy Department and other departments at Loyola University Chicago as well as a seminar on Hegel with Stephen Houlgate at DePaul University greatly expanded my horizons. Classes on African American Studies, African and Latin American Studies with Sterling Plumpp, Charles Branham, Ibrahim Sundiata, and Otto Pikaza at the University of Illinois at Chicago expanded my knowledge of the profound contributions of Africans, African Americans and Afro-Caribbeans to humanity. During my undergraduate years at UCLA, I also learned much from classes with feminist professors, Nancy Henley, Blanche Wiesen Cook, and Middle East scholar, Nikki Keddie. All of the above-mentioned classes and conversations were mind-opening and planted further questions to be explored over the course of the ensuing years.

Maggie Johnson, Senior Librarian at the Palms-Rancho Park Branch of the Los Angeles Public Library, and my supervisor, taught me a great deal about the intersection of race, gender, and class. For 15 years, she gave me creative ideas and full encouragement to organize author programs, book discussions, community panels, and philosophy classes, all of which also helped shape this book.

Wonda Powell of the Department of History at Los Angeles Southwest College offered enormously helpful suggestions in revising my syllabus for a community class series on "Socialist Feminism: From Analyzing Oppression to Theorizing Liberation" in 2018–19 at Art Share Los Angeles. I learned much from her participation in the series and from all the socialist feminism class participants. I am also indebted to Wonda for many illuminating conversations over the past nine years on African American history, philosophy, world politics, and Marx's *Capital*.

Michele Welsing and Yusef Omowale, directors of the Southern California Library, allowed me to host social justice panel discussions at the library, including a class series on the 150th anniversary of Marx's *Capital*, which also helped shape this book. Their seriousness, openness to international struggles, and commitment to human emancipation are very much appreciated.

Farzaneh Raji, former political prisoner and socialist feminist in Iran, collaborated with me in translating Heather Brown's *Marx on Gender and the Family*. In the process, we had some mind-opening exchanges via email. Ziba Jalali, publisher and founder of Shirazeh Press in Iran, courageously published the book in Persian and organized a public meeting on it at a bookstore in Tehran.

Farah Ghadernia, Iranian socialist feminist and friend, has exemplified the resistance of Iranian women in her own life and has written about the painful daily struggles of women factory workers, sex workers, and homeless women. Her interviews with homeless women about the gender violence that landed them on the streets, and the daily violence that they endure, kept reminding me of the shared pains and dreams of women around the globe.

Romarilyn Ralston, who endured 24 years of incarceration and became an abolitionist feminist scholar, activist and program director of Project Rebound at California State University, Fullerton, has shown me that Black Feminist Abolitionist thinkers and activists bring a dimension to the struggle that no one else does: the opposition to all forms of abuse and violence, and the affirmative vision of transformative justice. I am grateful to Romarilyn for helping me shape some of this book's discussion on intersectionality and Black Feminist Abolitionism, and for her depth, her words of wisdom, her generosity, her internationalism.

Lisbeth Gant-Britton of the Department of Social Sciences at Los Angeles City College and the Department of African American Studies at UCLA has taught me a great deal about Black women writers and activists, and African American history in general. She has been generous with her knowledge and her time.

Rosemary Gonzalez and Maria Remigio have taught me much about the experiences of Latina immigrant women and mothers who despite all odds, maintain their dignity, support their family, value education, and challenge misogyny.

I am grateful to Julia and Tiffany Wallace, Arielle Concilio, Emma Wilde Botta, and Eva Maria for sharing their experiences as socialist feminist activists in the United States today and to Manijeh Marashi and Fatemeh Masjedi for sharing their experiences as women political prisoners in Iran.

Librarian colleagues, Rita Romero, Tamiko Welch, Colleen Stretten, and Janice Batzdorff helped me in organizing a library study group on Black Lives Matter and Social Justice which also led to new insights that found their way into this book.

I have benefited from discussions at the Marxist Feminism conferences and exchanges with Nancy Fraser, Ariel Saleh, Diana Mulinari, and Nora Rathzel. Nancy Holmstrom of the Department of Philosophy at Rutgers University read the manuscript of this book and offered important insights from a Marxist Feminist point of view. I am grateful to her for her scholarship and her commitment to revolutionary socialist international-ism. The anonymous external readers of the manuscript for this book offered tremendously helpful and instructive comments and suggestions. I have incorporated their revisions to the best of my abilities.

Selin Cagatay of Central European University, and Jennifer Hernandez, a graduate of communication studies, read earlier drafts of this book and offered very helpful comments and suggestions.

Sam Brawand, my manuscript editor, has been meticulous, thoughtful, and has also offered the types of precious suggestions/comments that emanate from reading the text with interest and passion. Elaine Ross, copy editor for Pluto Press, also greatly benefited this text through her meticulous reading and corrections.

Cassandra Riveras, graduate of communication studies and educator in Spain, helped me with revising the Workbook for *Socialist Feminism*. This is available at www.plutobooks.com-socialist-feminism-workbook. She also helped with creating PowerPoint presentations for each chapter. Her creativity and deep interest in this subject has been invaluable. Touraj Rahimi has generously given me skillful technical support for many years.

I am also grateful to him for his encouragement and his commitment to social justice.

David Shulman, my editor at Pluto Press, originally contacted me at the Historical Materialism conference in April 2019 and asked if I had a manuscript for publication. Had it not been for his question, I might not have turned my accumulated work on socialist feminism into a book. The suggestions and ideas offered by David and the entire Pluto Press editorial board are very much appreciated.

I would like to thank my sisters Janet and Mona and my brother Kamran for being enormously loving and supportive in every way and always generously sharing their knowledge and experience. Janet, Mona, and Kamran all read earlier drafts of this book and offered extremely helpful suggestions. I would like to thank my niece Lena, for her love and for helping me during some challenging health crises. My great niece, Leila, taught me many lessons about child development, infinite human potential, and the challenges of childrearing.

My health care providers, including my uncle, Dr. Cyrus Pirnazar, have helped me overcome some difficult physical health challenges over the years. I am also grateful for the continuing support of Eleanor Rosenthal, Barbara Hauser and her partner Sandy Ramsey, as well as Huguette Kapinga, Dr. Zou and several other health care providers who have become personal friends over the years. Without their help, love and encouragement, I would not have been able to recover and write this book.

Frieda Afary
Los Angeles, California
April 10, 2022

Purpose of Workbook for *Socialist Feminism: A New Approach*

Socialist Feminism: A New Approach is a call to thoughtful action against the current global rise of authoritarianism and fascism. The author has provided a workbook consisting of key terms and concepts, discussion questions and ideas for activities related to each chapter. This workbook can help readers, including activists and teachers, to grapple with the key ideas of the book and take these ideas further both in theory and in practice. If you have any questions, you can also contact Frieda Afary at www.socialistfeminism.org

The free workbook for *Socialist Feminism* can be downloaded at www.plutobooks.com/socialist-feminism-workbook

Introduction: Rethinking Socialist Feminism to Find a Pathway Out of Authoritarian Capitalism and Develop a Humanist Alternative

This book begins by situating the context in which we live today: the COVID-19 pandemic's effects on women, children, and gender dynamics, the rise of the #MeToo Movement, contradictory developments in gender relations, the distinctive features of authoritarianism and capitalism/imperialism in the twenty-first century, the challenges of Black Lives Matter and global uprisings against authoritarianism, imperialist invasion/war and ecological catastrophe. Having an understanding of all these developments can help us engage in a rethinking of socialist feminism in order to find a direction forward, combat authoritarianism, militarism, and conceptualize an enriched emancipatory socialism with transformed gender relations at its heart. The many facts examined in this book show that the challenges we face are both objective and subjective, involving deep structures of class divisions, racism, sexism, heterosexism, as well as alienation. The assault on women, people of color, and people who do not *fit* into the gender binary has been ceaseless and is intensifying with the COVID-19 pandemic.

These developments compel us to re-examine and rethink socialist feminism's philosophical foundations and offer a humanist alternative to capitalist-racist-homophobic patriarchy in its twenty-first-century manifestations. In order to help develop such an alternative viewpoint, I will critically examine four foundational socialist feminist theories of gender oppression: (1) theories of social reproduction, (2) theories of alienation, (3) intersectionality, and (4) queer identities. I will then examine socialist feminist efforts to conceptualize an alternative to patriarchal and homophobic, as well as racist, capitalist, and imperialist forms of domination which continue to perpetuate the oppression of women and also destroy our ecosystem. Through a process of examination and discovery, this book hopes to draw out lessons from and for socialist feminist revolutionary theorizing, organizing, and international solidarity today.

The socialist feminism that I am advocating in these pages is informed by Social Reproduction Theory, Marxist-Humanism, Black Feminism, and Queer Theories. I attempt to offer a more expansive concept of socialist feminism that has been enriched by reflecting on these conceptual frameworks and the new challenges we are facing.

A BIOGRAPHICAL NOTE

I was born in an Iranian-Jewish family in Tehran, Iran. My parents and my extended family considered themselves modern. However, looking back at our lives, I recall how conservative and patriarchal they were when it came to women in our society. During my adolescence in the 1970s, nearly all the families in our upper middle-class neighborhood were concerned with how to raise modern educated daughters. Yet young women were expected to remain committed to the strict modesty rules of our society that confined a woman's life to having a husband and children, and often required her to endure domestic violence. One of the glaring contradictions which I faced during my adolescence was the division between the growing modernization of the urban middle and upper middle class and the deep poverty of the working classes and the newly arriving rural population who lived in shanty towns. Another contradiction was the contrast between living in a multicultural environment, with Muslim, Jewish, Christian, Zoroastrian, and Baha'i neighbors and classmates, and noticing that the stench of anti-Semitism and anti-Baha'ism was never far below the surface. The greatest problem was the reality of dictatorship. The whole population was living under the Pahlavi regime which paid lip service to modernity and liberalism but was highly authoritarian. At school, our teachers and administrators were constantly worried about the secret police and concerned about books that we might read. So many books were forbidden. Many youth were arrested and beaten up simply for reading forbidden books.

In 1978, shortly before a full-blown revolution emerged in Iran, my family emigrated to the United States. The revolution had a great impact on me, however. It involved students, women, workers, peasants, and professionals, many representing different national minorities. But it also included large segments of clerics and bazaar merchants who wished to turn the clock back on the modest social and cultural gains that had been made during the twentieth century. Both leftist and Islamic fundamentalist organizations vied for leadership of the revolution. Soon the latter forces decisively prevailed and the revolution turned into a brutal misogynistic and theocratic monstrosity that destroyed the Iranian Left, turned the clock back on the gains which urban middle-class women and religious minorities had made, and led to the migration of millions from the country.

Paradoxically, prior to its decimation, much of the Left had supported Ayatollah Khomeini as an "anti-U.S. imperialist" figure and insisted that everyone should unite under his banner since U.S. imperialism was "the main enemy." This support for Khomeini was so strong that the Left refused to challenge how the followers of Khomeini were trampling on the rights of women, as well as those of religious and national minorities, such as the Kurds. Most leftists refused to support the March 8, 1979 women's demonstrations against the Islamic fundamentalist takeover of the revolution, even though many of the women who organized and participated in these and other demonstrations were leftists themselves and were chanting, "we didn't make a revolution to go backward" (J. Afary, 2009).

The deep contradictions of the Iranian revolution made me search for explanations. In the United States, I started attending meetings of leftists who opposed Khomeini and the theocracy in Iran. An encounter with the writings of Raya Dunayevskaya on the Iranian revolution piqued my interest. Dunayevskaya was a feminist and founder of the philosophy of Marxist-Humanism in the United States. She strongly supported the March 8, 1979 Iranian women's demonstrations and pointed to the important role that Iranian women had played throughout Iran's modern history, starting with the 1906–11 Iranian Constitutional Revolution. She challenged the Iranian Left for its lack of comprehension of the critical moment they faced. She also addressed the possibility of creating a different society and explored the vision of a total transformation of human relations with new gender relations as its measure (Dunayevskaya, 1981). At a time when the Iranian Left looked either to the Soviet Union or Maoist China as saviors, Dunayevskaya called these regimes totalitarian state capitalists. She was asking Middle Eastern revolutionaries to reach out and learn about the depths of the Black struggle and the contributions of Africans and African Americans to emancipatory thought. She especially drew inspiration from nineteenth-century U.S. abolitionists.

My encounter with her intersectional Marxism encouraged me to read extensively about the Black struggle in the United States and the global history of feminist struggles. It also marked the beginning of my formal study of philosophy at university and my search for global international solidarity. All of these experiences helped me become a more critical thinker and a social activist. However, my formal study of philosophy in general, and feminist philosophy in particular, left me dissatisfied. I felt that in the case of Western philosophy, most academics were not interested in the experiences and ideas of people from the Global South. In the case of feminist philosophy, theorizing was often compartmentalized from international solidarity, and local perspectives were separated from global views.

During the past four decades, my study of philosophy, translations of philosophical texts into Persian, and translations of articles by Iranian dissidents, including feminist and labor activists, along with my experiences as an Iranian American activist, socialist feminist and public librarian, have all been an attempt to break these binaries. These experiences have also encouraged me to explore the question of a humanist alternative to capitalism, racism, sexism, heterosexism for the twenty-first century.

I hold on to the humanist designation because the #MeToo and the Black Lives Matter Movements and current global uprisings and protests against the rise of authoritarianism all show that despite the rise of populism and authoritarianism and the destructive impact of social media and disinformation on the human mind around the world, humans still have the *potential* for independent thinking and reasoning, in order to challenge dominant systems and to develop alternatives. These movements are crying out to be heard, comprehended, and further developed.

I hold on to the humanist designation, because, in the twenty-first century, we need an alternative to capitalism that challenges all forms of domination and transcends the oppressive models of the former USSR and Maoist China, as well as more recent claims to socialism as in Venezuela.[1]

WHY SOCIALIST FEMINISM?

This book argues that a critical re-examination and rethinking of socialist feminist thought and activism during the past century can help us find a way forward to reverse the global authoritarianism, and thereby, direct the conversation toward a deep transformation of human relations. Gender oppression today is the result of the intertwining of capitalism, patriarchy, and racism. None of these factors is autonomous. Rather, capitalism embodies both patriarchy and racism, forms of oppression that predate capitalism, which it uses for its benefit. At the same time, it is not sufficient to speak of capitalism as simply a mode of unequal wealth distribution, private property of the means of production, and market mechanisms. Capitalism is a system opposed to human self-determination and to nature. To the extent that it promotes individual freedom, it is an alienated, selfish, and utilitarian individualism that promotes the production of value but stands in opposition to collective emancipation and critical thinking. It objectifies and commodifies women and has consistently opposed women's control over their own bodies. Capitalism affects and alienates the mind and body and human relations in insidious ways that are not simply caused by private property and the market. Its alienated mode of labor affects all human relations and most deeply intimate and sexual relations. Socialist feminism addresses these questions.

Alternatives to capitalism, racism, sexism, and heterosexism are not created automatically and spontaneously. They require rootedness in history, philosophy, political economy, critical thinking, and national and international organization. That is why this book engages in critically analyzing twentieth- and twenty-first-century socialist feminist thinkers and their theories of oppression and emancipation as the basis for new global socialist feminist theorizing and organizing today. Each of the conceptual frameworks taken up in this book provides a *lens* (a term borrowed from Lise Vogel's (2014) *Marxism and the Oppression of Women: Toward a Unitary Theory*) for analyzing the particular oppression that women face as women. Each framework can enrich the other by posing questions about limitations or unaddressed issues. Each also opens the door to asking deeper questions about how to develop an alternative to capitalism, racism, sexism, and heterosexism. Toward that end, let's examine the structure of the book.

STRUCTURE OF THE BOOK

Chapters 1 and 2 explore the following question: What is new in the era of global authoritarianism, the #MeToo Movement, Black Lives Matter, and global uprisings?

Chapter 1, titled "The Pandemic, the #MeToo Movement, and Contradictory Developments in Gender Relations," explores how the COVID-19 pandemic is destroying decades of gains made by women around the world. At the same time, the #MeToo Movement which emerged as a global movement in 2017 has been growing against sexual violence and femicide and offers unique challenges from socialist feminist and abolitionist perspectives. I will examine contradictory developments in gender relations since the 1980s because we cannot move forward without full awareness of this new and contradictory objective reality.

Chapter 2, titled "Distinctive Features of Authoritarian Capitalism/Imperialism Today and the New Challenges of Black Lives Matter and Global Uprisings," begins with a Marxian explanation of why capitalism leads to authoritarianism. This chapter singles out the distinctive features of capitalist authoritarianism and multi-polar imperialism in the twenty-first century from a new form of state capitalism to mass incarceration and a high-tech assault on the mind. It also singles out some of the unique features and challenges of recent movements and uprisings against authoritarianism, imperialist invasion/war, ecological catastrophe. These include Black Lives Matter, uprisings or mass protests in Sudan, Algeria, Iraq, Lebanon, Iran, Belarus, Nigeria, Thailand, Indonesia, Hong Kong, Chile, Myanmar, India, Palestine, as well as the popular resistance within Ukraine against Russia's genocidal invasion.[2] In many of these protests, women have been in the forefront. The chapter ends with lessons that I have drawn from the 2011 Syrian uprising and the Occupy Wall Street Movement. These lessons pinpoint both the failure of the Arab leadership of the Syrian uprising to address class, gender, ethnic discrimination, and the reductive anti-capitalism of the Occupy Movement that often could not be distinguished from anti-globalist populism. Such a reductive anti-capitalism on the part of the Occupy Movement also led to a narrow anti-imperialism that only singled out Western imperialism and its allies while ignoring or siding with other global and regional imperialist powers such as Russia and Iran which helped to crush the Syrian uprising.

Chapters 3, 4, 5, and 6 discuss socialist feminist theories of gender oppression.

Chapter 3, titled "Women, Reproductive Labor, and Capital Accumulation: Theories of Social Reproduction," begins with a brief summary of the main theories of social reproduction from 1969 to today. Social reproduction looks at the everyday life of people under capitalism, paying special attention to reproductive labor and women's lives. It examines pregnancy, childcare, family life, health care, and education, as well as the manner in which capitalism uses the concepts of gender, race, and sexuality to further its exploitation and social oppression. This chapter examines works by Margaret Benston, Silvia Federici, Selma James, Mariarosa Dalla Costa, and Lise Vogel as well as more recent contributions to this discussion by Martha Gimenez, Tithi Bhattacharya, Susan Ferguson, and critiques by Angela Davis and Michelle Barrett. I attempt to shed light on some of their arguments by returning to the categories of value and surplus value, productive labor and accumulation of capital which they have borrowed from Marx's *Capital*, and by re-examining these categories. I also critically evaluate their arguments and attempt to draw out their assumptions and logical conclusions in order to find out to what extent their proposed suggestions can answer the questions and problems of today.

Chapter 4, titled "Alienated Labor and How It Relates to Gender Oppression," examines the view that gender oppression, under capitalism, is rooted in alienated labor. I begin by reviewing Marx's concept of alienated labor as it relates to gender in his *Economic and Philosophical Manuscripts of 1844* and *Capital*. I argue that Marx gave us signposts that illuminate the relationship between a capitalist mode of production and the specific oppression that women suffer—as women and not simply as workers. The chapter will then examine the ways in which various socialist feminists have explored or touched on the connections between gender oppression and Marx's critique of alienated labor. These socialist feminists include Angela Davis, Raya Dunayevskaya, Heather Brown, Ann Foreman, Nancy Holmstrom, Judith Grant, Marcia Klotz, Silvia Federici, and Gayatri Spivak. I end by arguing that a theory of gender oppression that is rooted in Marx's concept of alienated labor can illuminate questions raised by the #MeToo Movement today and the increased prevalence of sexual abuse and assault.

Chapter 5, titled, "Black Feminism and Intersectionality," draws out some key contributions of Black feminist intersectional thinkers and how their work can help redefine socialist feminism for the twenty-first century. First, it takes up the different articulations of Black feminist intersectional thought, beginning with the *Combahee River Collective Statement* and moving forward through the work of Audre Lorde, Angela Davis, Kimberlé Crenshaw, Patricia Hill Collins, bell hooks, Tracy Sharpley-Whiting, and Joy James. Then, it will briefly examine the ways in which Angela Davis and Ruth Wilson Gilmore have extended intersectionality to contemporary Prison Abolitionist Feminism. It acknowledges the importance of Beth Richie, Mariame Kaba, and Romarilyn Ralston's work on transformative and restorative justice, and the role of Black women in the leadership of the Black Lives Matter Movement, as well as challenges raised by Keeanga-Yamahtta Taylor. The chapter concludes by engaging with Ashley Bohrer's (2020) *Marxism and Intersectionality*. I will not examine intersectionality from the oft-repeated standpoint of socialists who argue that it does not see class exploitation as primary. Instead, my examination of intersectional thinkers aims to shed light on their view that oppression cannot be reduced to exploitation.

Chapter 6, on "Queer Theories," critically examines queer theories developed by Judith Butler, Rosemary Hennessey, and Holy Lewis. It also draws on the ideas of Nancy Holmstrom, Judith Grant, Marcia Klotz, and Heather Brown on the ways in which Marx's concept of human nature can help provide a fruitful ground for queer theory. I ask whether it is possible to develop a socialist feminist concept of sexual identity that is fluid but still relies on humanist conceptions of reason, universality, and solidarity. Toward that end, various critiques posed by Allison Weir, Nancy Fraser, Teresa Ebert and Sheena C. Howard's (2014) *Black Queer Identity Matrix* and her challenge to any replication of patriarchal gender norms in LGBTQ relationships are taken up.

Chapters 7 and 8 provide an in-depth analysis of socialist feminist alternatives to capitalism and relations of domination.

Chapter 7, titled, "Theorizing a Socialist Humanist and Feminist Alternative to Capitalism," begins by examining the ways in which works by Nancy Fraser, Ann Ferguson, Patricia Hill Collins, Maria Mies, Silvia Federici, and Kathi Weeks have attempted to pose a vision of an alternative to capitalism. The topic of ecofeminism is highlighted through a discussion of the ideas of Maria Mies. I also address some of the limitations of these works and ask whether a return to Marx can help socialist feminists develop an alternative to alienated human relations. Here I turn to insights from Audre Lorde who will be extremely relevant to our discussion. This chapter also briefly examines Raya Dunayevskaya's analyses of the former USSR and Maoist China as state capitalist societies in order to show us why we cannot consider what took place in the USSR and Maoist China as examples of socialism. I end with further questions and ideas about what theorizing a socialist humanist alternative to capitalism might mean today.

Chapter 8, titled "Overcoming Domination: Reconceptualizing the Self-Other Relationship," asks whether the dynamic of self-other always has to be about domination. How have socialist feminists analyzed this issue and sought to offer alternatives? I discuss the ideas of Simone de Beauvoir and Jessica Benjamin on the roots of domination, and then critically examine the ideas of Allison Weir, Raya Dunayevskaya, Frantz Fanon, and Audre Lorde on overcoming domination. The latter four thinkers all share a dialectical and humanist framework, and in the case of Weir, Dunayevskaya, and Fanon, they explicitly draw on Hegelian dialectics.

The Conclusion sums up the book and proposes ideas for organizing in the following areas: An opposition to war and imperialist invasion that does not limit itself to one pole of capital only; Building on the potential of the global #MeToo Movement to challenge capitalism's commodification and reification of human relations; Connecting the current global struggles and uprisings against authoritarianism, imperialist invasion/ war, with the Black Lives Matter and Prison Abolitionist Movement in the United States; Articulating a humanist alternative to capitalism's destruction of humanity and nature, and to all forms of domination.

This book is the product of four decades of study and social activism. I have translated and published some of the aforementioned authors in Persian. I have corresponded with some of them, developed syllabi and curricula for classes and workshops, worked with scholar and activist colleagues from various parts of the world, organized meetings and conferences in public and community libraries with grassroots movements, produced and edited collaborative papers and published book reviews in the process of writing this book. Every chapter of this book has been a journey of discovery for me. I hope it will also be a journey of discovery for the readers.

1

The Pandemic, the #MeToo Movement, and Contradictory Developments in Gender Relations

The COVID-19 pandemic has placed an unbearable pressure on women (Friedman, 2020; Lewis, 2020; Tharoor & Mellen, 2021). Hundreds of millions of women and girls have faced not only disease and death but also massive economic, social, physical, and emotional pressures. The United Nations Population Fund "warns that COVID-19 may lead to an additional 13 million child marriages around the world and some 47 million women being unable to get access to modern contraception" (Economist, 2020a, 2020c; Kristof, 2020a, 2020b). Everywhere in the world, women can have pregnancy complications because of the virus. Some have been turned away from hospitals upon delivery and died in childbirth because of lack of resources or attention (Turkewitz & Herrera, 2020). Many women have lost access to abortion. In the United States, in addition to all the hurdles that face women when seeking an abortion, some states deem abortion a "non-essential" service during shutdowns (Tavernise, 2020).

In China, women were often pushed out onto the front lines to combat the pandemic. Women who form approximately 40 percent of the physician workforce and 80 percent of the nursing workforce in South and East Asia (Boniol et al., 2019) continue to bear the brunt of the crisis of care. At the same time, Chinese government propaganda has buried women's major role in caring for the sick in Wuhan, where the pandemic started, and elsewhere (Wang, 2020).

Hunger, food insecurity, and the threat of eviction or actual eviction due to the inability to pay rent have also greatly harmed women and families (Mari, 2020). Globally, over 270 million people, especially in Africa, face life-threatening food shortages (Goldbaum, 2021). In the United States, which is the richest country in the world, out of a population of 333 million, 38 million are hungry or food-insecure. Twelve million of them are children (Abramsky, 2020; Feeding America, 2022).

Around the world, the majority of women who work outside of the home do not have the option of telecommuting. In the United States, only 9 percent of parents without college degrees get paid time off. Most employers, including federal and state governments, offer little or no childcare relief (extra pay or extra time off) to employees who are parents. Within those private companies that produce the highest value in the United States (for example, Facebook, Apple, Microsoft, Google), it is the highly educated who get the best benefits (Economist, 2021c).

At the same time, women who have had the option of working part time or of working from home have had to do triple shifts and massively reduce their sleep time which was not enough to begin with.[1] In addition to their paid job and the housework, they have also had to become teachers for their children who are out of school or out of day care centers. Parents and children face the digital divide that in many cases denies children access to online classes because they cannot afford to buy laptops or have proper access to the internet.

According to Vicky Smallman, Director of Women's Rights at the Canadian Labour Congress: "We know from research that women are more likely to reduce hours or leave work in order to care for kids or others. The outcome of this is reduced incomes and lifetime earnings for women, and a widened gender wage gap, poor mental health outcomes for those who continue to try and juggle paid work and remote learning" (Dolan, 2020; see also Cohen & Hsu, 2020; Schultz & Raj, 2020; Williams, 2020). By early 2021, over 2.3 million women in the United States, including one million mothers, had left the workforce because of the pandemic. Black, Latina, Asian American, and single women have been hit the hardest. They are physically exhausted, mentally under assault and crying for help (Dockterman, 2021, Hua, 2021; New York Times, 2021). Women in the United States have also been part of the "The Great Resignation" or the millions who have quit their jobs after the pandemic because they realized that they deserved more meaningful jobs, better treatment and better working conditions (Malone, 2022). Globally, 50 percent of working mothers who participated in a survey of office workers said that they wanted to work remotely most of the time (Goldberg, 2022).

Women, and especially women of color around the world, are more likely to be essential workers or have precarious employment which exposes them to the virus more often, whether on public transportation or in nursing homes, home care, agriculture, or industry (Coyle, 2021; Madgavkar et al., 2020). Women of color also get sick and die at a higher rate because they often live in multi-generational homes where physical distancing is not possible. They have more health problems related to poverty as well as malnutrition and limited access to health care. Often, they also face racism within the health care system. Women who are undocumented fear getting any aid for themselves or their families. In the United States, over eleven million mostly people of color are undocumented, a population that in some states does not go to health care providers and public institutions for fear of deportation.

The education of children has been disrupted. In 2020, over 872 million students in 51 countries were unable to head back to their classrooms. More than half of that number live in circumstances where remote learning is impossible because of poverty and lack of access to the internet (Tharoor, 2020). The United Nations also estimates that 24 million children have already dropped out of school, and millions more will be sucked into work to make a living (Gettleman & Raj, 2020).

Gender, family, and all relationships have been greatly strained by physical distancing, isolation, restrictions on hugging, touching, kissing, and any form of intimacy as well as restrictions on social gatherings. Many women and children around the world have also been subjected to more domestic abuse and violence because of the tensions rising from living in close quarters with their spouse, partner, and other family members (Bosman, 2020; Mlambo-Ngcuka, 2020; Stewart, 2020). This resulting rise in the rates of domestic violence has come to be known as "the shadow pandemic." Online sex exploitation of children has skyrocketed (Jakes, 2021). Sex workers are also forced to expose themselves to COVID-19 in addition to a whole host of sexually transmitted diseases.

Women prisoners, migrants, refugees and their children around the world have been exposed to COVID-19 because of the cramped and unsanitary conditions in which they live (*New York Times*, 2020a).[2] According to Ella Fassler (2020): "U.S jails and prisons, already death traps, have been completely ravaged by COVID-19. Crowded quarters, a lack of PPE, inadequate medical care, an aging population, and unsanitary conditions have contributed to an infection rate 5.5 times higher than the already ballooned average in the U.S." There are also reports that Latinas and Caribbean women in U.S. detention centers of the Immigration and Customs Enforcement (ICE) have been forcibly sterilized and given hysterectomies (Dickerson, Wessler, & Jordan, 2020).

The retrogressive impact of the pandemic has already pushed women back and destroyed some of our hard-fought achievements. (Tharoor & Mellen, 2021). What have been some of our achievements? Let's examine contradictory developments in gender relations in the twenty-first century.

THE #METOO MOVEMENT: ITS UNIQUE FEATURES FROM SOCIALIST AND ABOLITIONIST FEMINIST PERSPECTIVES

During the first 15 years of the twenty-first century, socialist feminists criticized second-wave feminists for abandoning the radical goal of liberation and for being lured by free-market capitalism and careerism in the era of neoliberalism. On the 15th anniversary of the publication of her landmark work, *Backlash*, Susan Faludi (2006) had argued that "as women near the finish line, we are distracted. We have dropped to gather glittery trinkets from an apparent admirer. The admirer is the marketplace, and the trinkets are the bounty of a commercial culture which has deployed the language of liberation as a new and powerful tool of subjugation" (p. 14). Nancy Fraser (2013b) had critiqued second-wave feminism for having become a "handmaiden of neoliberalism," and having "shifted its attention to cultural politics, just as a rising neoliberalism declared war on social equality" (p. 1). Kristin J. Anderson's (2014) *Modern Misogyny: Anti-Feminism in a Post-Feminist Era* had argued that the lure of neoliberal consumerism, marketplace "choice" and narrow individualism starting in the early 1980s was one of the main reasons for the "depoliticization of feminist goals" (p. 2).

The #MeToo Movement, which emerged as a global movement in 2017, has revealed that women, no matter how successful, whether in the corporate world or in academia, are still seen as sexual objects to be used and abused. It has the potential to dismiss the myth of capitalist "choice" and "empowerment" that did much damage to the women's movement in the 1980s and 1990s. It can point to the inseparability of capitalism and patriarchy.

Another critically important feature of the #MeToo Movement is that it was originally articulated by an African American woman, Tarana

Burke, and has also been further developed within the context of Abolitionist Feminism. Tarana Burke started her 2007 campaign with the aim of focusing on women of color, transgender folks, and people with disabilities, who experience the highest rate of sexual violence in the United States (Burke, 2021). Her preoccupation has been "real structural change" and transformative justice because:

> [M]any perpetrators are themselves survivors of sexual violence, particularly child sexual abuse. And that complicates a lot of things. We've got to get a clearer understanding of what justice is and what people need to feel whole. And if we're ever going to heal in our community, we have to heal the perpetrators and heal the survivors, or else it's just a continuous cycle. (Adetiba, 2017)

Abolitionist Feminism, a movement started in the United States by African American women, concomitant with their theorizing of and struggle against the prison-industrial complex, helps further articulate the goals and vision of the #MeToo Movement. Abolitionist feminist leaders, such as Tarana Burke, Angela Y. Davis, Ruth Wilson Gilmore, Joy James, Avery Gordon, Romarilyn Ralston, Mariame Kaba, Beth Richie, and Gina Dent, see gender violence as part and parcel of the racist, sexist, and heterosexist capitalist system which is carceral in its foundation. They oppose the capitalist dehumanization and commodification of Black people, all people of color, women, queer and trans people, and challenge relations of domination.

In *The Feminist and the Sex Offender*, Abolitionist feminists, Judith Levine and Erica R. Meiners (2020) also emphasize that gender violence cannot be separated from state violence. They argue that "Me Too is evidence that without thoroughgoing social change, the law does little to protect people from sexual harm" (p. 30). Furthermore, they state, "freedom from violence is not an end in itself but rather the atmosphere in which all can flourish" (p. 5).

This organic connection between the #MeToo Movement and the struggle against racism, police brutality, state violence, mass incarceration, and carceral capitalism offers the potential for the articulation of a profound vision of human emancipation on a global scale, based on the coming together of the #MeToo Movement and the Black Lives Matter uprising. In order to build on this potential, we need to further explore

14

the developments in gender relations and the distinctive features of capitalist authoritarianism, imperialism and the struggles against them in the twenty-first century.

CONTRADICTORY DEVELOPMENTS IN GENDER RELATIONS IN THE TWENTY-FIRST CENTURY

On the one hand, the rise of second-wave feminism since the late 1960s, and the phenomenon of globalization since the 1980s, have created more openness among the younger generations to changing sexual identities and gender roles and the idea that sexuality and gender need not be binaries (straight vs. gay or male vs. female). On the other hand, since the late 1970s and early 1980s, we have witnessed an anti-feminist backlash that has been strengthened by the expanding logic of capital accumulation and the high-technology depersonalization and dehumanization of human relations.

Today, millions of young people around the world are open to LGBTQ identities and orientations and are also opposed to capitalism. In the United States, 70 percent of young people oppose capitalism; 50 percent of U.S. millennials (people born between 1980 and the early 1990s) support gay rights, 20 percent identify as LGBTQ, and 12 percent are non-cisgender (that is, do not identify with the gender assigned to them at birth); 50 percent think gender is a spectrum, and 62 percent accept transgender bathrooms. In other words, U.S. millennials are overwhelmingly liberal and tolerant (Sexton, 2019, p. 239). In China as well, the Jiulinghou generation, born in the 1990s, stands out because "no generation has been more vocal in its support of LGBT and women's rights" (Economist, 2021b). In 2019, Taiwan became the first Asian country to legalize same-sex spousal rights. An increasing number of young college students around the world are taking gender studies classes along with ethnic studies classes that allow them to approach their experiences and reality as a whole in a thoughtful and critical way, and to challenge racism and sexism, and become better human beings.

In China, LGBTQ activists are fighting for the legalization of gay marriage and suing publishers for using language that treats homosexuality as a disorder. While discrimination against the LGBTQ community remains, and the government is promoting an official campaign to "prevent the feminization of male youths" (May, 2021), homosexuality has been decriminalized in China since 1997 and removed from the handbook of psychological disorders (Wee, 2020c).

Despite these developments, and perhaps in response to them, toxic masculinity and intense misogyny are growing around the world. The 2016 U.S. election of Donald J. Trump, even after the airing of his taped comments about enjoying sexually assaulting women, was a glaring manifestation of this trend. Even more tragic was the fact that 42 percent of all women who voted in the 2016 U.S. presidential election (or almost 25 million) voted for Trump (Tyson & Maniam, 2016). In the 2020 elections, approximately 33 percent of U.S. women voters (including 47 percent of white women voters) voted for Trump despite four years of his misogynistic, racist, anti-labor, and anti-immigrant presidency (Delmore, 2020). Even 25 percent of LGBTQ voters voted for Trump (Flores, Magni, & Reynolds, 2020). In various states in the United States, new laws banning abortion (see below) are going hand in hand with laws to prohibit classroom discussion about sexual orientation and gender identity in public elementary schools (Mazzei, 2022). Laws banning gender-affirming care for transgender youth have also been passed in various states (Conron et al., 2022).

In Africa, with the exception of South Africa which allows same-sex marriage, and Botswana which decriminalized homosexuality in 2019, homophobia has been on the rise among the young generation. Although over 80 percent of young Africans think that more should be done to protect the rights of ethnic minorities and over 60 percent believe that sexual harassment is a problem in their country, almost 70 percent do not support protecting the rights of LGBTQ people (Economist, 2021a).

In Hungary, all teaching related to "homosexuality and gender change" has been banned at public schools in the name of opposing pedophilia (Butler, 2021). In Poland, the government has been promoting a campaign of hatred against LGBTQ which it identifies with pedophilia (Pronczuk, 2021).

Let's explore more facts about the state of gender relations in the world, with the proviso that the COVID-19 pandemic is creating long-term regressive changes for which we do not yet have extensive published research.

In his *Man Out: Men on the Sidelines of American Life*, Andrew L. Yarrow (2018) claims that one in every four men in the United States feels "sidelined." He argues that the new misogyny in the United States is fundamentally a response to globalization, the Second Machine Age, and the rise of second-generation feminism. These transformations have led to ambiguity about gender roles, increasing alienation from work, the transactional relationships of the "hookup" culture, pornography, high rates of incarceration among men, and a lack of meaningful human relationships. According to Yarrow,

> Six things are new in the twenty-first century: 1. The changing demographic ratio of employed, educated men to women; 2. A grossly unequal economy producing bad jobs that couples can't survive on in the lower tiers of the socioeconomic scale; 3. The decline of work among men; 4. Heightened ambiguity about gender roles; 5. Online dating; and 6. Hookups. (Yarrow, 2018, p. 75)

The feminist and LGBTQ movements have certainly challenged gender roles and the concept of gender binary itself. These challenges, along with the fact that more and more women have been in a position to reject marriage or have much higher expectations from their partners, have created a new reality that many men cannot cope with. In the United States today, there are 3.5 million more women university students than male students. By age 27, there are one-third more women than men with bachelor's degrees. Thirty percent of wives have more education than their husbands (Yarrow, 2018, p. 138). Three out of eight women have bachelor's degrees or more advanced degrees while only three out of ten men attain that level (Yarrow, 2018, p. 70).

The rate of marriage in the United States has fallen drastically. Whereas in 1970, over 70 percent of U.S. adults were married, today less than 50 percent are married (Yarrow, 2018, p. 129). Fifty percent of marriages end in divorce. Over 70 percent of divorces are initiated by women. Not getting married is no longer a stigma. The unmarried figure includes those who cohabit either with a member of the opposite sex or a member of their own sex. Seven percent of U.S. adults currently cohabit, the duration of which is typically a little more than one year (Yarrow, 2018, pp. 132, 138; see also Graf, 2019; Stepler, 2017). Ten percent of LGBTQ adults are married to each other. The large majority of women in the lowest income categories in the United States and Britain are not married (Economist, 2017c). On a global scale, marriage is "becoming less hidebound, less dutiful and less obligatory." The average age of marriage has increased. Couples place more emphasis on conjugal love and commitment. Divorce is more acceptable (Coontz, 2006; Economist, 2017b). These figures are partly related to women having more control over their lives, partly related to financial constraints which do not allow people with low income to get married, and partly related to alienation as well as trauma experienced in women's and men's own family lives while growing up (Yarrow, 2018, p. 134). In the West, those with a college degree and higher income are much more likely to get married and stay married, in comparison to those without a college degree and economically disadvantaged.

In the words of a Pew Research Center (2010) study: "A marriage gap and a socioeconomic gap have been growing side by side for the past half-century and each may be feeding off the other." At the same time, Yarrow (2018) argues that the decline of middle-class, blue-collar jobs is only one contributing factor to the class-based decline of marriage. The more enduring factor, in his view, is that adult single life without marriage has taken deep roots in cultural norms and the return of manufacturing jobs will not change that (p. 137).

In the United States, more than 60 percent of married women work outside of the home. Expectations of marriage have also changed. Economic security and children are still important reasons for marriage. However, love, commitment, and companionship are cited as the first three reasons (Pew Research Center, 2010). In general, women are more independent and seek higher-quality companionship.

> The old line is that men don't want to make a commitment, but it's divorced women who don't want to get remarried, and a lot of never-married women are not in any great hurry to marry. Women tend to be less satisfied than men with marriage, and initiate nearly 70 percent of all divorces, a proportion that has barely changed during the last century. (Yarrow, 2018, p. 138)

"Men who are married are generally the lucky ones, economically, psychologically and in terms of health and self-esteem" (Yarrow, 2018, p. 138; see also Economist, 2015).

In China, since 2015, the government which for over 30 years advocated the one child only policy, has been pushing women to get married, have more children, and balance career and family. However, when women get pregnant, they are fired by their employers. At the same time, the divorce rate is 50 percent (Stevenson & Chen, 2019; Qin, 2019). Some provinces are tightening access to abortion and making it more difficult to get divorced (Meyers & Ryan, 2018). Sometimes even severely battered women cannot use evidence of gender violence as grounds for divorce unless the husband agrees (Wee, 2020a).

In China, there is also a shortage of women as a result of the government's one child policy (from 1980 through 2015) and a patriarchal culture that led to couples using ultrasound to determine the sex of a fetus and abort the girl fetuses or give up baby girls for adoption or kill them after birth. Thus, China is missing more than 60 million girls and women (Economist, 2017a, 2021b). On the one hand, urban Chinese women, especially the millennials who are more educated, have more choices when it comes to marriage. Divorce rates are also on the rise (Chen & Wee, 2021). On the other hand, in Xinjiang province, the Chinese government is organizing the systematic rape and forced marriages of Uyghur women to Han men (Economist, 2020d). There is also an epidemic of prostitution, and abduction of girls throughout China (Economist, 2017a).

In India, marriage is still much more about binding families and much less about personal choice and fulfillment. Most women are still expected to live with their in-laws after marriage. However, since a quarter of youth go to university and half of university students are women, young people are having more say now about whom they marry, especially among the urban middle classes (Economist, 2017d).

In South Africa, 60 percent of university graduates are women. The average age for marriage for women is 31 years old. The divorce rate is 44 percent and most divorces are initiated by women (Wasserman, 2019). Across West Africa, there has been a surge in divorces initiated by women, not only women who are educated and have jobs that support them, but also by rural women who expect more from marriage and demand love and respect (Mvulane, 2020; Searcey, 2019).

In Iran, despite over 40 years of the repressive and misogynistic Islamic Republic, women have continued to resist and to develop themselves. They constitute 60 percent of university graduates. Although the legal age for marriage is 13 years old, the average age for marriage is 24 years old. Cohabitation is also becoming more common, although not openly (Afary & Faust, 2021). The fertility rate is 1.9, and for every three marriages, there is one divorce (Deutsche Welle, 2019; Hein, 2020; Pursaleh, 2020). While a large majority of women work to earn money to help their family, they are mostly restricted to the informal labor market. The patriarchal laws and practices of the Islamic Republic make it very difficult for them to enter the formal labor market in which they only have a 16 percent participation rate (Afary, 2020b). They also face openly discriminatory practices in the formal and informal labor market.

In general, throughout the world, with the exception of some countries in Africa, the fertility rate has gone down after a century of growth and especially after the 2008 economic crisis. With more access to birth control and education, more women have delayed or abandoned childbirth in face of the pressures of doing it all in a crisis-ridden world (Cave, Bubola, & Sang-Hun, 2021; Wee, 2021).

In the United States, prior to the pandemic, there were more women working than ever before, and they are more educated than ever before. There are more women college graduates than men college graduates. In fact, women with post-graduate degrees who are childless and are in fields such as science and math can get even more pay than men. But the class divide among women is growing: on the one hand, a thin sector of high-skilled, high-paid women, and on the other hand, the masses of women in lower paid and lower skill positions (Foroohar, 2012).

The gender gap in pay also persists. On paper, a woman doing the same job for the same employer in the United States earns 98 cents to one dollar paid to a man. However, in reality in the United States, a woman earns a shocking 49 cents for every one dollar a man earns, because women have to take much more time off to take care of children or the elderly or the sick (Chalabi, 2017; Newburger, 2018).

Other very alarming facts reveal the ways in which the automation and mechanization of our work and lives are specifically affecting sexuality and reproduction. The use of pornography among men around the world is booming because technology has made it much cheaper or free of charge. In order to compete with free pornography sites and blogs, the pornography industry is producing more extreme sex scenes. Young people are watching these scenes, developing unrealistic expectations, misogynistic mindsets, and also becoming addicted to pornography (Economist, 2015). The addiction to pornography among men is leading to an epidemic of impotence, including among young men, because normal sex no longer arouses them. In the United States, one-third of men under the age 40 years have erectile dysfunction or low sexual desire (Spitz, 2018).

Yarrow's (2018) *Man Out* shows that one in every five men in the United States is disconnected from work, family, children, civic and community-life, and relationships. They are angry, not only with the government and employers but also with women. These angry and alienated men include working-class, middle-class, and upper-class men, and young men of every race, ethnicity, and sexual orientation, from every part of the United States (p. xii). "A vocal minority are unabashed misogynists" (p. xv).

Some men use names of sex organs to call women, and also assault and shoot women for denying men sex and making them "involuntary celibates." Some have joined the "men's rights movement" and the "manosphere" and promote the views of Robert Bly's *Iron John*, the evangelical Promise Keepers, Louis Farrakhan, or the National Council For Men (Yarrow, 2018, p. 81). Some claim that most sexual assault charges are lies and most domestic violence is committed by women. Some like the "Red Pillers" call men "the oppressed gender" and encourage men to rape women (Wachtell, 2017; Yarrow, 2018, p. 82).

Conversely, only 30 percent of men aged 18 to 44 years in the United States call themselves "completely masculine" (Yarrow, 2018, p. 65). There is also a "pro-feminist Men's Movement" based in Amherst, Massachusetts, that publishes the quarterly magazine, *Voice Male* that aims to show "a way for men to live that is centered not on their masculinity but on their humanity" (Yarrow, 2018, p. 83). Yarrow argues:

> Although feminism has enabled women to make huge advances and also has done many good things for men … its effects on men have been much more ambiguous. A "cultural lag between the genders" has opened up, with women developing a new, more defined set of beliefs and greater ambition, and men unable to figure out how to respond to these changes and how to act. (Yarrow, 2018, p. 68)

As male identity has become more fluid, "behavioral norms have become rife with contradictions and minefields" (Yarrow, 2018, p. 68).

Jared Yates Sexton (2019), author of *The Man They Wanted Me to Be: Toxic Masculinity and a Crisis of Our Own Making*, also offers important insights on these questions. As a *New York Times* columnist and Professor of Creative Writing, he speaks from the vantage point of his own experiences as someone who was raised by a single mother in extreme poverty in the state of Indiana in the United States, and who suffered great hardships as he and his mother were both physically and emotionally abused by various men in their lives.

He argues that with the 2016 U.S. election of Donald J. Trump, "It was like all of the troubling, frightening things that'd been saved for private spaces, kept behind locked doors had suddenly exploded into the public arena" (Sexton, 2019, p. 123). "At its core, the Trump phenomenon was a movement a long time in the making ... finally metastasized into a political identity" (Sexton, 2019, p. 212). Sexton pinpoints the patriarchal beliefs within the U.S. white working class with which he grew up and the deadly impact of patriarchal and misogynistic views promoted in online groups collectively known as the manosphere which promote the views of Alt Right figures such as Richard Spencer or figures like Jordan Peterson who advocate patriarchy as the natural order and call on men to "take responsibility." While Sexton focuses on white supremacist patriarchal ideologues, it is important to note that in the United States, the language calling on patriarchal men to take responsibility is also promoted by figures such as Louis Farrakhan of the Nation of Islam and many other leaders in various ethnic and religious communities.

Jared Yates Sexton's (2019) main message, however, is that patriarchy is unhealthy for men and does not make them strong but damages them physically and mentally. If men want to be healthy and strong, he argues, they need to be thoughtful, evaluate and analyze issues and vulnerabilities, show feelings, take care, and promote communal well-being (pp. 250–2).

Kristin J. Anderson's (2014) *Modern Misogyny*, published two years before the election of Trump, has focused more on subtle forms of misogyny that present themselves under the veneer of women's equality. Thus, she argues that the lure of neoliberal consumerism, marketplace "choice" and "empowerment" in the sense of narrow individualism starting in the early 1980s led to the "post-feminism" of the 1990s. This post-feminism moved away from the second-wave feminist goals of collective action for transforming capitalism and control over our bodies, and pay equality. Instead, it promoted narrow individualism, consumerism, and reduced choice to "choos[ing] to be sexualized and objectified" (p. 12).

Such an attitude, Anderson argues, normalized the sexual objectification of women in mass media and advertisements. It reduced sexual liberation to sexual self-objectification. It also facilitated the capitalist drive to make the sex industry mainstream, more pervasive and acceptable, and led to an uncritical attitude toward or even embrace of porn culture (p. 14). Instead of promoting women as "*subject* of their sexuality," it promoted women as "objects of someone else's desire" (p. 14). Thus "hard-core porn is now the primary form of sex education in the Western world" (p. 16).

Anderson also examines the effects of the heightened militarism following the September 11, 2001 terrorist attacks on the New York City Twin Towers, and the U.S. invasion of Afghanistan that year and of Iraq in 2003. Pointing out the heavy promotion of hypermasculinity in the United States following these events, she demonstrates "the swiftness with which progress … reverts to traditional patriarchal patterns … during times of crisis" (p. 28). Examples of such retrogression in gender roles that are promoted include the focus on policemen, firemen, and male first-responders as hypermasculine men coming to the aid of women who were presented as *damsels in distress*. In addition, *chick flick films* encouraged women to choose family over career, and *purity balls* celebrated teen women pledging their chastity to their father until the day of their marriage. Militarism also included the general assault on civil rights, press freedom, and the vilification of immigrants as *the other*. Thus she argues that the U.S. government's intensified promotion of militarism following the September 11 attacks "enhanced and accelerated a conservative agenda already in place in the U.S" that had "begun in the early 1980s" (Anderson, 2014, p. 42).

That conservative agenda that aimed to roll back women's hard-fought rights was seen most clearly in the attacks on abortion rights after the 1973 U.S. Supreme Court case, *Roe v Wade*, made abortion legal up until the end of the sixth month of pregnancy. In her *Without Apology: The Abortion Struggle Now*, Jenny Brown (2019b) argues that the current assault on abortion rights in the United States is rooted both in racist concerns about the low birth rate of white women, and in the fear of women's independence and sexuality. She takes us through the step-by-step effort by the conservative Right to nullify the 1973 *Roe v Wade* Supreme Court decision. This reversal effort started with the 1976 *Hyde Amendment* which denied federal Medicaid funding for abortion. It continued with the gag rule preventing adolescent school sex education classes from mentioning abortion, followed by parental consent and notification laws, imposing time limits, waiting periods, mandatory ultrasounds, mandatory statements to discourage women from having abortions, establishing unusually strict standards for abortion clinics and providers in order to force them to close down, assassinating abortion providers, heckling women entering abortion clinics, restricting the availability of the abortion pill RU486 and demanding that it be administered in a clinic, and allowing employer-provided health care plans to not cover abortion and certain forms of birth control. Furthermore, in 2014, the passage of the federal *Unborn Victims of Violence Act* meant that any act causing the death of embryos and fetuses would be a separate crime from the harm caused to a pregnant woman. This law in turn allowed some states to subject women to imprisonment if they had a poor pregnancy outcome or a stillbirth (Brooks, 2018; Brown, 2019b, p. 146; Pollitt, 2015, p. 142). A new Texas law upheld by the U.S. Supreme court in September 2021 bans any abortion after the sixth week of pregnancy. Furthermore, it authorizes vigilantes to collect bounties of at least $10,000 from the state for filing lawsuits and hunting down any person anywhere in the United States who directly or indirectly aids a woman with having an abortion in Texas (Walker, 2021).[3] On October 2, 2021, over 250,000 women marched throughout the United States against this law. The marches, however, were not nearly as large as those which brought out millions for abortion rights during the Trump presidency (Lerer & Robertson, 2021). Anti-abortion laws including laws that ban or restrict the use of abortion pills are now being passed by multiple state legislatures around the United States (Levenson, 2022; Zernike, 2022). An Oklahoma law signed in April 2022 criminalizes abortion at any stage and allows for sentencing abortion performers to up to ten years in prison (LeBlanc & Stracqualursi, 2022). On June 24, 2022 the U.S. Supreme Court took away women's constitutional right to abortion and gave states full authority to ban abortion.

Brown (2019) challenges the abortion rights movement in the United States to not take the ground of the anti-abortion movement by calling abortion a tragic decision. Instead, she argues, we need to proudly recognize that abortion too is a right and a form of birth control and should always be an option for women. "The feminist position is that you must have absolute control over whether you take on this massive effort [pregnancy and child birth] or you are not free" (p. 116). She also calls on the reproductive rights movement to not limit itself to the language of *choice* but learn from the Reproductive Justice Movement, which was pioneered by the Black feminist organization Sister Song in the early 1990s. The Reproductive Justice Movement views abortion rights as part of a broader struggle including social justice, universal health care, and education. According to Loretta Ross and Rickie Solinger (2017), authors of *Reproductive Justice: An Introduction*, reproductive justice is about "the right *not* to have a child" or "the right to have a child" and to "parent children in safe and healthy environments" (p. 65).

In her *Pro: Reclaiming Abortion Rights*, Katha Pollitt (2015) also shares these views and expands on them. She challenges the misogynistic roots of the anti-abortion movement's claim that "life begins at conception." This view, she argues, reduces women to mere vessels for carrying fetuses, and gives a fetus a right to rent a woman's body without her consent, simply because a woman had sex (p. 91). She argues that "the ability to determine the timing and number of children undergirds the modern ideal of egalitarian, intimate marriages based on love, companionship, and mutual sexual delight. It makes for marriages that are less rigidly role-bound and more democratic—and better for children" (Pollitt, 2015, p. 113). In this statement, Pollitt echoes an earlier statement by Adrienne Rich (1986):

> Procreative choice is for women an equivalent of the demand for the legally-limited working day which Marx saw as the great watershed for factory workers in the nineteenth century. The struggles for that "modest Magna Carta" as Marx calls it … did not end capitalism, but they changed the relation of the workers to their own lives. (p. 21)

Furthermore, Pollitt (2015) argues that it is the anti-abortion side that devalues motherhood. It treats motherhood lightly with no understanding of all the pain and work that it involves. On the one hand, it demonizes single mothers on welfare who receive meager public assistance funds to survive. On the other hand, if a single woman opts to have an abortion to avoid the rigors of single motherhood, she is told that motherhood is a breeze.

The glaring proof of the inhumanity of the "pro-life" movement is the lack of concern for Black women and poor women of color. In the United States, Black women are twice as likely than white women to die from complications of pregnancy and child birth (Sgaier & Downey, 2021). Indeed the United States has the highest maternal mortality rate in the developed world (Rabin, 2021). The Black infant mortality rate is also more than double the white infant mortality rate (Gaither, 2020; Saad, 2020, p. 88). One in three women of color in the United States who give birth in a hospital report experiencing disrespectful care or mistreatment (*New York Times*, 2018). In the words of Keeanga-Yamahtta Taylor (2017), "Black feminists identified reproductive justice as a priority, from abortion rights to ending the sterilization practices that were common in gynecological medicine when it came to treating working-class, Black and Puerto Rican women in the United States" (p. 9).

The struggle for abortion rights has also brought out millions of women in protests in Ireland, Argentina, other countries in Latin America, and Poland in the last decade. In 2018, Irish voters decided by a landslide to repeal one of the world's most restrictive abortion bans (Freytas-Tamura, 2018). In Argentina, in December 2020, a strong feminist movement which includes the wide participation of working-class women, pushed the legislature to legalize abortion on demand up until the 15th week of pregnancy (Politi & Londoño, 2020).[4] In Mexico, abortion was decriminalized in September 2021 and in Colombia, it was legalized in February 2022, thanks to the efforts of feminist activists. While there have been some abortion rights victories in Latin America, abortion continues to be criminalized and banned under all circumstances in Nicaragua, El Salvador, Honduras, Haiti, Dominican Republic, and Suriname (McDonnell & Linthicum, 2021). In Poland, in October and November of 2020, hundreds of thousands of women protested against widened restrictions on abortion and forced a government delay in the enforcement of the more restrictive regulations. However, on January 28, 2021, the Polish government put the near total ban on abortion into effect. Women protesters have vowed to continue to fight the ban (Kwai, Pronzuk, & Magdziarz, 2021; Majewska, 2020).

Around the world, the objectification, dehumanization, and commodification of women, especially poor women and children of color, are most glaringly seen in the massive increase in trafficking. Of the approximately 40 million enslaved people around the world today, an estimated 50 percent are women over the age of 18 years; 23 percent are girls under the age of eighteen years; 21 percent are men over the age of eighteen years; and 7 percent are boys under the age of eighteen years (United Nations Office on Drugs and Crime, 2018b). The trafficking of women and girls as sexual slaves is booming. Human trafficking earns global profits of roughly $150 billion a year for traffickers, of which $99 billion comes from commercial sexual exploitation (Human Rights First, 2017; International Labor Organization, 2017).

Trafficking can include forced labor, forced marriage, prostitution, and organ removal (International Labour Organization, 2017). Regional wars and conflicts have made people more vulnerable to trafficking. Traffickers also use online social media platforms to recruit and to advertise targets of human trafficking. The average age when a teenager enters the sex trade in the United States is 12 to 14 years old. Many victims are girls who were sexually abused as children and have run away from home (Do Something, 2020). Tens of thousands of women and girls of color including 70,000 Black girls were reported missing in the United States in 2020 (Robles, 2021).

Women who are trafficked and experience sexual violence are also much more likely to contract HIV (Wirth et al., 2013). Globally, there are approximately 18 million women currently living with HIV. Female sex workers are 14 times more likely to be infected with HIV. Young women and adolescent girls (ages 15–24 years old) are particularly affected especially in sub-Saharan Africa (United Nations Women, 2020).[5]

It is true that world powers often close their eyes to atrocities against women, including most recently the rape and mass incarceration of Uyghur Muslim women in Xinjiang by the Chinese government, the rape and ethnic cleansing of Rohingya Muslim women by the Myanmar government, and the rape and assault on women in Congo, Somalia, and Ethiopia's Tigray Region mostly by government forces.

In Afghanistan, however, in 2021, the U.S. government and other occupying NATO allies practically handed over power to the Taliban, a misogynist, racist, and jihadist army that they claimed their occupation had originally sought to uproot (Afary, 2022a). The Taliban is an army that is in many ways similar to ISIS and to the Ku Klux Klan in its extremism and brutality (Achcar, 2021; Cole, 2021). Since their second takeover, the Taliban have assaulted women's protests, beaten and censored reporters, stopped girls over the age of 12 from attending school or university, forced girls and women to marry Taliban fighters, forced most employed women to stay home, reinstituted complete gender segregation, and replaced the Department of Women's Affairs with their morality police known as "the Department of Promotion of Virtue and Prohibition of Vice" (Engelbrecht & Hassan, 2021; Nebehay & Farge, 2021; Pal, 2021).

In Ukraine, Vladimir Putin's genocidal invasion in 2022 has devastated the whole nation and women in particular. Russian soldiers have raped and sexually abused women, children and men (Sidner et al., 2022). As of this writing in May 2022, millions of women have joined the resistance, including tens of thousands who have taken up arms against the Russian army (Bloom & Moskalenko, 2022). Millions of women and children have become internally displaced people or refugees in neighboring countries. Some refugees have become victims of sex traffickers (Fallon, Cundy, & Crean, 2022).

The contradictory developments in gender relations in the twenty-first century are clearly staggering. These trends matter because they reveal an immense challenge, new possibilities, and the dire need for an emancipatory alternative. Building on the progressive possibilities, however, requires rootedness in socialist feminist concepts and categories. It also requires full awareness of the distinctive features of capitalist authoritarianism in the twenty-first century and a comprehension of the new dimensions of the various global uprisings against it.

2

Distinctive Features of Authoritarian Capitalism/Imperialism Today and the New Challenges of Black Lives Matter and Global Uprisings

It can be argued that capitalism in its essence is authoritarian. If we begin with Karl Marx's *Das Kapital* (*Capital*), and his *Economic and Philosophical Manuscripts of 1844*, we will learn that capitalism is not simply an unjust mode of *distribution*. It is a mode of *production* based on alienated labor, an extreme mental and manual division of labor that turns work into a meaningless, undifferentiated, monotonous activity, and turns the human being into a cog in a machine. Capitalist labor alienates us not only from the products of our labor but also from our potential for free and conscious activity and from other human beings (Marx, 1961, 1976).

Based on Marx's *Capital*, we can sum up the logic of capital in the following way: alienated labor (not limited to factory or manufacturing labor) produces value, and leads to a system in which the goal becomes the expansion of value as an end in itself. To meet this goal, capitalism introduces more and more machinery and technology to increase labor productivity and extract more and more surplus value from human or living labor. This process also leads to the concentration and centralization of capital in fewer hands to the point where within a single country, Marx anticipated, capital could even be accumulated in the hands of a single capitalist or a single capitalist corporation.[1]

At the same time, this process leads to an imbalance for capitalism itself. Relatively more and more technology and machines are used at the expense of living human labor which is the only source of value. This imbalance leads both to an increasing rate of unemployment relative to investment and a tendency toward a decline in the rate of profit and periodic economic crises. These crises can lead to war between competing capitalist entities or states.

Even without an outright war, in order to overcome crises, capitalism needs to resort to more and more authoritarian means, physically and ideologically, to extract more surplus value from labor and to quell the dissatisfied unemployed. These means can be seen in the use of slave labor, a prison-industrial complex, more policing, and in general, greater militarization of society in life and in thought.

However, there is more to why capitalism leads to authoritarianism (Afary, 2018). The logic of capital also promotes authoritarianism by devaluing critical and independent thinking. Its reduction of the concept of time to value-production time, devalues the time spent on thinking, analyzing, and performing labor that is outside the context of the accumulation of capital. It reduces thought itself to mathematical formulas or computer algorithms. It reduces human reason to the application of formulas and to calculation for pure and narrow self-interest or what the sociologist Max Weber (1978) has called "instrumental" rationality (pp. 24–5).

Marx thought that capitalism, by bringing workers together, would create the *conditions* for national and international solidarity among them to uproot the capitalist system and to replace it with a humanist alternative of which he had given us some signposts in his work (Hudis, 2012). At the same time, as a Hegelian dialectical philosopher, he was able to see that reality develops in contradictory ways, that capitalism can be very resilient and that racism, sexism, intra-class divisions, and ideological conditioning are also used to divide the working class and all those who suffer from the ills of capitalism. We can still learn from his writings and activities to address these issues and to offer solutions. In that spirit, let's analyze some of the distinctive features of authoritarian capitalism in the twenty-first century.

THE DISTINCTIVE FEATURES OF CAPITALIST AUTHORITARIANISM IN THE TWENTY-FIRST CENTURY

From Neoliberalism and Globalization to Protectionism and Regionalization

According to the Marxist economist, Michael Roberts (2016), author of *The Long Depression*, after the first three decades of the post-World War II boom in economic growth in the 1940s, 1950s, and 1960s, a crisis of profitability caught up with the Western economies. This, he argues, is what led to what we know as the neoliberal reforms starting in the early 1980s. Neoliberalism included an assault on labor rights and regulations, and massive cuts in social services through the privatization of the state sector of the economy which provides these services. It also included globalization: the flight of capital to Mexico and then mostly to China, India, and South East Asia in search of cheaper labor costs and higher profits (Roberts, 2016).

Roberts (2016) shows that capitalism's incessant drive to cut labor costs and increase the rate of profit is also the basis for what some economists have called the "Second Machine Age" (Brynjolfsson & McAfee, 2016). Computers and robotics are being used to replace living human labor on a scale much greater than before. However, he argues that this phenomenon will lead to deeper crises of profitability for capitalism (pp. 257–63). In the Western economies, these changes since the mid-1970s through the early 1980s have been accompanied by a massive decline in formerly "good paying" manufacturing jobs, as well as longer recessions characterized by rising unemployment and underemployment, and a sense of increasing alienation and hopelessness on the part of the working class.

The 2008 global economic crisis was a major turning point for capitalism. It showed that even neoliberal reforms were not sufficient to generate high enough profits to overcome the depth of the crisis of profitability (Kliman, 2011). In its never-ending search for a higher rate of profit, capitalism has now discovered that there is much more value to be made from the proximity of production to research and development. According to Ryan Avent (2016), in *The Wealth of Humans*, that is why some U.S. and European multinational companies, which had gone to China to benefit from the cheap labor and lack of regulations, are now *returning* to build or to reopen manufacturing plants in their home countries (pp. 173–7).

Avent (2016) admits that this proximity of production to research and development will not lead to renewed mass employment in manufacturing in the economically developed countries, because the new jobs created are too high-skilled and relatively too few. Thus, what he anticipates as the future for Western economies is that a small sector of high-skilled professionals will benefit from the return of manufacturing jobs. The low-skilled laid-off workers, however, will continue to compete for low-skilled work (pp. 45–6).

Although the trend away from globalization began after the 2008 economic crisis, it has also been intensified by the COVID-19 pandemic, which has broken many of the existing global supply chains. According to *The Economist*, "the pandemic will not end globalization but will reshape it." While the economic appeal of protectionism and economic self-sufficiency will grow, and the globalization of goods and services will be reduced, we will see more regional blocks for trade in goods and services, especially digital trading. "South America will supply cheap digital services to North America; Africa to Europe, and South-East Asia to North-East Asia." This is what *The Economist* has called "slowbalization," by adopting a term coined by the Dutch writer, Adjiedj Bakas (Economist, 2019a, 2020g).

State and Monopoly Capitalism

For much of the Left, since the 1980s, *neoliberalism* has been an all-encompassing term to identify the character of contemporary capitalism. Since the 2008 economic crisis, however, with the collapse of the neoliberal model or Washington Consensus, some leftist as well as liberal analysts have argued that this concept is not adequate for defining the current character of global capitalism (Dunn, 2017; Economist, 2012; Khader, 2016). It does not explain the statist character of the emerging economies and, most recently, the rise of authoritarian statism in some Western countries. Thomas Piketty's (2017) *Capital in the Twenty-First Century* also argues that today, states have more influence over the global economy than ever before (p. 473; see also Afary, 2016).

Today, the capitalism that we see on the rise is no longer neoliberalism with the language of choice and "liberation." Capitalism no longer finds liberalism useful. It does not attempt to hide its brutality, racism, and misogyny. In fact, neoliberalism was never really an adequate explanation of capitalism. Neoliberalism is simply a form in which capitalism expressed itself from the early 1980s and faced a demise beginning with the 2008 economic crisis.

In his *State Capitalism: How the Return of Statism Is Transforming the World*, Joshua Kurlantzick (2016) defines state capitalism as state ownership or significant influence over more than one-third of the 500 largest companies (by revenue) in a country. Indeed, today, eight out of the ten largest corporations around the world are state-owned. Twenty-first-century state ownership or control is not limited to sectors such as energy, defense, and communications. It is not based on isolation from the world market, but is open to global trade and technological innovation. It also uses modern management techniques similar to any multinational giant, and fires managers who do not promote profitability.

Kurlantzick (2016) argues that although states have interfered in their economies for centuries, state intervention has become far more extensive on a global scale since the late 1990s. This intervention is not limited to state spending and work projects, protecting domestic industries (through tariffs and subsidies) and controlling strategic industries. It is not an emergency measure such as the 2008 bailout of bankrupt companies in the United States and state ownership of General Motors. It is also not aimed at autarky or creating a pure state-owned economy. Instead, this new state capitalism combines statist strategies with aspects of free-market strategies used by multinational companies. He writes, "Thus it may have a better chance of surviving over the long term compared to strategies pursued by Maoist China, The Soviet Union and even a more democratic state capitalism in the 20th century like France" (Kurlantzick, 2016, p. 22).

This state capitalism is also not monolithic but is better understood as a "continuum" (Kurlantzick, 2016, p. 7). Based on Kurlantzick's (2016) definition, China is the most prominent state capitalist country in the world. However, the state capitalist designation also covers Singapore, Malaysia, Thailand, and less efficient ones such as Turkey, United Arab Emirates, Qatar, South Africa, Brazil, Indonesia, India, Vietnam, Argentina, Kazakhstan, Venezuela, Russia, Saudi Arabia, Iran, Uzbekistan, Egypt, and Algeria.

In the United States, a form of state capitalism was dominant during the New Deal in the 1930s and continued as a welfare state through the mid-1970s when the 1973–74 economic crisis severely damaged the economy and set the stage for massive cuts in the public sector. Today, the state continues to play a major and growing role in the U.S. economy and collaborates with private monopoly capitalism.

Prior to the pandemic, U.S. technology titans, Apple, Amazon, Alphabet (Google), Microsoft, and Facebook were already making astronomical profits. Now, the pandemic and the increased reliance of a larger share of the population on these companies for performing their job duties, communication, and shopping "has lifted them to new heights, putting the technology industry in a position to dominate American business in a way unseen since the days of railroads" (Eavis & Lohr, 2020; see also Mac-Millan, Whoriskey, & O'Connell, 2020; Ovide, 2021). Apple is the first U.S. company to reach $3 trillion in value (Manjoo, 2022). Together, the tech titans constitute 20 percent of the U.S. stock market's total worth, a level not seen from a single industry in at least 70 years. They have done so through massive mergers and an enormous concentration and centralization of capital, which substantially reduces costs of production and allows them to outdo competitors, including startups. At the same time, Big Tech firms also rely on their collaboration with the U.S. military and police, including U.S. Immigration and Customs Enforcement (ICE) with whom they have signed highly profitable contracts (Conger et al., 2019; Economist, 2016; Khan, 2017; Roose, 2019). The fact that the Pentagon is soliciting multibillion dollar bids from Amazon and Microsoft for cloud computing means that the Pentagon also has much say in determining the direction of Amazon and Microsoft (Conger & Sanger, 2021).[2] NASA has also given a $2.9 billion contract to monopoly capitalism in the form of the rocket manufacturing company SpaceX in Texas (whose owner, Elon Musk, also owns the Tesla electric car company) in order to develop a large reusable spacecraft, Starship, to land astronauts on the moon in 2024, as part of NASA's permanent moon outpost, Artemis (Economist, 2021d).

Prior to the pandemic, increasing state intervention within the U.S. economy could also be seen in the role of the U.S. military as the world's largest employer. It employs over three million people who also include over 732,000 civilians. In addition to training soldiers for war, it employs people in a variety of fields including construction, engineering, science, health care, and transportation. The U.S. government also aids large companies through deregulation and stimulus funds. Of the roughly $4 trillion post-pandemic relief packages in the spring and summer of 2020, the larger portion was spent on large companies as well as the purchase of U.S. bonds to prevent the U.S. economy from collapsing. The funds given to large companies also required government ownership shares of those companies in exchange. U.S. President Joseph Biden's proposed multitrillion dollar infrastructure plan—even if not ratified in its entirety—puts the state in charge of the U.S. economy in a manner unprecedented since World War II (Tankersley, 2021). In the words of British socialist feminist and economist, Grace Blakeley (2020), "What has happened as a result of 2008 and 2020 is that both financial and now also non-financial institutions—in other words, the entirety of the 'monopoly-finance' hybrid—have collapsed into the arms of the state, and appear set to become wholly and permanently reliant upon it" (p. 23).

This does not mean that state intervention in the economy in the Global North and the Global South are currently the same. However, it can be argued that we are facing a new model of state capitalism with the state and military having more and more control over the direction of companies even when there is no direct full ownership. China is setting the direction for the rest of the world. The 2008 economic crisis and the pandemic have facilitated that direction in the West as well.

More Imperialist Powers: West and East

Whereas in the twentieth century, it was Europe, the United States, the USSR, and states backed by them, which played the role of imperialist powers, today, China and the new Russia, and states supported by them, are also playing important roles as global or regional imperialist powers around the world.

Despite its military and economic strength, U.S. imperialism has become weaker in the twenty-first century because of the global competition from China as well as the United States' wars in Afghanistan and Iraq, and the 2008 economic crisis. Under the Trump administration, the United States strengthened its assault on Iran and its support for Israel and Saudi Arabia. But it also withdrew most of its forces from Syria and largely reduced its troop presence in Iraq and Afghanistan. The Biden administration withdrew U.S. troops from Afghanistan, following a Trump administration deal with the Pakistan-backed Taliban which in effect left power in the Taliban's hands.[3] The United States has thus also allowed for an increased role for both Russian and Chinese imperialism and for Iranian and Turkish sub-imperialism in Syria, Afghanistan and the region as a whole.

Both under the Obama administration and under the Trump and then Biden administrations, the United States has been shifting its military focus to the Pacific. There, it has been challenging China's military exercises and claims to Taiwan and the South China Sea (Buckley & Lee, 2021) through military exercises of its own with South Korea, the sale of nuclear submarines to Australia (Sanger & Kanno-Youngs, 2021) and threatening moves in the South China Sea, and in defense of Taiwan's independence from mainland China. It has also engaged in a trade war and diplomatic war with China (Sanger, 2021a, 2021b).[4]

Since 2013, China's massive $17.7 trillion state capitalist economy has initiated the Belt and Road Initiative under Xi Jinping. This project, also known as the New Silk Road, involves anywhere from $400 billion to $6 trillion of financing in grants, but especially in loans already spent or about to be spent in more than 160 countries around the world that contain three-fifths of the world's population. The amount spent and projected is much larger than the post-World War II's U.S. Marshall Plan (also known as European Recovery Program), which in today's money would equal $130 billion. The Belt and Road Initiative is a strategic program aimed at gaining critical supplies of natural resources to drive economic growth inside China, and to develop ports and gain dominance in the global shipping industry in order to allow China to project its naval power around the world. "By rolling out infrastructure across the Eurasian land mass, China becomes the indispensable power in an emerging supercontinent. Crucially, the state directs state enterprises to do the national bidding and state banking institutions to provide the financial firepower" (Economist, 2020f). Through this global imperialist infrastructure investment project, China has placed not only Africa, Latin America, and much of Asia, but also Europe and Australia in debt to itself. Furthermore, China, after Japan, is the second largest holder of the United States' debt in the form of $1.07 trillion in U.S. Treasury bonds, and is thus a major force in maintaining the U.S. economy (Amadeo, 2020).

Russia's state capitalism, though economically much weaker than the United States or China, promoted proxy warfare in Eastern Ukraine, annexed Crimea in 2014 and launched a full-scale genocidal invasion of Ukraine in February 2022. This invasion which has faced massive popular resistance within Ukraine continues as of this writing (May 2022). Russia became the main imperialist power in Syria in 2015. In the name of attacking ISIS, it started launching massive aerial attacks against the progressive and moderate opposition zones in order to crush a popular uprising against the authoritarian regime of Bashar al-Assad. Russia has played a strong role in Iran and Saudi Arabia through the sale of arms and nuclear plants. It has also conducted extensive cyberattacks on state and private networks in the United States (Sanger, Perlroth, & Barnes, 2021).

Russia counts on its new political, military, and economic alliance with China to protect its capitalist and imperialist interests (Wright, 2022).

Whether in the United States, Russia, China or elsewhere around the world, most notable has been an increased state and military role in policing, prisons, and the commanding heights of the economy (energy, transportation, communication, etc.).

Mass Incarceration and Policing

Since the early 1980s, there has been a massive increase in the U.S. prison, jail, and detention center population. At 2.3 million, this prison population constitutes the largest in the world (K. Afary, 2009; DuVernay, 2016; Pillischer, 2012). In China, there are over two million prisoners and detained people, over one million of whom are ethnic minority Uyghurs held in "re-education camps" in Xinjiang province. Russia has an estimated prisoner population of 875,000. In the Middle East, the largest official prison and jail populations are in Iran (240,000), Turkey (over 200,000), the Assad regime's prisons in Syria (at least 128,000), and Egypt (120,000) (Afary & Al-Kateb, 2020; World Prison Brief, 2021). After China, the highest prison execution rates in the world are in Iran, Egypt, Iraq, and Saudi Arabia (Hubbard, 2021).

U.S. feminist abolitionist thinkers, Angela Y. Davis (1998) and Ruth Wilson Gilmore (2007), whose work I will discuss in Chapter 3, have theorized that the relationship between capitalist crises, globalization, racism, and the prison-industrial complex is based on a system of social control. It is partially about profit extraction from the work of prisoners and partially a source of job creation for prison guards and for communities where prisons are built. In *The New Jim Crow: Mass Incarceration in the Age of Colorblindness*, Michelle Alexander (2020), U.S. civil rights attorney and legal scholar, has categorized the disproportionate rate of imprisonment of African Americans as part of a New Jim Crow system of racial segregation and disenfranchisement in the United States.

The rise of mass incarceration in the United States has also gone hand in hand with an unprecedented expansion in the scope and intensity of policing and the militarization of the police since the early 1980s. Alex Vitale's (2017) *The End of Policing* has documented the very origins of policing as an effort to promote the interests of capital in its drive to extract more labor from enslaved people, workers, immigrants, people of color, and the colonized, and to manage the inequities of race and class. He has specifically tied the massive increase in policing in the United States to a backlash against the gains of the civil rights movement and labor struggles in the United States in the 1960s and early 1970s.

China and Russia have a history of repression of dissidents and the use of forced labor camps and gulags that were started under the rule of Joseph Stalin in Russia and Mao Zedong in China. The new "re-education camps" in Xinjiang province in China are set up not only to extract labor and punish dissidents but also to destroy the Uyghur Muslim ethnic minority as a people. Out of a population of 12 million Uyghurs in Xinjiang, over one million have been put in camps, prisons, and detention centers. In addition, approximately 885,000 children have been separated from their parents and put in orphanages. At schools, they are not allowed to speak their language and are taught to worship Xi Jinping's Thought. Women are systematically raped through the government policy of sending hundreds of thousands of Han officials and civilians to stay in Uyghur homes, and also through forcing Uyghur girls to marry Han men (Buckley & Ramzy, 2019, 2020; Economist, 2020h). At the same time, many Uyghur women who are having children with Uyghur men have been forced to have abortions or have been sterilized (Stavrou, 2021; Qin, 2021).[5]

The prisons of the Assad regime in Syria, which contain the large majority of Syria's approximately 128,000 detainees, are also known as some of the most brutal in the world. Their main purpose is to crush any civil resistance (PBS, 2019). The state arrests, tortures, and executes people on a mass scale. Those arbitrarily arrested since the 2011 popular uprising have included children, women, and men of different backgrounds, including the Kurdish minority and leftists. According to the Syrian Network for Human Rights, there are currently 127,916 people detained (Barnard, 2019; Syrian Network for Human Rights, 2021).[6]

However, given government secrecy and limited access to official records, the number is believed to be much higher. Methods of torture include starvation, daily beatings, sexual violence against women, men, and trans people, genital mutilation, forced sterilization, and acts of degradation. According to a former prison survivor from Syria, Omar Alshogre, the intent of torture in prisons is to break the human spirit (100 Faces of the Syrian Revolution, 2020). In 2016, Amnesty International published a report detailing the extrajudicial execution of 13,000 prisoners (Amnesty

International, 2016). The release of the Caesar Photos showing the industrial-scale brutality of the Assad regime's prison system have pointed to at least 6,500 torture-related deaths (Human Rights Watch, 2015). The Syrian Network for Human Rights reports that between March 2011 and June 2021, over 14,000 people have been killed due to torture mostly by the Syrian regime (Masri, al-Issa, & al-Mahmoud, 2021; Syrian Network for Human Rights, 2021). In 2019, the Syrian regime released 700 death certificates of prisoners to the public, reaffirming its ability to brutalize a people with impunity. Today, in the midst of the COVID-19 pandemic, overcrowding, limited access to water or adequate medical care, many prisoners face widespread contagion and diseases.

Gaza, a Palestinian territory occupied by Israel for the past 50 years, and home to a population of 1.9 million Palestinians, has been called "the world's largest open air prison" (Hovring, 2018). For the past ten years, it has been blockaded by Israel, Egypt, and by the Fatah-led Palestinian Authority. Its water and power facilities have been damaged and destroyed by Israeli raids. In a manner similar to the brutal and authoritarian regime of Syria, Israel's raids have also targeted hospitals and health clinics as well as residential buildings. The people of Gaza suffer from Israeli colonialism/racism, as well as the authoritarianism of the Palestinian Authority and Hamas.

Another feature of mass incarceration today is the existence of a global refugee and displaced population worldwide which is the largest since World War II. Of the more than 100 million forcibly displaced people around the world as of early 2022, the majority came from Syria, Venezuela, Afghanistan, South Sudan, and Myanmar (United Nations Refugee Agency, 2021 and 2022). As of April 2022, millions of Ukrainians fleeing Russia's brutal invasion of their country have been added to that list. While Ukrainian refugees have been mostly welcomed and supported in Poland, the welcoming attitude has not been offered to refugees from other countries. As victims of authoritarian regimes, religious fundamentalism, and ethnic cleansing, many have fled in search of a better life. However, in refugee camps and refugee detention centers, whether in the East or the West, North, or South, they are subjected to racism, gender violence, torture, hunger, misery, unsanitary conditions, and the forced use of drugs. Most refugees are also turned into the Other by extremist racist forces in various countries who aim to stoke hatred and deflect attention from each country's own internal class, race, and gender inequities. As a result, many refugees attempt suicide (Shahabi, 2020). In addition to all the above, the world's prison and refugee population is being disproportionately affected by the COVID-19 pandemic, and thereby facing catastrophic consequences with the spread of the disease and death.

In discussing the distinctive features of authoritarianism in the twenty-first century, I have so far enumerated objective factors, such as the move from globalization to regionalization, the increasing monopolization and statification of capital, and the rise in mass incarceration and intensification of policing, all of which promote an authoritarian mindset. I would also like to highlight the impact of the current mode of capitalist production on the functioning of the human brain itself.

High-tech Unreflectiveness, Disinformation, Fake News, and Post-Truth

Although social media have created amazing new possibilities for learning and for communication with human beings around the world, they have also been used to promote disinformation, fake news, and con-spiracy theories (Girish, 2020). In the words of Jamelle Bouie (2020), "like industrial age steel companies dumping poisonous waste into waterways, Facebook pumps paranoia and disinformation into the body politic, the toxic byproduct of its relentless drive for profit" (see also Roose, 2020).

In her *Reader, Come Home: The Reading Brain in a Digital World*, Maryanne Wolf (2018), Professor of Education and social justice advocate for children, argues that "as society becomes increasingly dependent on digital reading, fissures are appearing in our most sophisticated cognitive and emotional processes, from critical analysis and empathy to contem-plation" (p. 11). Furthermore "in a milieu that continuously confronts us with a glut of information, the great temptation for many is to retreat to familiar silos of easily digested, less dense, less intellectually demanding information" (p. 11).

While this latter point has been argued by many analysts who have commented on the dangers of social media, Wolf's (2018) argument about the impact of digital reading itself on the brain is new. She shows that whereas reading print mediums gives the brain more time to absorb the content and reflect on it, switching to full reliance on digital mediums changes the circuitry of the brain and makes us unreflective and unempathetic (also see Flatow, 2018).

Changing this course, Wolf argues, demands a return to "deep reading" of great books of literature and philosophy to foster our ability to form analogies and inferences, and to develop critical thinking, reflection, and empathy (quoted in Flatow, 2018). This, she insists, cannot be done so long as digital mediums or screen reading constitute the bulk of reading. Reliance on print mediums is necessary in order to slow us down and make us reflect more on what we read. Furthermore, Wolf (2018) argues, this does not mean that we should abandon digital mediums. It means that we need to be as proficient in reading print mediums as we are in reading digital mediums and be concerned not only about what we read but how we read and why we read. Reading critically and with these questions in mind in turn, she argues, demands having an overall humanist conceptual framework inculcated in human beings through a system of education that values science and the humanities.

This does not mean, however, that we need to return to an uncritical capitalist view of science, objectivity, and humanism. It does mean that these concepts need to be reclaimed. Casey Williams (2017), in an opinion piece in the *New York Times*, argues that "For decades, critical social scientists and humanists have chipped away at the idea of truth. We've deconstructed facts, insisted that knowledge is situated and denied the existence of objectivity." He further argues that while these critiques have raised valid concerns about the limitations of formal logic and capitalism's claim to objectivity, Trump and the populist Right's assault on truth and objectivity should make us pause. "Not all assaults on the authority of facts are revolutionary" (Williams, 2017). Williams does not go as far as reclaiming the concepts of objectivity and of truth. However, his admission that the populist Right has seized on and weaponized key concepts in poststructuralist thought should make us ponder.

It can be argued that reversing the populist Right's dangerous assault on facts and its rewriting of history would not be possible without rethinking the concepts of objectivity, reason, and truth. It cannot be done without the type of "deep reading" that Maryanne Wolf calls us to engage in. It is possible to critique capitalism's "instrumental rationality" and the limitations of positivist and capitalist versions of reason and objectivity, without falling into mere relativism and the dangerous concept of "post-truth." Some socialist feminist thinkers discussed in this book can help us in this regard. It is in the context of all that has been discussed so far that we need to examine the global uprisings against authoritarianism in the twenty-first century.

WHAT ARE THE NEW FEATURES AND CHALLENGES OF RECENT GLOBAL UPRISINGS AGAINST AUTHORITARIANISM?

The role of women in the Black Lives Matter Movement in the United States has been most notable. Keeanga-Yamahtta Taylor, Professor of African American Studies at Princeton University and author of *From #BlackLivesMatter to Black Liberation* reminds us that Black women have always played an integral role in the Black freedom struggle:

> Today, though, the face of the Black Lives Matter movement is largely queer and female. ... Across the United States, 1.5 million men are "missing", snatched from society by imprisonment or premature death. ... Women have stepped into leadership roles because of the devastating impact of policing and police violence in Black people's lives. But whatever the reasons, their presence has contributed more than just gender balance. (Taylor, 2016, pp. 165–6)

Black women have exposed police brutality as part of a much larger system of oppression. In the words of Alicia Garza: "Black queer and trans folks bearing a unique burden in a hetero-patriarchal society that disposes of us like garbage and simultaneously fetishizes us and profits off of us is state violence" (Garza, 2014).[7]

The work of African American woman journalist, Nikole Hannah-Jones, has also been an important contribution of the broader movement for Black lives. She conceived and produced the Pulitzer Prize-winning "The 1619 Project," of the *New York Times* (2020b), published on the 400th anniversary of the entry of the first African enslaved person into Jamestown. This special 1619 issue of the *New York Times* magazine started new debates about the racist and anti-Black foundations of the United States and its legacy of slavery.

In 2019, uprisings in Sudan, Algeria, Hong Kong, Iraq, Lebanon, Chile, and Iran, as well as mass protests and labor strikes in France, Haiti, and elsewhere, led many analysts to compare the year to 1968 (Economist, 2019b), when a wave of revolutionary protests took place around the world. For the first time in 50 years, a large, mostly young population around the globe was in revolt against political repression, poverty, corruption, police brutality/state violence, ethnic and racial discrimination, gender violence, and environmental destruction. The protests were mostly spontaneous and leaderless. Women were active participants, and in some cases, in the forefront.

In Sudan, women's mass participation and leadership were unprecedented in the country's political history. Women fought against police brutality, Shari'a law, the morality police, and the dress code. Feminist organizations were part of the leadership of the uprising, especially during a long sit-in, which was held in front of the army headquarters. However, after a bloody assault by the military regime and its militias upon the protesters in June 2019—one that included sexual assaults and rapes targeting women—a power-sharing deal ensued between the Sudanese opposition and the military. This agreement kept the military in power through a joint, military-civilian government (Abbas, 2020; Mustafa & Abbas, 2020). On October 25, 2021, the military arrested the representative of the civilian part of the power-sharing deal, declared a state of emergency, and reverted to complete military rule. Mass protests against the coup and against any compromise with the military have ensued despite the brutal repression (Walsh, Dahir, & Marks, 2021).

In Algeria, during the 2019 uprising, women fought against patriarchal practices promoted by both the secular military regime and the religious fundamentalist opposition. They have opposed the country's Family Code which discriminates against women and treats them as minors. However, over two years after the start of the uprising, the military government is still in power, and Algerian opposition activists say that "we are moving backward fast" (Nossiter, 2020).

In Iraq, women's main demands in the protests that started in October 2019 included the separation of religion and state, job creation, and rights for women. They have also held literacy classes for protesters. The most important concerns among women participants have been femicide, child marriage, illiteracy, and women's lack of access to formal employment, even when they are educated. Activist women oppose sex segregation, temporary marriage, and the pressure to wear the *hijab*, all of which have been imposed on them since the United States overthrow of the brutal Saddam Hussein, in 2003, and as a result of Iranian intervention. They also oppose proposed changes in the constitution that take away some progressive legal clauses from the 1950s on marriage and child custody.[8]

In Lebanon, similar to Iraq, feminist activists have been demanding an end to femicide and to family laws that are based on one's religion. Women want the right to pass on their citizenship to their children, the right to child custody, and the right to abortion. They want jobs that offer security and benefits, such as health care. Many also defend the rights of migrant workers and refugees. Some have challenged nationalist symbols such as the flag used by protesters (Akram-Boshar, 2020; Alliance of MENA Socialists, 2019; Arab Reform Initiative, 2020; Bitar & Younes, 2019; Nasser, 2019).

In Iran, women's participation in the 2017 and 2019 uprisings were not limited to the middle class but involved the broad participation of working-class women often leading (Afary, 2020c). The brave acts of "Girls of Revolution Avenue," who were women stepping up on electric posts and removing their headscarves in public, showed that opposition to the compulsory *hijab* pervaded all social classes. Women activists demand the criminalization of "honor" killings or femicide, the separation of religion and state, and call for the right to equal inheritance, child custody, travel without the permission of a male guardian, as well as secure employment with benefits in the formal economy (Afary, 2020b; Rahrovan, 2021). All women activists demand the release of political prisoners, many of whom are women. A recent documentary, *Nasrin*, about imprisoned feminist human rights attorney, Nasrin Sotudeh, produced by U.S. feminist and social justice activists, Jeffrey Kaufman and Marcia Ross, beautifully and movingly depicts her life and work as the embodiment of Iranian women's struggles (Kaufman, 2020; see also Amos, 2020; Ross, Kaufman, & Afary, 2020, Sepehri Far, 2020). The work of Narges Mohammadi, imprisoned Iranian feminist and activist against the death penalty and solitary confinement, is also gaining international attention with her documentary, *White Torture*, based on her recent two-volume collection of interviews with mostly women political prisoners who have been subjected to solitary confinement (Mohammadi, 2021).

The Chilean uprising had the most explicit and active feminist dimension. As part of the widest nationwide protests since the end of the Augusto Pinochet dictatorship in 1990, young women and men were in the forefront of the struggle against police brutality and neoliberalism through spontaneously created popular local councils. In the words of Chilean socialist feminist, Juliana Rivas, "The Feminist Uprising in Chile began in 2018 over the issue of sexual assault in universities and unequal relations of power" (quoted in Wilde Botta, 2020; see also Alliance of MENA Socialists, 2019). Since then, young women have also started feminist discussion groups in high schools to talk about reproductive rights, abortion, domestic violence, and police violence. The Chilean women's song and dance, "A Rapist in Your Path" (now adopted by feminists in other countries), has been an expression of opposition to the severe police abuse and sexual assault experienced by women and children from the state, and from society at large. Chile has also legalized same-sex marriage (Bonnefoy & Londono, 2021) At the same time, the Chilean extreme Right has been able to expand its base by appealing to misogyny, and hatred for indigenous peoples and refugees from Haiti and Venezuela. Nevertheless, in the December 19, 2021 presidential election, the leftist, pro-labor and pro-feminist candidate, Gabriel Boric received 55 percent of the popular vote and defeated the fascist candidate José Antonio Kast, largely thanks to an increasing number of votes from pro-feminist Chilean women (Luna & Goodman, 2021).

In Hong Kong, many young women, as well as women in the unions of nurses and flight attendants, and women who consider themselves housewives, participated heavily in the 2019 mass protests against authoritarianism. The main focus of the 2019 protests was opposition to police brutality (Chi Leung, 2019, 2020; Loong-Yu, 2020). For women, that also meant opposition to sexual violence (Choi, 2020). With the passage of the National Security Law and imposition of full authoritarian rule by the mainland Chinese government in July 2020, Hong Kong democracy activists were muzzled and imprisoned.

In 2020, despite the rise of the COVID-19 pandemic, new uprisings emerged in Belarus, Thailand, Indonesia, and Nigeria. In this wave of protests as well, common features were, on the one hand, opposition to police brutality and state violence, and on the other hand, the presence of women in the forefront, and often raising feminist demands.

In Belarus, in the summer of 2020, women were in the forefront of mass protests against the authoritarian and misogynist rule of Alexander G. Lukashenko. The opposition is led by three women, Svetlana Tikhanovskaya, Veronika Tsepkalo, and Maria Kolesnikova, who organized large rallies across the country. Hundreds of women also held hands in Minsk to confront the police (Nechepurenko, 2020). They demanded the release of all political prisoners and an end to the Lukashenko regime through free elections. According to Ukrainian socialist feminist, Hanna Perekhoda (2021), although feminist demands were not raised, the very coming together of women in these protests created new possibilities for an "awareness among women of their interests and strengths."

In Nigeria, nationwide mass protests of youth against police brutality and sexual harassment were spearheaded by women in the autumn of 2020. The Feminist Coalition, a group of young Nigerian feminists, collectively mobilized all facets of the #EndSARS protests against the Special Anti-Robbery Squad police (Maclean, 2021; Ndifon, 2020). Indeed, these protests were "against Nigeria's police and armed forces. Against its leaders and the system" (Internationalism From Below, 2020; Maclean & Ezeamalul, 2020). During the past few years, women have also protested against the Nigerian government's inaction or slow action in the face of the Islamic fundamentalist extremist group, Boko Haram's terrorizing of the population in Northeastern Nigeria since 2009. These terrorist attacks include the abduction of 276 schoolgirls in Chibok and several hundred other girls and boys from other schools (Maclean & Alfa, 2020; Mbah, 2019; Strochlic, 2020).

In Thailand, young women led pro-democracy protests of tens of thousands of mostly student youth against the military, the monarchy, the Buddhist monkhood. They raised specific demands against patriarchy and for abortion rights, LGBTQ rights, and an end to school rules that force girls to conform to strict definitions of femininity. They also challenged male opposition leaders who degrade women and promote views about female inferiority. Some activists have been arrested, charged with sedition, and face prison sentences (Beech & Suhartono, 2020; Internationalism from Below, 2020).

In Indonesia, in the autumn of 2020, more than a million people, including tens of thousands of workers, protested and struck against a new law that slashed protections for workers and the environment (Anderson, 2020a). Women are most affected because the law brought an end to paid maternity and menstruation leave, along with pay cuts and replacement of permanent employees with contract workers. Some of the same protesters had demonstrated successfully in 2019 against a law that banned same-sex relations (Sijabat & Paddock, 2020).

In Myanmar, since February 2021, hundreds of thousands of people have taken to the streets or struck in protest against a military coup.

Women have led protests including members of ethnic minority groups. Thousands have been arrested and killed. Although Aung San Suu Kyi, the deposed civilian head of the government, has denied the ethnic cleansing, mass rapes, and genocide of Rohingya Muslims by the government/military in Buddhist-majority Myanmar (Simons & Beech, 2019), the women leading the protests against the coup have opposed the military's repression of ethnic and religious minorities and its systematic gang rapes. Many women protesters have also defied gender stereotypes by challenging traditional religious hierarchies and using women's sarongs to protect protest zones in a country where walking under sarongs worn by women is considered an affront to men's virility (Beech, 2021; Internationalism From Below, 2021; Iranian Progressives in Translation, 2021b). Myanmar has now become a war zone with the military bombing cities and villages through air raids and sealing neighborhoods. The people are resisting by forming civilian defense forces especially with the help of ethnic minorities (Pierson & Hsan Hlaing, 2021).

In India, hundreds of thousands of farmers protested around New Delhi after November 2020, to oppose agricultural laws that do away with a minimum government-set price for their crops. Women farmers were on the frontlines. Mostly from the rural and very patriarchal states of Punjab, Haryana, and Uttar Pradesh, women started to pour in at protests in large numbers after the government told them to go back home. They were welcomed by women's rights activists who offered messages about women's equality and held discussions about women's social and economic contributions. Many women's rights activists have also protested against a new citizenship law which discriminates against Muslims (Bhowmick, 2021).

In Palestine, in May 2021, a new Intifada against the Israeli government's settler colonialism and apartheid system began among Palestinians in East Jerusalem, West Bank, and Gaza with young women in the forefront (Iranian Progressives in Translation, 2021a). Although it was repressed by the Israeli army, racist Jewish mob attacks, and the Palestinian Authority, Palestinians feel that they have gained a new consciousness which seeks to transcend the Palestinian Authority and Hamas.

The year 2022 has seen the continuation of popular struggles against authoritarianism as well as efforts by authoritarian rulers to crush these struggles with military might and with disinformation. In January 2022, in Kazakhstan, a short-lived nationwide popular uprising involving miners' strikes was brutally crushed by the government with the help of Russian government troops and Russia's regional allies.

On February 24, 2022, Vladimir Putin launched a full-scale invasion of Ukraine and a campaign of mass murder against the Ukrainian people, their right to self-determination, and their desire for a democratic existence. As of this writing in May 2022, the courageous resistance of the Ukrainian people against Russia's invasion continues. Women and feminist activists are an active part of the resistance (Afary, 2022c and Internationalism From Below, 2022). Thousands of Russians, including many women and mothers inside Russia, have been arrested for protesting against this invasion. There have been efforts to organize a Russian feminist anti-war resistance (Afary, 2022b and Internationalism From Below, 2022). However, protests inside Russia have been mostly silenced for now through severe legal penalties and disinformation.

How can all the above movements and struggles connect with each other, with Black Lives Matter and the global #MeToo Movements, and also challenge capitalist authoritarianism? In order to move in that direction, we need to be mindful of what went wrong when an opportunity for global international solidarity emerged a decade earlier and was tragically lost.

LESSONS FROM THE ARAB SPRING AND THE OCCUPY MOVEMENT

In 2011, the world was abuzz with the spirit of the Arab Spring, a revolutionary movement for social justice, freedom, and human dignity, which aimed to overthrow authoritarian states in the Middle East. This movement seemed to come out of nowhere but was actually the result of decades of deep mass dissatisfaction with worsening poverty and political repression under authoritarian regimes such as those of Tunisia, Egypt, Libya, and Syria.

The Arab Spring was really a Middle Eastern Spring that involved non-Arabs and even extended to protests against poverty and corruption in Israel. It was also preceded by the Iranian Green movement, a mass protest movement against the fraudulent Iranian presidential election in 2009, which lasted several months before it was brutally crushed by the Iranian government.

The revolts in Tunisia and in Egypt involved the participation of youth and women as well as large labor unions. They led to the overthrow of the dictators Ben Ali in Tunisia and Hosni Mubarak in Egypt. The uprising in Syria against the regime of Bashar al-Assad had the most diverse composition, involving youth, workers, women, and not only the Sunni Arab majority but also the Kurds, an oppressed national minority, as well as members of the Alawite Muslim minority, Christians, Assyrians, and the Druze Shi'a community.

It was the spirit of the Middle Eastern Spring that many consider to have been the inspiration for the Occupy Movement, which was also a response to the 2008 global economic crisis (Saba, 2011). The first Occupy protest to receive widespread attention was Occupy Wall Street in New York City's Zuccotti Park in September 2011. It became a global movement which spread to 30 countries and all the continents, and stated that it was anti-capitalist. It focused on opposing the influence of corporations in politics, and called for a more equitable distribution of income and for tax reform. Its defining slogan became: "We are the 99%."

More than ten years later, the masses of both Tunisia and Egypt are worse off economically, face greater corruption, and higher unemployment than they did before 2011. In Egypt, after the election of Mohammad Morsi of the Muslim Brotherhood as president, and after the ensuing mass dissatisfaction, a military coup by General Al-Sisi restored the old regime. In Tunisia, authoritarian one-man rule has re-emerged (Yee, 2021).

In Syria, the diverse and powerful mass protests for social justice, democracy, and human dignity were brutally crushed by the Assad regime. Between 2011 and 2016, the majority of the Syrian people continued to resist Assad's death machine which directly or indirectly killed over 500,000 innocent people and caused the displacement of 12 million, or half the population, close to six million of which have become refugees in other countries. The Syrian revolutionaries, under siege mostly by the regime, also faced counter-revolutionary religious fundamentalist forces, including Al-Qaida and The Islamic State of Iraq and Syria (ISIS), some members of which had been let out of prison or let into the country by the Assad regime. The revolutionaries were also assaulted by military intervention from Iran and Russia, countries that support the Assad regime. The Gulf states intervened to promote religious fundamentalism and to destroy the revolution. Turkey intervened to crush the Kurdish struggle for self-determination in the Rojava region and to promote religious fundamentalism. Although the United States and European governments offered some help to the anti-Assad opposition, they eventually decided to let the regime stay in order to maintain "stability" in the region. Their imperialist logic would have never allowed them to support the genuine revolutionaries. In, 2014 however, when ISIS began to pose a real threat to the stability of U.S. interests in the region, the United States directly intervened under the Obama administration, to destroy ISIS (Yassin Kassab & Al-Shami, 2016).

Why couldn't the global Occupy Movement forge alliances with revolutionaries in the Middle East on the basis of a thorough challenge to the capitalist system? First, it has to be acknowledged that the revolutionary movements that became known as the Arab Spring had many internal contradictions, namely, class bias, sexism, various forms of ethnic and religious prejudice, homophobia, and the lack of an alternative to capitalism (Hubbard & Kirkpatrick, 2021). Although the uprising in Syria involved the participation of Kurds and religious minorities, it was not able to offer a banner that was truly inclusive. Most Arab leaders of the Syrian revolution did not welcome any talk of Kurdish self-determination or federalism. Hence, the Assad regime was able to take advantage of the class and ethnic divisions that already existed within the Syrian society. The Kurdish Rojava region, in northern Syria, was able to offer a model that included secularism and the recognition of some rights for women as well as the strong and heroic participation of women guerrillas in the struggle against ISIS (Knapp, Flach, & Ayboga, 2016; Moradi, 2018). However, the Rojava leadership—the Democratic Union Party, PYD or YPG—also embodied certain authoritarian practices and views, and engaged in off and on non-aggression pacts with the Assad regime (Daher, 2019).

What about the Occupy Movement? What were its defects? I would argue that its main defect was that it reduced anti-capitalism to simply being against income inequality, big corporations, Wall Street, and neoliberalism. Another major defect of the Occupy Movement was that it limited imperialism to simply Western imperialism. Hence, although the Occupy Movement was inspired by the Arab Spring, many of those on the Left who called themselves anti-imperialist supported the Assad regime in Syria because it claimed to be against U.S. imperialism and its regional imperialist backers, Israel and Saudi Arabia. Some leftists also openly supported Russian imperialist intervention in the Middle East and Ukraine, as well as Iranian regional imperialist intervention in Syria and in Iraq. This unprincipled and inhumane attitude, this failure of those who claim to be against capitalism to see the connection between capitalism and the rise of imperialist powers other than those in the West, was another one of the factors that led to the destruction of the Syrian revolution (Hensman, 2018).

Thus, in 2011, even though humanity had an unprecedented chance to launch a global anti-capitalist movement, that chance was lost. It was lost both because of counter-revolutionary forces, such as repressive regimes, imperialist intervention, and religious fundamentalism in the Middle East, and because of defects within the revolutionary movements in the Arab Spring and within the Occupy Movement in the West. The movements in the East and the West failed to connect because of the lack of an affirmative, humanist alternative to capitalism (Afary, 2017).

As a result, the capitalist drive for profitability, which had encountered a major crisis in 2008, was able to use the language of anti-globalization, and appeal to racism, sexism, and homophobia to win over parts of the global working class. Thus, we saw the victory of Donald J. Trump in the 2016 U.S. presidential election. Thus, authoritarian state capitalist regimes, such as those in China and Russia which were treated as exceptions to capitalism, have now become the image of the future for the rest of humanity.

* * *

In 2022, there is a chance to learn from these mistakes and to forge a powerful alliance between the Black Lives Matter Movement, the #MeToo Movement, and a new wave of global uprisings against authoritarianism (Economist, 2020e). What is different about the current movements and uprisings is that feminist demands especially opposing gender and state violence are being explicitly put forth by many women participants. Black Lives Matter is putting the issue of opposition to anti-Black racism, and indeed any form of racial or ethnic discrimination, on the agenda of world struggles. Ecological demands to cleanse and to preserve nature, and to tackle climate change are being made explicitly. At the same time, a tendency to reduce capitalism to neoliberalism, private property and the "free" market remains. There is also much confusion about the realities of imperialism in the twenty-first century.

Any effort to create revolutionary international alliances needs to challenge the intertwining of capitalism, imperialism, racism, sexism, and heterosexism, and to develop an affirmative humanist alternative. It is toward this aim that this book's rethinking of socialist feminism for the twenty-first century has been centered.

3

Women, Reproductive Labor, and Capital Accumulation: Theories of Social Reproduction

This chapter begins with socialist feminist theories of social reproduction, by which I mean theories that explain gender oppression by focusing on the relationship between domestic or reproductive labor and the creation of value under capitalism. These theories remain highly relevant in a world in which 75 percent of unpaid care and domestic work is done by women (Charmes, 2019).

I come to this subject with deep empathy. My Iranian grandmothers and great-grandmothers were child brides who endured multiple pregnancies, miscarriages from overwork, and loss of children. They spent a significant portion of their lives nursing and caring for multiple children as well as tending to their husband and in-laws and in some cases baking bread and selling it door to door to earn a living. Most women around the world are still suffering from a similar fate.

In 2018, a study by the British Office for National Statistics determined that if a monetary value were to be placed on a year's worth of women's household chores such as washing dishes and taking care of children, that value would amount to "1.2 trillion pounds a year, about 1.6 trillion dollars" in Britain (Yeginsu, 2018). A global study by the Oxford Committee for Famine Relief (Oxfam) supposed paying women and girls a minimum wage for their 12.5 billion hours per day of unpaid household and care work. It estimated the value of that work at 10.8 trillion dollars for the year 2019, with women in India doing the largest share (Oxfam, 2020; Wezerek & Ghodsee, 2020). Another recent official study has determined that in the United States, a woman earns only 49 cents for every dollar that a man earns. This figure is far less than the commonly stated figure of 80 cents for every dollar, because it takes into account all the time that women take to care for children and elderly members of their families (Newburger, 2018). Another study, by feminist economist Nina Banks (2020), has put a value on the historically overlooked and uncompensated work of community activism by Black and other marginalized women (see also Nelson, 2021).

First, let's begin with a brief summary of the main theories of social reproduction from 1969 to today. Next follows a review of some of the categories that these theories borrow from Karl Marx's *Capital*. Finally, I present a critical evaluation of the main arguments of Social Reproduction Theory, with an attempt to draw out their assumptions and logical conclusions in order to examine their relevance for the twenty-first century.

SUMMARY OF THE MAIN THEORIES OF SOCIAL REPRODUCTION

The year 2019 marked the 50th anniversary of the publication of Margaret Benston's (1969) essay, "The Political Economy of Women's Liberation," which was published by *Monthly Review* and articulated the Marxist discussion of what came to be known as the "domestic labor debate." Benston, Professor of Chemistry, Computing Science, and later Women's Studies, at Simon Fraser University in Vancouver, British Columbia, was a respected feminist and labor activist.

In her 1969 essay, Benston argued that in a society in which receiving money for work is the measure of the value of that work, the material basis of the inferior status of women is that their household labor lies outside the money economy. Household labor, she emphasized, is in the pre-market stage and thus produces only simple use-values, not exchange-value. The solution she offered was to industrialize housework, that is, convert the private production of housework into public production, and do so without the profit motive and in a socialist society.

Three years later, in 1971, Selma James, a U.S. socialist feminist anti-racist activist and Mariarosa Dalla Costa, an Italian socialist feminist, co-wrote the pamphlet, *The Power of Woman and the Subversion of the Community*, which came to be known as the founding document of the International Wages for Housework Campaign (1972) and later the Global Women's Strike (2000) (see Dalla Costa & James, 1971).

Like Benston, they claimed that the material basis of women's specific oppression was unwaged housework. They went on to argue that demanding wages for housework from the state, as the representative of collective capital, "must be our lever of power" in the struggle against capitalism (James, 2012, p. 45).

They differed from Benston because they believed that under capitalism, women's domestic and reproductive labor produces not only simple use-value but also exchange-value (James, 2012, pp. 50–1). Hence, they concluded that a movement of women refusing to do domestic labor could be "a fundamental lever of social power" against capitalism, and that "the role of the working-class housewife ... is *the* determinant" (p. 54). Women should not only refuse to do housework and destroy the role of housewife but also "refuse the myth of liberation through work" outside the home and reject the capitalist mode of labor altogether because, they argued, it was based on control and regimentation (p. 59).

In her work, *Revolution at Point Zero: Housework, Reproduction, and Feminist Struggle*, Silvia Federici (2012), an Italian feminist academic/activist and the founder of the U.S. branch of Wages for Housework, identified the main influences that led to the creation of this campaign. Federici (2011) wrote: "Women who launched Wages for Housework [in 1972], came from a history of militancy in Marxist-identified organizations filtered through the experiences of the anti-colonial movement, the Civil Rights Movement, the Student Movement and the [Italian] 'Operaist' [workerist] movement" (p. 6). They saw the home and housework [not only housewives] as foundations of the factory system because "capitalism requires unwaged reproductive labor to contain the cost of labor power" (p. 8). Hence, the Wages for Housework theorists believed that "a successful campaign draining the source of this unpaid labor would break the process of capital accumulation and confront capital and the state on a terrain common to most women" (pp. 8–9).

In another work, *Caliban and the Witch: Women, the Body and Primitive Accumulation*, Federici (2004) suggested that the rise of capitalism in the 1500s and 1600s relied heavily on the imposition of a new reign of patriarchy, based on the devaluation (de-waging) of women's reproductive work and an assault on women's knowledge of the significance of women's own reproductive power.

Wages for Housework also broadened its focus to include the reproductive labor of all mothers, subsistence and family farmers, people on welfare, those with disabilities, sex workers, and prisoners.

An effort to critically appropriate and expand the work of Benston, on the one hand, and Selma James and Mariarosa Dalla Costa, on the other hand, can be seen in Lise Vogel's (1983/2014) *Marxism and the Oppression of Women: Toward a Unitary Theory*. Vogel specifically aimed to respond to socialist feminists who espoused a "dual systems theory," that is, socialist feminists who made a clear distinction between women's oppression through patriarchy and women's exploitation through capitalism. Vogel challenged the view of patriarchy as an autonomous system. Instead, she built on theories of social reproduction to develop what she called a "unitary theory" of women's oppression.

Vogel (2014) argued that women's reproductive labor does not produce exchange-value in the capitalist sense (p. 192). However, women's reproduction of the labor force, especially through generational replacement (that is, having and raising children), creates a portion of what Marx calls "necessary labor" or the labor that is needed to produce the basic needs of the worker. Thus, although women's labor is outside capitalist production, it indirectly contributes to capitalist accumulation (Marx, 1976, quoted in Vogel, 1983, p. 152). In the later 2014 edition of her work, Vogel made a correction and stated that from a capitalist standpoint, women's reproductive labor does not create a portion of "necessary labor" because reproductive labor is not a cost to the capitalist. However, she argued that women's reproductive labor still contributes to necessary labor in an indirect way.

Vogel further argued that although the domestic component of necessary labor might be reduced to a minimum by capitalism, it can never be completely socialized under capitalism. Since the process of childbearing will continue to be the province of women, capitalism faces a contradiction. On the one hand, women's giving birth to children is essential for capitalism because it produces labor power. On the other hand, women's childbearing limits the availability of women's labor power. Therefore, Vogel (1983) wrote, "over the long term, the capitalist class seeks to stabilize the reproduction of labor power at a low cost and with a minimum of domestic labor" (p. 156). The alternative to capitalism that she advocated was a society based on the abolition of private property, with a planned economy, and with public or social production that would lessen the burdens of domestic labor and allow domestic partners to share that labor. In this process, she argued, the family, patriarchy, and the oppression of women would wither away (Vogel, 1983, pp. 174–5).

In the later 2014 edition of her book, Vogel clarified that reproduction of labor power can also take place through migration and slavery. She also called attention to the role of Assisted Reproductive Technologies (ART) in the twenty-first century: "[R]eproduction of labor power is not invariably associated with the private kin-based household as the domestic labor debate commonly assumed. In particular, it does not necessarily entail … heterosexuality, biological procreation, family forms and generational replacement" (Vogel, 2014, p. 189).

Up to now, we have established that there are two main branches within Social Reproduction Theory. First, there are those who argue that unpaid domestic and reproductive labor produce use-value which indirectly contributes to the capitalist process of production. Second, there are those who argue that this labor produces not only use-value but also exchange-value, and hence contributes directly to the process of capital accumulation.

In order to critically evaluate these claims, let's return to Marx's *Capital*, for a direct encounter with the categories that social reproduction theorists have borrowed from him. How does Marx explain value, use-value, exchange-value, surplus value, productive labor, and the accumulation of capital, in his own words?

REVISITING THE CONCEPTS OF VALUE, PRODUCTIVE LABOR, AND THE ACCUMULATION OF CAPITAL IN MARX'S *CAPITAL*

In chapter 1 of *Capital*, Marx (1976) explains that the most important feature distinguishing capitalism from previous economic systems is: "the production of value. Nothing can be a value without being an object of utility" (p. 131). Value, however, he argues, is the expression of a particular mode of labor which is specific to capitalism. The "substance" of value is mechanical, general, "abstract," that is, undifferentiated human labor (p. 131). It is a type of labor that was not dominant prior to the rise of the capitalist mode of production in the 1500s in Europe.

In his earlier work, the *Economic and Philosophical Manuscripts of 1844*, Marx (1961) had described this type of labor under capitalism as one which was alienated from its product, from its activity, from other human beings, and from the human potential for "free conscious activity" (p. 101). He had emphasized that the worker "does not develop freely his mental and physical energies but is physically exhausted and mentally debased … . His work is not voluntary but imposed *forced* labor.

It is not the satisfaction of a need but only a *means* for satisfying other needs" (p. 98).

Later in the first chapter of *Capital*, he further expanded this idea by discussing what he called the "dual character of labor" under capitalism. He counterposed "abstract," general, undifferentiated labor to "concrete," purposeful, differentiated labor. He also made a similar distinction between *labor power as a commodity* and *labor as an activity*.

On the one hand, all labour is an expenditure of human labour-power in the physiological sense, and it is in this quality of being equal, or abstract human labour that it forms the value of commodities. On the other hand, all labour is an expenditure of human labour-power in a particular form and with a definite aim, and it is in this quality of being concrete useful labour that it produces use-values. (Marx, 1976, p. 137)

He explains this distinction further:

While therefore with reference to use-value, the labour contained in a commodity counts only qualitatively, with reference to value it counts only quantitatively, once it has been reduced to human labour, pure and simple. In the former case, it was a matter of the "how" and the "what" of labour, in the latter of the 'how much', of the temporal duration of labour. (Marx, 1976, p. 136)

In the first chapter of *Capital*, Marx also makes a distinction between the "substance" of value explained above and the "form of appearance" of value which is exchange-value or money (Marx, 1976, p. 139; see also Khosravi, 2017). In his view, money is simply the expression of this general, homogeneous, abstract, undifferentiated, alienated human labor which is specific to the capitalist mode of production. Although money in the form of coins had been used since the sixth century B.C.E. and in other forms since centuries before (Nova, 1996), money and exchange of commodities had not started to become widely used prior to the rise of capitalism in Europe in the 1500s.

Marx (1976) also defines the "magnitude" of value as time, but not time in general. Rather, what he calls "socially necessary labour time" or the amount of time required to produce a use-value based on average skill and average intensity of labour (p. 129). In other words, under capitalism, since labor has a dual character, both concrete labor and abstract alienated labor are reduced to something mechanical, general, and homogeneous. Their measure becomes a socially average amount of time, or socially necessary labor time.

Now that the basic understanding of the concept of value as the expression of alienated labor has been outlined, let's go on to explore the concept of surplus value.

In part 2 of *Capital*, "The Transformation of Money into Capital," Marx (1976) argued that the capitalist (whether an individual or a corporation or the state as capitalist) becomes rich by buying a commodity called labor power which, in the process of production, produces a value greater than itself. The capitalist buys labor power at its value, that is, the value (based on socially necessary labor time or socially average time) of the means of subsistence necessary for the production and reproduction of this worker and their family. These necessities include food, clothing, fuel, housing, transportation, education, etc. However, the manner in which these needs are satisfied differ in each country and are based on the physical peculiarities, customs, and level of historical development of each country (p. 275). Therefore, buying labor power at value in the United States, where there is for the most part a higher standard of living than the developing nations, is not the same in cost as buying labor power at value in China or in India where the standard of living for the majority of the population is much lower.

Marx (1976) demonstrates that since the goal of capitalism is the valorization of value, it is not enough for the worker to produce a value that is equivalent to the value of their wages. If it takes half the working day to produce a value equivalent to a worker's wages, the other half of the working day produces surplus value for the capitalist. The value of the worker's labor power (that is, the worker's wage) will be less than the value of the goods and services which the laborer produces. Marx (1976) emphasized that now "The trick has at last worked: money has been transformed into capital" (p. 301).

If we compare the process of creating value with the process of valorization (or surplus value creation), we see that the valorization process is nothing but the continuation of the process of creating value beyond a definite point (Marx, 1976, p. 302). That is, beyond the point at which the worker has made the equivalent of their wages.

Another way of looking at this process is through using the categories,"necessary labor" and "surplus labor." If a worker works 12 hours per day, and if it takes six hours to produce the daily customary necessities of the worker and their family, or the equivalent of the value of the worker's wages, then these six hours constitute "necessary labor." The remaining six hours constitute "surplus labor" (Marx, 1976, p. 325).

Marx demonstrated that from the standpoint of capitalism, the only labor that is considered "productive" is the labor that produces surplus value. That is because capitalism is a mode of production based on the production of value, and its goal is therefore the valorization of value or expansion of value as an end in itself. Although from a moral and ethical standpoint and certainly from the standpoint of Marx's humanist philosophy, domestic and reproductive labor is valuable, it is not considered value producing from a capitalist standpoint. The time that a woman spends on cooking a nutritious meal for her family, tending to her children and her husband, and to their daily physical and emotional needs, results in no surplus value in so far as the capitalist is concerned.

However, reproductive labor, if sold for the purpose of producing surplus value and subject to socially necessary labor time and the laws of the global market, can be considered "productive" from a capitalist standpoint. Marx (1976) gives the example of a school teacher at a for-profit school whose labor would be considered "productive." He argues that from the vantage point of capitalism, a teacher who instructs students is not a productive worker. However, a teacher whose work increases the profits of the "knowledge-mongering institution" is a "productive worker" (p. 644). We can also offer other examples. For instance, a woman worker who cleans an office, a cook who makes food for a company, a caregiver in a for-profit hospital, or a sex worker who sells her services to an enterprise which makes profit from her labor, all produce surplus value. In contrast, when the same type of work is performed in a domestic setting and for one's children and husband, there is no surplus value.[1]

Finally, another category that social reproduction theorists have borrowed from Marx (1976) is "accumulation of capital" or what he calls "expanded reproduction." Marx emphasized that what takes place in the capitalist process of expanded reproduction is that an increasing portion of the surplus value generated by laborers goes toward expanding the means of production (machinery, tools, buildings, roads) at the expense of wages, and more broadly at the expense of humanity and nature.

Capitalism is obsessed with expanding the means of production at the expense of humanity and nature because more efficient means of production (faster machines, for example) allow capitalists to increase the rate of extraction of surplus value from workers and make them produce more in less time or work more intensely. That is why Marx argued that the goal of capitalism and the logic of capital is the expansion of value as an end in itself. For capitalism, humans and nature are simply a mere means for the expansion of value, and not ends in themselves (pp. 735–7). The worker as a human being has no value for the capitalist. If they died as a result of sheer exhaustion from work they performed, they could be replaced with a younger worker. There was thus no value in trying to protect the worker's life.

In addition, Marx's (1976) *Capital* demonstrated that capitalism, from its beginnings and throughout its existence, has relied on various forms of slave labor. Capitalism transformed slavery from a patriarchal institution into a commercial one in which the exploitation of slaves was greatly increased to produce value.

Now that some of the main categories in Marx's *Capital* have been clarified, let's return to the social reproduction theorists described earlier, and to more recent theorists in this field, in order to critically examine their views.

CRITICALLY EXAMINING SOCIAL REPRODUCTION THEORIES

We began this chapter by summarizing the two main branches of Social Reproduction Theory. One branch argued that women's domestic and reproductive labor for the family produced use-value only. Another branch argued that domestic and reproductive labor under capitalism produced use-value as well as exchange-value.

In examining Marx's definitions of value, surplus value, productive labor, and the accumulation of capital, we learned that from a capitalist standpoint, labor is considered "productive" or "value" producing if it has a dual character (abstract/concrete), is measured by socially necessary labor time, and is produced for the market (domestic or global).

Some of the latest articulations of Social Reproduction Theory by Marxist feminists, such as Tithi Bhattacharya and Susan Ferguson, can help us appreciate why this distinction between "productive" and "non-productive" labor is important, and at the same time why the role of reproductive labor in capitalist production cannot be ignored.

Tithi Bhattacharya (2020) has argued that although women's domestic and reproductive labor outside the market do not create value and surplus value, they do represent a "nonmonetary set of social relations" which prepare labor power for reproductive work. In that sense, capitalism's "productive labor" depends on women's reproductive labor (see also Elson, 1994). She has emphasized that socialist feminists need to begin with the question of *who* produces labor power and under what conditions. Domestic and reproductive labor produce labor power. Therefore, capitalism has an interest in maintaining the heteronormative family form as well as a public sector that includes educational, health care, recreational facilities or even slave forms of labor (Bhattacharya, 2020).

Social Reproduction Theory, in her view, "restore[s] to the 'economic' process, its messy, sensuous, gendered, raced and unruly component" (Bhattacharya, 2017, p. 70). It also explores how the logic of capital accumulation does or does not affect the production of human beings away from the site of production of commodities (p. 72). It considers the role that "such spaces play in organizing against capital" (p. 91).

Susan Ferguson (2019) has brought to our attention issues raised by some Black feminists: "That not all housework is unpaid and not all women see the work that they do to maintain the households (and communities) as inherently oppressive" and also that "women are oppressed in ways that have nothing to do with housework" (p. 106).

Rather than focusing on unpaid housework as the explanation of women's oppression, Ferguson (2019) has presented oppression as capitalism's "devaluation of life-making" (p. 111). Building on Lise Vogel's (1983, 2014) work, she has argued that "neither the gender division of labor, nor the family itself constitute the material basis of women's oppression." Instead, women's oppression under capitalism is rooted in "the necessary but contradictory relation of the reproduction of labor power to capitalist accumulation" (p. 113). In other words, "the point is that all processes of social reproduction (not just those in individual households) come up against capitalism's hostility to life" because resources for reproducing life are "owned by capital and the capitalist state" (p. 114). Capitalism needs laborers to produce value. For this reason, it needs to minimize the portion of value that goes into developing and maintaining living laborers (p. 111).

Ferguson (2019) has also built on the work of Silvia Federici, Maria Mies, and Sadie Alexander, and has similarly emphasized that capitalism is "developed through a reliance upon those social oppressions that divide and subjugate bodies according to 'race,' gender, sexuality and more" (p. 115).

For all the above reasons, Ferguson (2019) has concluded that "social reproductive labor is the coercive underbelly of capitalist value creation" (p. 121). Value creation requires both "productive" and "non-productive" labor. However, this does not mean that domestic and reproductive labor indirectly create value. In contrast to Leopoldina Fortunati (1995), who has argued that social reproductive labor has a dual character (abstract/concrete) and indirectly creates value because its ultimate product, labor power, is a commodity (pp. 105–11), Ferguson (2019) has argued that social reproductive labor is not abstract/undifferentiated and is mostly not produced for the market (p. 124). She has emphasized that although workers' control over the content, pace, and timing of work is considerably less among paid social reproductive workers who are subject to the disciplining logic of capital accumulation, capital's domination of these jobs is often less direct among public sector teachers and care providers. "The production of life regularly requires resisting the subsumption of life to capital" (Ferguson, 2019, p. 128). Thus teachers and personal support workers need to take more time with students or clients. In this process, social reproduction workers "establish connections with others that cut against the alienating tendencies of capitalism" (Ferguson, 2019, p. 129).

Bhattacharya and Ferguson have addressed some important questions with regard to the role of women's labor and its relation to capitalism. However, some unresolved questions remain. All social reproduction theorists assume that the private kin-based family is not the only site of reproduction of the working class. However, most argue that capitalism can never stop relying on the private family to reproduce the working class. In the 1983 edition of her *Marxism and the Oppression of Women*, Vogel argued that the family "cannot be completely socialized in a capitalist society. The main barrier is economic for the costs are extremely high in such areas as child rearing and household maintenance … . The basic physiological process of childbearing will continue to be the province of women" (Vogel, 1983, pp. 155–6). In the 2014 edition of her *Marxism and the Oppression of Women*, however, Vogel changed her view and argued that the reproduction of labor power does not necessarily require any form of the family (Vogel, 2014, p. 189).

Silvia Federici (2004, 2011) has argued that doing away with unpaid domestic labor would be too costly for capitalism and would seriously affect its rate of accumulation of capital. In addition, in an interview, she has pointed out that capitalism needs unpaid domestic labor in marriage to divide men and women and to "pacify men, giving them a servant on whom to exercise their power" (Federici, Souvlis, & Čakardić, 2017).

Joan Smith (1977, 1978), author of the two-part "Women and the Family," agrees with this analysis. She has argued that

> because of the importance of the Family as a cheap means of reproducing wage-labour, the abolition of the family system in any *one* Capitalism could only be accomplished by the abolition of the family system in all capitalisms .... If, however, it is argued that all Capitalisms can abolish the family at a stroke and institute a "Brave New World" or "1984" of test-tube babies, baby farms, etc., then, the question we must look at is the nature of free wage-labour. (Smith, 1977, p. 25)

In other words, Smith (1977) has argued that in such a society we will no longer have a capitalist system of "free wage-labour" in the sense of workers selling their labor power. Instead, we will move away from capitalism and return to a pre-capitalist society that re-establishes a modern form of slavery as the mode of production.

Similarly, Martha Gimenez (2018) has argued that the continued socialization of family, under capitalism, and the reproduction of labor power on a highly advanced capitalist basis, would destroy the material basis for the production of free individuals, autonomous and responsible for their own success or failure, which constitute the cornerstone of a capitalist social and market relations (p. 75).

Michele Barrett (1980), in her *Women's Oppression Today: The Marxist-Feminist Encounter*, does not see the gender division of labor as an essential part of capitalism. She has argued that although capitalism has historically benefited from the sexual division of labor, women's domestic labor and the separation of the domestic sphere from the realm of wage labor, "it is more difficult to argue that gender division *necessarily* occupies a particular place in the class structure of capitalism. It has not, at least as yet, been demonstrated that the sexual division of labour forms not simply a *historically* constituted but a *logically pre-given* element of the class structure [of capitalism]" (p. 138).

In order to prove this claim, Barrett (1980) has argued that with the widespread use of computers, the separation of the domestic sphere from the sphere of wage labor is no longer necessary for capitalism. This separation, which was a characteristic of industrial capitalism, is no longer "a functional prerequisite of capitalist production" (p. 175). Furthermore, she has pointed out that under capitalism, it is possible to socialize domestic labor and childrearing to a much greater extent. In other words, in Barrett's (1980) opinion, reorganizing capitalist relations of production without the need for women's domestic labor and the nuclear family is entirely possible (p. 211). Because, she states, "I am not convinced that this household structure is potentially the most beneficial for capital" (p. 221). "[T]his particular form of household and its accompanying ideology of women's dependence is not the only possible form for an efficient reproduction of labor power in capitalist relations of production" (p. 249).

Angela Y. Davis (1983) has also argued that

housework cannot be defined as an integral component of capitalist production. It is rather related to production as a *precondition*. The employer is not concerned in the least about the way labor power is produced and sustained. He is only concerned about its availability and its ability to generate profit. In other words, the capitalist production process presupposes the existence of a body of exploitable workers. (p. 234, emphasis in the original)

Davis's (1983) discussion of male worker dormitories in South Africa under apartheid has provided a very illuminating example. She writes: "The social architects of Apartheid have simply determined that Black labor yields higher profits when domestic life is all but entirely discarded. Black men are viewed as labor units whose productive potential renders them valuable to the capitalist class. But their wives and children 'are superfluous appendages'" (p. 235). South Africa established an apartheid system, where women and children were relegated to Bantustans. Other capitalist countries, such as the Gulf states, achieve the same through the exploitation of migrant workers who live in sex-segregated hostels and work 16–18 hours per day for five years or more, leaving their families behind in their native land (Amnesty International, 2020b; Economist, 2020i). The above debate and examples are critically important in light of the global rise of a capitalist authoritarianism that leaves no room for workers' unions and has blurred the boundary between "free labor" and slave labor.

SOCIAL REPRODUCTION THEORY AND THE CHALLENGE OF CAPITALIST AUTHORITARIANISM

When Marx (1976, 1981) defined the capitalist wage-laborer as being "free," he meant that one is free from the means of production and formally free to sell one's labor. However, he emphasized that this "freedom" was another form of slavery. The capitalist mode of production, based on alienated labor and the domination of dead labor (machines) over living labor (human beings), was in fact not free at all. Marx also argued that capitalism used slavery not only in the stage of "primitive accumulation" or "original accumulation" but in all its stages.[2]

Although Marx (1976) saw the world market as an essential feature of capitalism, his discussion of capitalist accumulation emphasized capitalism's drive toward the greater concentration and centralization of capital in fewer hands and even in the hands of "a single capitalist or a single capitalist corporation" in a given society and within the context of the world market. Marx (1976) concluded that

> In any given branch of industry, centralization would reach its extreme limit if all the individual capitals invested there were fused into a single capital. In a given society this limit would be reached only when the entire social capital was united in the hands of either a single capitalist or a single capitalist company. (p. 779)

One can argue that Marx anticipated the emergence of an authoritarian state capitalism as the direction of global capitalism. However, he did not theorize that concept or its relation to the family.

Today, the realities of global capitalism in the twenty-first century compel us to seriously address the possibility of authoritarian state capitalism taking charge of all aspects of life, including the family. Consider phenomena such as the factory/dormitory in China or the practice of putting migrant workers or oppressed ethnic or racial minorities in camps such as in Xinjiang province and placing their children in orphanages, or the mass incarceration of African Americans in the prison-industrial complex in the United States, or the new technological experiments with altering genes in fetuses and research on ectogenesis (Alexander, 2020; Economist, 2020i; Sedgwick, 2017a). All point to ominous directions that need to be analyzed by socialist feminists.

We should, therefore, consider the possibility that reproductive labor could be fully socialized through state capitalist industrialization of domestic and reproductive activity. Since capitalism's goal is the self-expansion of value as an end in itself, it has proven to be very dynamic. Thus, it is entirely possible to have a state capitalist society that would separate adult members of the working class from their small children, placing the children in 24-hour childcare centers to be raised as future workers, and forcing the adult members of the working class, of all genders, into work camps where they would work, eat, and sleep.

At the same time, given the changing nature of production in our time, and the ways in which the COVID-19 pandemic has massively increased the reliance of capitalism on distance work, especially for white-collar workers, the clear distinction between the domestic sphere and the value production sphere, which many definitions of capitalism have taken for granted, is fast eroding. Today's Second Machine Age, with its gig economy and distance work through the use of information technology, means that domestic and reproductive labor in the home can be done more frequently alongside work for pay done at home. The COVID-19 pandemic has also shown that this transformation in capitalism can easily lead to an even more intense and stressful work life, as well as sleep deprivation, especially for women.

Furthermore, in the twenty-first century, capitalism's dangerous scientific experimentation with genetically engineering human reproduction is now manifest in gene editing. Gene editing has been used by a scientist, Ha Jianhui, in China, and possibly by others, to genetically modify embryos. This technology can be used and is most likely already being used to create humans with superior skills or desired physical features (Kolata, Wee, & Belluck, 2018). Its use to alter natural embryos, a practice which many other scientists in the field have strongly condemned, has some very dangerous ramifications. In addition to being used for racist, sexist, and capitalist purposes, it can lead to the creation of unexpected mutations, which are then passed on to the next generation.

Ectogenesis, or the invention of an artificial external womb, is also seriously on the horizon and could completely change the nature of human reproduction within a few generations. In April 2017, researchers at the Children's Hospital of Philadelphia announced that they had developed an artificial womb, which they called the "biobag" (Cohen, 2017). The biobag is intended to improve the survival rates of premature babies and is a significant step forward from conventional incubators. Researchers at Cambridge University have also kept a human embryo alive outside the body for 13 days by using a mix of nutrients that mimic conditions in the womb. Researchers state that the embryo could have survived longer than 13 days but had to be destroyed because of medical ethics laws (Johnston, 2016). Thus, as the technology to keep an embryo alive develops further and the incubator technology improves (Kolata, 2021), the idea of developing an embryo and fetus entirely outside the mother's womb comes closer to reality.

In the words of Helen Sedgwick (2017b), the author of *The Growing Season*, a novel about ectogenesis, this technology could give women more choices and dismantle the gender hierarchies within our society, but it could also be used for harvesting spare parts and taking away abortion rights, "with women forced to have their fetuses extracted and gestated outside the body" (2017a). We are not so far from the realm of science fiction where such a technology, in combination with gene editing, could also be used to harvest human beings for whatever purpose capitalism finds profitable, whether as slaves or as super-humans.

CONCLUSION

In this chapter, both branches of Social Reproduction Theory have been presented and discussed. Both those who argue that reproductive work produces exchange-value and those who argue that it produces only use-value agree on one point: that the fundamental basis of gender oppression under capitalism is the devaluation of women's reproductive labor.

For Benston (1969) and Vogel (1983, 2014), women's specific oppression in capitalism is rooted in the fact that women's domestic and reproductive labor fall outside the labor market. Hence, such labor is devalued. The solution they offer is to socialize domestic and reproductive labor, to bring women into the labor market to join the class struggle against capitalism, and to create a socialist society where reproductive work would be fully socialized.

For James (2012), Dalla Costa and James (1971), Federici (2004, 2011), and other proponents of Wages for Housework, the foundation of women's specific oppression is that capitalism, from its inception, has de-waged women's domestic and reproductive labor, and thereby, has created an unequal power relationship between women and men. They have advocated wages for housework in order to "denaturalize" house-work as women's work and also to allow domestic and reproductive workers to join the class struggle and oppose capitalist domination and hierarchy, whether they work inside or outside of the home. Bhattacha-rya (2017, 2020), Ferguson (2019), and others have applied aspects of Social Reproduction Theory to the situation of both unwaged and waged domestic and reproductive workers on a global scale.

But one can also ask the following question: Is it adequate to theorize women's oppression on the basis of capitalism's unequal distribution of wealth? Does that lens (I am using Vogel's term) help us come up with a unitary theory that does not separate patriarchy from capitalism and oppression from exploitation?

In the next chapter, I will examine a different theory of gender oppression, one that is based on alienated labor under capitalism and views alienation as a phenomenon that affects all spheres of life, including family and love relationships. Also examined will be Marx's claim that the capitalist mode of production, rooted in alienated and mechanical labor, destroys nature, *thingifies* or *reifies* human relationships, and therefore, makes them utilitarian, and that capitalist alienated labor also creates resistance and the quest for new human relationships.

4

Alienated Labor and How It Relates to Gender Oppression

> In the relationship with *woman*, as the prey and handmaid of communal lust, is expressed the infinite degradation in which man [*Mensch*] exists for himself.
>
> —Marx (1961), *Economic and Philosophical Manuscripts of 1844*

Can alienated labor be seen as the foundation of gender oppression under capitalism? Let's begin by briefly reviewing Marx's (1961, 1976) concept of alienated labor in his *Economic and Philosophical Manuscripts of 1844*, and in *Capital* in order to see if Marx provided us with signposts that might illuminate the relationship between the capitalist mode of production and the specific oppression of women. Next, let's look at the views of Angela Y. Davis, Raya Dunayevskaya, Heather A. Brown, Ann Foreman, Judith Grant, and Marcia Klotz on this question.

Socialist feminists, who are discussed in this chapter, argue that instead of focusing on the role of women as producers of labor power, we need to address the relationship between alienated labor and alienation in gender and sexual relationships. They draw on Marx's concept of alienated labor to ask how the capitalist mode of production itself, and not only its unequal distribution of value, promotes and intensifies objectified, distorted gender relationships.

WHAT IS ALIENATED LABOR? EXPLORING MARX'S 1844 MANUSCRIPTS AND CAPITAL

In his *Economic and Philosophical Manuscripts of 1844*, also known as the Humanist Essays, Marx expresses his critique of capitalism and of classical political economy, not by beginning with money, the private property of the means of production, capitalist competition, and monopoly, but by beginning with labor or what he calls "alienated labor." He argues that "although private property appears to be the basis and cause of alien-ated labor, it is rather a consequence" (Marx & Fromm, 1961, p. 106). He further explains, "in speaking of private property, one believes oneself to be dealing with something external to humankind. But in speaking of labor, one deals directly with humankind itself. This new formula-tion of the problem already contains its solution" (Marx & Fromm, 1961, p. 108).[1]

Marx's goal is to get to the root of the problems of exploitation and of oppression under capitalism. In order to do so, he defines four character-istics of alienated labor. While he used the pronoun "he" because he lived in the nineteenth century, what he wrote is just as relevant to women and transgender people:

(1)
The *alienation* of the worker in his product means not only that his labor becomes an object, assumes an *external existence*, but that it exists independently, *outside himself*, and alien to him, and that it stands opposed to him as an autonomous power. The life which he has given to the object sets itself against him as an alien and hostile force. (Marx and Fromm, 1961, p. 96; emphasis in the original)

(2)
[This] alienation appears not only in the result of labor but also in the *process of production*. ... The work is *external* to the worker ... it is not part of his nature ... he does not fulfill himself in his work but denies himself, has a feeling of misery rather than well-being, does not develop freely his mental and physical energies but is physically exhausted and mentally debased. The worker therefore feels himself at home only during his leisure time, whereas at work he feels homeless. His work is not voluntary but imposed, *forced labor*. It is not the satis-faction of a need, but only a *means* for satisfying other needs. Its alien character is clearly shown by the fact that as soon as there is no physical or other compulsion, it is avoided like the plague. (Marx and Fromm, 1965, pp. 98–9; emphasis in the original)

Elsewhere and in further explicating this concept, he writes "This is *self-alienation* as against the above-mentioned alienation of the thing" (Marx & Fromm, 1961, p. 100, emphasis in the original).

(3) The "species character" of human beings or what distinguishes us from other animals is our ability for "free, conscious activity" (Marx & Fromm, 1961, p. 101). Unlike animals who produce only what is strictly necessary for themselves or their young, and produce in a single direction, humans produce universally and also in accordance with standards of beauty. Alienated labor does not only make the objects and activity of our labor alien, but also alienates humans from their ability for free, conscious activity. Thus, it turns human life into a mere "means of physical existence" (Marx & Fromm, 1961, p. 103).[2]

(4) A direct consequence of the above-described characteristics of alienated labor is that humans also become alienated from other human beings.

Having established the four characteristics of alienated labor, Marx argued that this type of labor leads to relations of domination and coercion in all aspects of life:

> If he is related to his own activity as to unfree activity, then he is related to it as activity in the service, and under the domination, coercion and yoke of another man. Every self-alienation of man, from himself and from nature, appears in the relations which he postulates between other men and himself and nature. (Marx & Fromm, 1961, p. 105)

Thus, "the relation of the worker to work also produces the relation of the capitalist (or whatever one likes to call the lord of labor) to work" (Marx, 1961, p. 105). This is why Marx concluded that "*Private property* is therefore the product, the necessary result of *alienated labor*, of the external relation of the worker to nature and to himself" (Marx & Fromm, 1961, p. 106, emphasis in the original). It is *not* the cause but the *consequence* of alienated labor.

The wage system was also "a necessary consequence of the alienation of labor" (Marx & Fromm, 1961, p. 106). "An enforced increase in wages … would be nothing more than a *better remuneration of slaves,* and would not restore, either to the worker or to the work, their human significance and worth" (Marx & Fromm, 1961, p. 106, emphasis in the original). Equality of incomes was one of the main issues on the platform offered by Pierre Proudhon that Marx found inadequate. Marx argued instead that the equality of incomes "would only change the relation of the present-day worker to his work into a relation of all men to work. Society would then be conceived as an abstract capitalist" (Marx & Fromm, 1961, p. 107). In other words, equality of incomes would not change the alienated nature of labor itself. It would only universalize that labor.

The connection that Marx discerned between alienated labor and other relations of domination explains why he believed that the emancipation of labor or emancipation from alienated labor was the key to the emancipation of humanity as a whole. This is why he argued that "All human servitude is involved in the relation of the worker to production, and all the types of servitude are only modifications or consequences of this relation" (Marx & Fromm, 1961, p. 107).

When Marx referred to the relationship of worker to production being a determinant for all the types of human servitude, he was not speaking of income inequality or the male proletariat leading the women. Rather, he was referring to the four types of alienation discussed earlier. One can argue that for Marx, so long as alienation from the product of one's labor, from the process of labor, from one's potential for free, conscious activity, and from other human beings continues to exist, servitude will also exist in various forms including racial, gender, and ethnic terms.

In fact, in his *Economic and Philosophical Manuscripts of 1844*, he tried to show the relationship between alienation and the oppression of women. Here he wrote,

In the relationship with *woman*, as the prey and the handmaid of communal lust, is expressed the infinite degradation in which man exists for himself; for the secret of this relationship finds its *unequivocal*, incontestable, *open* and revealed expression in the relation of man to woman … . From this relationship man's whole level of development can be assessed. It follows from the character of this relationship how far *man* has become, and has understood himself as, a *species-being*, a *human being* … and consequently how far the other person, as a person, has become one of his needs. (Marx & Fromm, 1961, p. 126, emphasis in the original)[3]

Here too, it is necessary to pay attention to the emphasis on the relationship between alienated labor, alienation, and the oppression of women. Marx was arguing that it is the infinite degradation in which

73

man exists that comes through in the relationship to the woman as an object of sexual abuse. Specifically, he was arguing that in a man-woman relationship that has a sexual component, men cannot hide their alienation. The effects of alienated labor and alienation will come through in this relationship in the most revealing way. Furthermore, Marx was not only saying that the relationship between man and woman is the measure of how much progress a society has made in human relationships. He was also arguing that the measure of one's humanity is the treatment of the other, not as a mere means or object for use and pleasure, but as an end in itself.

In *Capital*, where Marx (1976) used the term "abstract labor" instead of "alienated labor," he argued that under the capitalist mode of production, with its extreme mental/manual division of labor, the objects of our creation come to dominate our lives in the form of commodities, and human relations take the form of relations between things. He called this "the fetishism of the commodity and its secret" (p. 163). Marx's point was that so long as the labor process remains alienated, this *thingification* or reification of human relations would remain and the mode of distribution would also be unjust. That is why he called not only for ending the private property of the means of production but also for abolishing alienated labor and creating the conditions for people to flourish and to have conscious, transparent, and ethical relationships with their fellow human beings and with the rest of nature. At the same time, in Marx's (1961) *1844 Manuscripts* he emphasized that abolishing alienated labor was only the beginning. Marx's goal was human development as an end in itself.

HOW HAVE SOCIALIST FEMINISTS ANALYZED THE RELATIONSHIP BETWEEN MARX'S CONCEPT OF ALIENATED LABOR AND WOMEN'S OPPRESSION?

In her "Women and Capitalism: Dialectics of Oppression and Liberation," Angela Y. Davis (2000) takes up Marx's *Economic and Philosophical Manuscripts of 1844*. In her view, these essays reveal that for Marx the male-female bond or sexual activity was a "central ingredient of the social complex which must be overturned and remolded by the revolutionary process" (Davis, 2000, p. 151). Furthermore, Davis (2000) has argued that these essays challenge any essentialist view of women's "nature" and instead expose such a view as an ideological construct (p. 148). Davis singles out the following passage from Marx to show how he illuminated the relationship between alienated labor and the specific oppression that women experience:

> We arrive at the result that man (the worker) feels himself to be freely active only in his animal functions—eating, drinking and procreating, or at most also in his dwelling and in personal adornment—while in his human functions he is reduced to an animal ... Eating, drinking and procreating are of course also genuine human functions. But abstractly considered apart from the environment of other human activities and turned into final and sole ends, they are animal functions. (Marx, 1961, p. 99)

Davis (2000) points out that the woman who tends to the man's needs "is reduced to the status of mere *biological* need of man" (p. 152, emphasis in the original). She concludes that an unmistakable reference of Marx's early theory of alienation is that "a critical and *explicit* mission of communism must be to shatter and recast sexual and marital relations, as production itself is transformed" (p. 152, emphasis in the original). Thus, Davis (2000) writes, it is only when "a new, more human, more creative posture toward external nature" is adopted, and at the same time when women are no longer defined as "a natural prolongation of man" that "she and man [can] come together on a new basis both experiencing an equal and authentically human need for one another" (p. 152).

Davis (2000) also expands on Marx's dialectical critique of capitalism as it affects family and gender relations. She argues that capitalism offers an "equalization-repression dialectic." On the one hand, it offers the potential of equality for women, inherent in the apparatus of production. On the other hand, it promotes the "inevitable domination of women implied in but not confined to the family" (p. 163).

Another Marxist feminist, Raya Dunayevskaya, founder of the philosophy of Marxist-Humanism, has argued that Marx's critique of alienated labor and of the oppression of women, when put in the context of his writings as a whole, and his later study of pre-capitalist and primitive societies, helps to illuminate the roots of women's oppression even in primitive societies. She writes:

Marx strongly opposed patriarchy, calling for the "abolition" of the patriarchal family. He held: "The modern family contains in embryo not only slavery [servitus] but serfdom also …. It contains within itself, in miniature, all the antagonisms which later develop on a wide scale within society and its state." And "all the antagonisms" extended from "ranks" that began in communal life and led to the division between the chieftain and the masses, class divisions in embryo, "in miniature." (Dunayevskaya, 1991, pp. 105–6)

Dunayevskaya connects Marx's (1961) insights on alienation and women's oppression in his *Economic and Philosophical Manuscripts of 1844* to his critique of women's oppression in his last studies of non-Western societies, which included a study of gender relations in Native American and Indian primitive communal societies among others. As the first Marxist feminist to take up Marx's *Ethnological Notebooks* from the last decade of his life (Marx & Krader, 1972), she discerns fundamental differences between the views of Marx and those of Friedrich Engels's (1972) *Origin of the Family, Private Property and the State*, and emphasizes that these differences are important for redefining socialist feminism for our time. She argues that from Marx's standpoint, "The elements of oppression in general and of woman in particular arose from *within* primitive communism and not only related to change from 'matriarchy' but began with the establishment of ranks—relationship of chief to mass—and the economic interests that accompanied it" (Dunayevskaya, 1991, p. 180, emphasis in the original). From Engels's (1972) standpoint, however, primitive societies were free of any oppression, and it was only with the production of a surplus in the newly emerging agricultural societies and the private ownership of this surplus by men that the origins of oppression arose.

Heather A. Brown's (2012) *Marx on Gender and the Family* agrees with Dunayevskaya's arguments and further explores them by examining other works of Marx. Brown demonstrates that for Marx, the roots of women's oppression could not simply be traced back to economic class inequality, but rather were related to the beginnings of the social division of labor that preceded economic inequality. She singles out Marx and Engels's (1932) discussion of the division of labor in *Die deutsche Ideologie* (*The German Ideology*), co-authored in early 1846, and the priority which this work gave to the mental/manual division of labor as the first class division in human society. Brown (2013) argues, "the division of labor only becomes oppressive when the worker loses control over the creative process, which necessarily occurs with the division between mental and manual labour" (p. 41). That is why *The German Ideology* discerns the "nucleus" of class division in the "latent slavery" of the patriarchal family in which the patriarch controls the power to dispose of the labor power of others (Brown, 2013, pp. 52–3).

Brown shows that although *The German Ideology* was co-authored by Marx and Engels, these insights concerning the mental-manual division of labor as the basis of class and gender oppression were not carried through and developed in Engels's (1972) *Origin of the Family*.

Brown (2013) also cites passages from Marx's *Ethnological Notebooks* that pinpoint the limitations of women's decision-making rights in primitive communal societies, their subordinate position vis-à-vis the chief, or the fact that despite being in charge of the household and food supply, and despite having the right to divorce her husband, a woman would have been severely punished if she slept with a man other than her husband. According to Krader's translation, the husbands demanded "chastity of the wives *under severe penalties* [which the husband might inflict], but [he did not admit the] reciprocal obligation ... *polygamy* [was] universally recognized as the right of males, [although the] practice was limited from inability to support the indulgence" (quoted in Brown, 2013, p. 160, emphasis in the original; see also Marx & Krader, 1972). Brown (2013) adds: "Even among the relatively egalitarian communal society of the Iroquois, women's sexuality was still controlled by men who did not have to adhere to the same standard" (p. 160). Brown therefore argues that socialist feminists can draw a great deal from connecting Marx's *Ethnological Notebooks* to his 1844 insights, and his writings as a whole, which also include insights on a whole range of issues such as prostitution, rape, incest, sexual abuse, and suicide.

Anne Foreman has also tried to theorize the specificity of women's oppression under capitalism, based on her understanding of the concepts of alienation and of reification in Marx. In Foreman's (1977) *Femininity as Alienation: Women and the Family in Marxism and Psychoanalysis*, she argues that the capitalist mode of production accomplished two things with regard to gender: on the one hand, it separated the sphere of labor from the domestic sphere, and on the other hand, it turned labor into an activity devoid of creativity which destroyed the individuality of the producer. With the intensification of alienation at work, humans attempted to express themselves outside the workplace and in spheres such as the family, and also in their gender identities such as femininity and masculinity. "In a world of chaos and change, gender appears as the one element of continuity to which individuality can be attached" (Foreman, 1977, p. 78).

Foreman argues that Freud's understanding of the sexual drive, as the main factor in social and political relations, is really only true in a capitalist system based on alienated labor and reified human relations. Capitalism, in contrast to prior systems, emphasized human individuality. But this individuality expressed itself in alienated ways and was based on the separation of pleasure from consciousness. Foreman (1977) writes: "In our understanding, the structuring of the psyche into a conscious and unconscious area is dependent on the process of reification in capitalist society. If men were to overcome reification, then the dynamic for this form of mental structuring would cease" (p. 108). As a result, the predominant understanding of sexuality, and the importance of strict and binary forms of masculinity and femininity would wane. Sexuality would still be important, but it could be expressed in a conscious and polymorphous form. In other words, Foreman thinks that the structuring of the psyche into a Freudian conscious and unconscious arena, where some forms of desire are relegated to the unconscious, is itself the product of a system where humans cannot live consciously and establish a healthy relationship between mind and body or reason and desire. The establishment of such a relationship will not signify the disappearance of desires but lead to a more conscious way of expressing them.

Judith Grant (2005) has similarly argued that socialist feminists and queer theorists need to build on Marx's Humanism, his understanding of the socially and historically constructed nature of gender relations, and specifically, his critique of alienated labor, as well as his view of an alternative free, conscious and reflective "species-being," "as part of [a] dynamic vision of an everchanging humanity" (p. 61). In concert with Marx, she argues that the alienated character of work under capitalism dehumanizes us and makes us pursue eating, drinking, and sex as ends in themselves and not as components of thoughtful human relationships/ friendships based on equality and mutual respect. Grant (2005) emphasizes that "To the extent that man treats woman as an object of his mutual desire, neither he nor the woman can be authentically human species-beings" (p. 68). She thus also emphasizes Marx's view on how the male/female relationship can indicate the extent to which our potential human essence has or has not become second nature to us. The man-woman relationship becomes a measure of how far or how close humans are to their potential for a free and conscious existence.

Grant (2005) argues that Marx's vision of "species-beings" as thoughtful and equal moral agents can only become real when labor itself becomes a thoughtful activity. However, she also points out that transforming gender relations and the denaturalization of gender are themselves a part and measure of this humanist revolution. We will revisit Grant's views in more depth in Chapter 6 on queer identities and theories.

Marcia Klotz (2006) argues that Marx posits a parallel between sexuality and labor as two modes of human productive activity that are both subject to alienation under capitalism. However, she thinks that "a contemporary analysis of sexual alienation within the modern capitalist socialist order, ought to begin not with a discussion of its role in production or even in the reproduction of the labor force, but rather with its role in consumption" (p. 409). Furthermore, Klotz emphasizes that the alienation of sexuality does not apply only to women. No one can escape the capitalist commodification of sexuality. In the manner of Grant, Klotz believes non-alienated labor needs to go hand in hand with a non-alienated sex, the emancipation of all human senses and attributes. This means transcending a strictly utilitarian approach to other human beings and to nature, and understanding our interconnectedness. That is why Klotz considers Marx's Humanism as central to redefining socialist feminism and queer theory.

Klotz (2006) concludes that what Marx envisions as the alternative to alienated labor and alienated sexuality is "nothing less than the abolition of the cartesian mind/body split" (p. 412). Thus being human means a mode of being in a post-capitalist world in which "intersubjectivity comes to take the place of individual subjectivity" (p. 412).

The transformation of labor is of course at the heart of the revolutionary project by which humanity comes to a fundamentally different understanding of itself and its role within the universe. And yet this process cannot be conceived without an equally thoroughgoing transformation of that other mode of productive human activity—sexuality. (p. 412)

Silvia Federici, who is not a proponent of Marx's Humanism, has offered some important insights on the relationship between the rise of capitalism and what Michel Foucault called the "disciplining of the body." In her *Caliban and the Witch: Women, the Body and Primitive Accumulation*, Federici (2004) agrees with Marx that the alienation of mind from body is a distinguishing trait of capitalist-work relations (p. 135). She points out that it was seventeenth-century European philosophers, such as Thomas Hobbes and René Descartes, who theorized the subordination of the body "to a work process that increasingly relied on uniform and predictable forms of behavior" (Federici, 2004. p. 139). She further argues that the attacks on women as witches, which took place in sixteenth- and seventeenth-century Europe, were also part of capitalism's drive to discipline the proletarian body and take away any control that women had over their sexuality and reproductive ability (pp. 163–217). Federici (2004) argues that the capitalist effort to turn the human being into a machine was in her paraphrased "Marx's terms," part of the process of creating "an 'abstract individual' constructed in a uniform way as a social average and subject to a radical decharacterization, so that all of its faculties can be grasped only in their most standardized aspects" (p. 146). Hence, the proletariat was not to be seen as capable of reason, just as women were to be seen as weak and irrational.

Gayatri Spivak who is also not a proponent of Marxian Humanism has argued that Marx's concept of alienation is more relevant to feminism than a strict economic analysis of women's oppression. She writes:

> From a feminist point of view, "the idea of externalization (Entausserung/Verausserung) or alienation (Entfremdung) is of greater interest. Within the capitalist system, the labor process externalizes itself and the laborer or worker as commodities. Upon this idea of the fracturing of the human being's relationship to himself and his work as commodities rests the entire ethical charge of Marx's argument." (Spivak, 1978, p. 243)

CONCLUSION: CAN MARX'S CONCEPT OF ALIENATION HELP THE #METOO MOVEMENT?

Today, misogyny is on the rise on a global scale: in the family, at the workplace, in the public sphere, and in society at large. Women experience sexual harassment, abuse, assault, and rape in both low-paid and precarious jobs as well as in the upper echelons of corporations, academia, and the arts. The #MeToo Movement has exposed highly educated men, who might have publicly supported feminism and women's rights but continue to sexually harass, abuse, and assault women. The following passage from Narges Imani (2020), a young Iranian socialist feminist translator and researcher living in Tehran can help explain what is new about the questions posed by the #MeToo Movement:

> But there is an important and partially contradictory point which has received less attention: explanations based on patriarchy as a mental construct ... argue that educating more and more men to respect women's rights, is the solution to confronting the lack of culture leading to sexual harassment. In fact, however, the main perpetrators of the current assaults are "very cultured" men, some of whom are famous figures in the fields of art or science or ideas. Fundamentally, one of the main reasons for the shock brought about by the recent exposes is not so much the mere fame of these assaulting figures but the damage which these exposes have done to "the cultural explanation of patriarchy."[4]

Imani (2020) argues that neither lack of education, nor the aim of directly exploiting a woman for material gains can explain why so many men sexually harass and abuse women. She emphasizes that the impact of the logic of capital on the body and the mind needs to be addressed. Specifically, she refers to the ways in which capitalism uses both pre-capitalist forms of domination, such as "masculine-centeredness" and religion, or more modern forms of domination such as pornography, to discipline the body or to shape our desires, in order to commodify and instrumentalize human relations.

Many women within the Left know from their own experience that it is entirely possible for a man to claim to be a feminist and expound beautiful theories about human emancipation but also treat his girlfriend or wife or partner in an instrumental and abusive manner.

While Marx's own life was not free of contradictions, the signposts that he has given us in connecting alienated labor to alienated gender and sexual relations, and the work that socialist feminists have embarked upon in theorizing this connection, can shed light on these questions.

We can argue that since the capitalist mode of production is based on an extreme fragmentation of the human being and of the labor process, of mind and body, mental and manual labor, even those whose work is not purely mechanical, but rather involves creative and intellectual endeavors, suffer from the extreme fragmentation of mind and body, or what Anne Foreman (1977) has called the separation of consciousness and pleasure. Under capitalism, humans are alienated from their potential for free conscious activity. In the absence of a thoughtful existence and meaningful labor in which the mind and the body are in dialogue with each other, and in which humans are allowed to develop their natural and acquired talents in a holistic and multidimensional manner, humans turn to addiction. Men especially, turn to alcohol, drugs, and sex as an addiction. They see women as only sexual objects. The plethora of pornography and images and commercials commodifying women's, men's, and trans people's bodies in our society also intensify sexual addiction and objectification. When men's exposure to sex is through pornography, their expectations in real life relations with women become unreal.

Under pre-capitalist forms of human organization as well, the rift between mind and body, and the objectification and exploitation of humans existed. However, capitalism, with its extreme fragmentation of the human being and the labor process, greatly increases this alienation. It also turns human relations into mostly utilitarian ones, and commodifies them. Human relationships, in all spheres under capitalism, are affected and shaped by these dynamics and hence suffer from an impersonal form of domination.

The #MeToo Movement's opposition to sexual harassment and violence has certainly shown that neither economic explanations concerning the devaluation of women's reproductive labor nor cultural explanations are enough to explain the phenomenon of alienation as seen in gender relations.

In the next chapter we will examine another socialist feminist effort to explain the connections between gender, racial, and economic oppression. Let's see how Black feminist intersectionality offers a conceptual framework that seeks to transcend both economic and cultural determinism.

5

Black Feminism and Intersectionality

Intersectionality is much more than the simple pronouncement that race, gender and class might relate. ... If we are to actually think expansively, sensitively and concretely about the actual organization of really existing capitalism, revealing relations of domination must be the beginning point.

—Bohrer, *Marxism and Intersectionality*[1]

Black feminist intersectional thought is not monolithic. It constitutes a rich and varied body of writings with a historical range extending back to Maria Miller [Y.] Stewart, who in 1831, declared "How long shall the fair daughters of Africa be compelled to bury their minds and talents beneath a load of iron pots and kettles?"[2] This chapter seeks to draw out some of the key contributions by Black feminist intersectional thinkers and their importance for redefining socialist feminism for the twenty-first century. It will take up their challenge to the erasure of women of color, and Black feminism's effort to articulate a deeper and more meaningful concept of human emancipation.

First, I will take up the different articulations of Black feminist intersectional thought, beginning with the Combahee River Collective Statement and through the work of Audre Lorde, Angela Y. Davis, bell hooks, Patricia Hill Collins, Kimberlé Crenshaw, Tracy Denean Sharpley-Whiting, and Joy James. Then, I will briefly examine the ways in which Black feminist thinkers such as Angela Y. Davis and Ruth Wilson Gilmore have extended intersectionality,[3] to prison abolitionism, and the ways in which abolitionists such as Mariame Kaba, Romarilyn Ralston, and Beth Richie have begun to articulate alternatives such as transformative justice. Keeanga-Yamahtta Taylor's work will also be considered as an effort to provide theoretical-historical grounding for the Black Lives Matter Movement. Finally, I will draw out some points from a recent book on Marxism and intersectionality by Ashley J. Bohrer. As Bohrer points out, intersectionality is about far more than stating the interconnections of race to gender and class. It is a challenge to relations of domination within the struggle.

DIFFERENT ARTICULATIONS OF BLACK FEMINIST INTERSECTIONAL THOUGHT

Although the term intersectionality was coined by the legal scholar, Kimberlé Crenshaw (2000) to whom we will return, the first conscious political articulation of the concept of intersectionality can be traced back to the statement of the Combahee River Collective, written in 1977, where we see the outpouring of ideas from three Black lesbian socialist feminist activists and thinkers, Barbara Smith, Beverly Smith, and Demita Frazier. As active participants in the Black liberation movement, the anti-Vietnam war movement, and the newly emerging feminist movement of the time, they found that none of these movements addressed the simultaneity of forms of oppression that Black women experienced. The authors argued that a socialist revolution that was not also feminist and anti-racist could not guarantee Black women's liberation (Taylor, 2017, p. 20). Toward that aim, they sought to further advance Marxism by proposing new concepts such as "interlocking systems of oppression" and "identity politics."

What they meant by "identity politics" or "focusing upon our own oppression" (Taylor, 2017, p. 19) was not the exclusion of other struggles, but rather the refusal to subsume the struggle against racism, sexism, heterosexism, and class oppression in the name of unity. That is why they argued that "If Black women were free, it would mean that everyone else would have to be free since our freedom would necessitate the destruction of all systems of oppression" (Taylor, 2017, pp. 22–3). Barbara Ransby (2003), historian and author of *Ella Baker and the Black Freedom Movement*, argues that the Combahee River Collective Statement "debunks the notion that so-called identity politics represents a narrowing rather than a broadening of our collective political vision. The document is anti-racist, anticapitalist, anti-imperialist and anti-hetero-patriarchy. That is CRC's Black feminist agenda" (Ransby, quoted in Taylor, 2017, p. 180). What the Combahee River Collective Statement meant by "interlocking systems of oppression" was that the authors "find it difficult to separate race from class from sex oppression because in our lives they are most often experienced simultaneously" (Taylor, 2017, p. 19).

In their effort to articulate their struggle against interlocking systems of oppression, they drew on the ideas and experiences of Sojourner Truth, Harriet Tubman, Frances Harper, Ida B. Wells Barnett, Mary Terrell, and thousands upon thousands of African American women "who had a shared awareness of how their sexual identity combined with their racial identity to make their life situation and the focus of their political struggles unique" (Taylor, 2017, p. 16). They also emphasized that "the liberation of all oppressed peoples necessitates the destruction of the political-economic system of capitalism and imperialism as well as patriarchy" (Taylor, 2017, p. 19).

Barbara Smith, Beverly Smith, and Demita Frazier explicitly stated their opposition to the capitalist system as an economic system of exploitation because they believed that "work must be organized for the collective benefit of those who do the work and create the products, and not for the profit of the bosses. Material resources must be equally distributed among those who create these resources" (Taylor, 2017, pp. 19–20). They stated that they agreed with Karl Marx's theory as it related to economic relations, and wanted to extend his analysis further.

They also argued that their focus on Black women's oppression arose from the fact that Black women, and especially Black working-class women, have been the most oppressed sector of U.S. society and hence "our freedom would necessitate the destruction of all the systems of oppression" (Taylor, 2017, p. 23). They called for a socialist revolution that was anti-racist, anti-sexist, and internationalist.

The Combahee River Collective Statement promoted international revolutionary solidarity and saw Black women's struggles as part of the struggles of developing countries' peoples from Africa to Asia to Latin America as well as all working-class people. It was especially committed to struggles in which race, sex, and class were simultaneous factors in oppression.

It can be argued that while the Combahee River Collective Statement offered the first conscious *political* articulation of the concept of intersectionality, Audre Lorde's work offered a *philosophical* articulation of the message embodied in the statement of the Combahee River Collective and thus took it further. In an essay for the *Black Scholar*, Lorde's (1979) "The Great American Disease" challenged Black men who disparaged

Black feminists and lesbians and who continued to treat women in sexist and patriarchal ways. She called on them to turn their rage toward capitalism and argued that "Black men are also diminished by sexism which robs them of meaningful connections to Black women" (see Lorde, 1984, p. 65). She called on Black men to not recreate the master-slave racist relationship in their relationships with Black women. Lorde (1984) further developed this challenge in her essay, "Man Child: A Black Lesbian Feminist's Response":

> I wish to raise a Black man who will not be destroyed by, nor settle for those corruptions called power by the white fathers who mean his destruction as surely as they mean mine. I wish to raise a Black man who will recognize that the legitimate objects of his hostility are not women, but ... the particulars of a structure that programs him to fear and despise women as well as his own Black self ... . Men who are afraid to feel ... deny themselves their own essential humanity, becoming trapped in dependency and fear. (Lorde, 1984, p. 74)

Lorde (1979) also sharply critiqued white feminists who took Black women for granted, who did not make a conscious, consistent, and persistent effort to reach out to Black women to learn about their experiences and contributions, or did not engage them in a dialogue on liberation. In Lorde's (1979) famous essay, "The Master's Tools Will Never Dismantle the Master's House" she challenged a concept of difference that is limited to pluralism and does not go beyond legitimizing domination.

> Advocating the mere tolerance of difference between women is the grossest reformism ... . Difference must be not merely tolerated but seen as a fund of necessary polarities between which our creativity can spark like a dialectic ... . Within the interdependence of mutual (nondominant) differences lies that security which enables us to descend into the chaos of knowledge and return with true visions of our future. (Lorde, 1984, p. 111)

Anything short of this was to Lorde, an "oversimplified approach" and an "incomplete vision" (Lorde, 1984, p. 77). Thus, when Lorde (1984) wrote that "without community there is no liberation," she qualified that statement by saying that

Those of us who have been forged in the crucibles of difference—those of us who are poor, who are lesbians, who are Black, who are older—know that *survival is not an academic skill.* It is learning how to stand alone, unpopular and sometimes reviled, and how to make common cause with those others identified as outside the structures in order to define and seek a world in which we can all flourish. (Lorde, 1984, p. 112, emphasis in the original)

When Lorde (1984) wrote that "The Master's Tools Will Not Dismantle the Master's House," she emphasized that in the struggle to develop an alternative to capitalism, racism, sexism, homophobia, we need to address and to overcome the internal contradictions of the movement and not merely focus on opposing the outside power structures: "For we have, built into all of us, old blue prints of expectation and response, old structures of oppression, and these must be altered at the same time as we alter the living conditions which are a result of those structures" (p. 123). Lorde's challenge to all socialist feminists, and the depth and breadth of her vision, are truly an inspiration and must be grappled with over many encounters in order to gain a deeper understanding of the concept of intersectionality as it relates to feminism and universal human emancipation.[4]

I argue that she articulated a philosophical expression of intersectionality because she went beyond refusing to separate class struggles from the struggle against race and gender discrimination. She provided us with a concept which revealed that emancipation cannot be achieved without a continuous grappling with and overcoming of the ever-developing internal contradictions within our movements and struggles. Lorde's philosophic contribution on the relationship of self to other and identity to difference will be further addressed in Chapter 8.

Another landmark work in Black feminist intersectional thought is Angela Y. Davis's (1983) *Women, Race & Class.* It can be argued that Davis offers a *historical* expression of the concept of intersectionality in her examination of U.S. history from the nineteenth-century anti-slavery movement to the late twentieth century. Davis pointed out that the first wave of U.S. feminism arose in the 1840s out of the Abolitionist Movement against slavery, and it made gains when white feminists and Black women and men in the South came together during the Reconstruction and established the first public school system. However, later, when white women in the leadership of the first wave of U.S. feminism realized that white men would not grant them the right to vote, they separated the struggle for women's suffrage from solidarity with anti-racist and labor struggles. They even retrogressed to the level of using anti-Black racism to gain support from white men for women's suffrage.

Davis also challenged the second wave of U.S. feminism in the 1960s for making the same mistake that the first wave had made and for separating themselves from Black women, anti-racist, and labor struggles. Thus, she argued that social progress in the United States is not possible without solidarity between white and Black women and the recognition of the inseparability of the struggles against racism, sexism, and class exploitation. We will return to Davis later in this chapter.

The term "intersectionality" itself was first coined by Kimberlé Crenshaw (2000), a U.S. legal scholar who focused on its *legal* expression. She argued that the experience of being a Black woman cannot be understood by considering being Black and being a woman independently of each other. Rather, we must include the interactions between the two experiences which reinforce each other. Hence, Crenshaw has focused on how the law should respond when faced with issues that involve the intertwining of gender and race discrimination.

In Crenshaw's (2002) essay, "Background Paper for the Expert Meeting on the Gender Related Aspects of Race Discrimination," published by the United Nations in 2000, and later published by *Revista Estudos Feministas*, she argued that racism, patriarchy, and class oppression "often overlap and cross each other creating complex intersections at which two, three or four of these axes meet … . Racialized women and other multiply burdened groups who are located at these intersections by virtue of their specific identities must negotiate the 'traffic' that flows through these intersections" because "intersectional injuries occur" (quoted in Grzanka, 2014, pp. 17–18).

Crenshaw focused on the entire range of human rights violations that were obscured by the failure to fully address the intersectional vulnerabilities of marginalized women and marginalized men. These included racially motivated rape, racialized gender stereotypes, forced sterilization, exclusion from jobs and education, as well as structural adjustment policies that increase the burden of community care on women.

The challenge to these cases of "structural intersectionality," Crenshaw (2002) argued, was "political intersectionality" or the ways in which women in communities that are racially, culturally or economically marginalized have actively organized in large and small ways to challenge the conditions of their lives. Within this political intersectionality, she especially pointed out that "women who insist on pursuing their rights against certain abuses that occur within their communities risk ostracism or other forms of disapproval for allegedly betraying or embarrassing their communities" (quoted in Grzanka, 2014, p. 22).

In Crenshaw's (2000) "Demarginalizing the Intersection of Race and Sex: A Black Feminist Critique of Antidiscrimination Doctrine, Feminist Theory and Antiracist Politics," her classic essay on intersectionality, she challenged both white feminists who were insensitive to the experiences of Black women and Black men who promoted sexism. She cited a passage from nineteenth-century Black feminist, Anna Julia Cooper, who anticipated the message of the Combahee River Collective Statement, seeing the liberation of Black women as the liberation of society as a whole. Cooper wrote, "Only the Black women can say, when and where I enter ... then and there the whole Negro race enters with me" (quoted in Crenshaw, 2000, p. 229).

Similar to the thinkers discussed so far, Patricia Hill Collins (2000) also placed emphasis on the ways in which Black women's shared experiences of oppression and resistance gave them a particular standpoint and interpretation of reality that was different from those of the dominant groups (p. 184). She argued that such a standpoint could be best developed by an Afrocentric feminist epistemology rooted in an African value system that existed prior to and independent of racial oppression (p. 190). This value system gave priority to relational nexuses, contextual rules, and emotions (p. 194). At the same time, Collins (2000) pointed out that "social class introduces variations among Black women in seeing, valuing and using Afrocentric feminist perspectives" (p. 191). Thus, Collins advocated a combination of an Afrocentric and a feminist epistemology that would challenge, race, class, and gender divisions:

> Black feminist thought challenges prevailing tendencies to categorize everyone in either/or boxes of being either oppressor or oppressed ... . Most of us experience contradictory positions. We are oppressed by someone and then we oppress someone else. This is what happens with African American men who clearly experience racial oppression but who also enjoy a degree of gender privilege especially in the home

.... In this way, Black Feminism identifies important themes that need to be addressed. (Collins, 2012, pp. 14–15)

Collins also helped to articulate intersectionality by arguing that it was "a way of understanding complexity in this world, in people and in human experience ... shaped by many factors in diverse and mutually influencing ways" (Collins & Bilge, 2016, p. 2). Furthermore, she pointed out that the "major axes of social division" by which she meant class, race, gender, sexuality, and issues of disability and age do not operate as "discrete and mutually exclusive entities but build on each other and work together" (Collins & Bilge, 2016, p. 4).

In her book, *Black Feminist Thought: Knowledge, Consciousness, and the Politics of Empowerment*, Collins (1990) emphasized that understanding the special oppression experienced by Black women requires an understanding of the concept of "the other" which is expressed in the objectification of Black women as the mammy, the matriarch, the welfare mother, or the sexually aggressive woman (p. 67). An Afrocentric feminist consciousness, she argued, allowed women to be self-defined through self-respect, self-reliance, family and friendship relationships, art, music, and literature (pp. 91–113). "Autonomy and not separatism" was, in her view, the "foundation for principled coalitions with other groups that are essential for institutional transformation" (p. 145). Afrocentric Feminism allowed Black women to embrace a paradigm of race, class, and gender as interlocking systems of oppression, and also to avoid an overarching theory of oppression which would be "positivist." Instead, Afrocentric Feminism promoted a combination of pragmatism and humanism (p. 224).

For Collins (1990), the view that the most oppressed groups can have a deeper vision of liberation was a standpoint approach, and an outcome of Marxist social theory, which she argued invoked positivism or the idea that human behavior can be reduced to predictable rules (p. 235). Instead, Afrocentrism emphasized women's tendency toward justice-seeking and ethical responsibility. Collins further argued that class, race, and gender oppression mutually shaped and constructed each other. Her Afrocentric feminist consciousness was an alternative that promoted love, a humanist vision of community, justice, an ethics of personal accountability, and the recognition that each group by itself can only achieve partial perspectives and not a universal vision. Dialogue, however, was critical in address-ing power inequalities and "decentering" the dominant groups (Collins, 1990, pp. 236–7).

bell hooks (2000) offers a Black feminist standpoint theory that is more complex. hooks has argued that since Black women have no institution-alized "other" to oppress:

> Our world view differs from those who have a degree of privilege … . It is essential for continued feminist struggle that Black women rec-ognize the special vantage point our marginality gives us and make use of this perspective to criticize the dominant racist classist sexist hegemony as well as to envision and create a counterhegemony… . We have a central role to play in the making of feminist theory … a libera-tory feminist theory and praxis. (hooks, 2000, pp. 144–5)

Furthermore, hooks (1984) has challenged the cooptation of feminism by capitalism and its academic institutions. She has argued that feminist theory needs to be reshaped both in relationship to the experiences of Black women and toward a revolutionary vision that truly challenges sexism, racism, and class divisions. Specifically, in the United States, "it is only by analyzing racism and its function in capitalist society that a thorough understanding of class relationships can emerge. Class struggle is inexorably bound to the struggle to end racism" (hooks, 2000, p. 133).

In her view, part of the challenge for socialist feminists is to distin-guish the difference between a theory of individuality that recognizes the importance of individuals, and an ideology of individualism that assumes a competitive view of the individual (hooks, 1984, p. 138). At the same time, socialist feminists must demonstrate the difference between an ideology that imprisons the mind and an emancipatory theory that is open to analyzing new developments, criticizes, questions, and re-exam-ines and explores new possibilities (hooks, 1984, pp. 139–40).[5]

Another Black feminist thinker, Tracy Denean Sharpley-Whiting (1997), has further articulated the questions of identity, difference, and emancipation by drawing on the works of Linda La Rue, Frances M. Beal, and Frantz Fanon in her *Frantz Fanon: Conflicts & Feminisms*. All three of these thinkers called for revolutionary transformation and saw women's emancipation as its yardstick. In the words of Francis Beale, "Unless women in any enslaved nation are completely liberated, the change cannot be called a revolution" (quoted in Sharpley-Whiting, 1997, p. 86).

What Sharpley-Whiting (1997) has singled out in the thought of Frantz Fanon is his concept of "a new humanism" which she defines as an "unwavering eye toward total human freedom, irrespective of class, race, sexual orientation and gender" (p. 95). She points out that this concept is further illuminated in Fanon's discussion of "the pitfalls of national consciousness" in his *Wretched of the Earth*, and his critique of African anti-colonial revolutionaries for falling short of creating new egalitarian relations in the postcolonial nations.

In Sharpley-Whiting's (1997) view, Frantz Fanon's new humanism needs to be reclaimed as a challenge to the rejection of the concept of universality which has led to a narrow focus on particularity and a move away from a concept of total human emancipation. She writes,

> The current pitfalls of postmodern academic feminisms lie essentially in their consistent inability to connect, address and represent the hopes, needs and interests of women within (e.g. professoriate to professional and custodial staff) and outside of the academy. This inability has led academic feminism to a turning in on itself that does not recognize the importance of a philosophy of social, economic and political change. (Sharpley-Whiting, 1997, p. 99)

Joy James, similar to Sharpley-Whiting, and hooks, advocates a revolutionary Black feminism that envisions the total transformation of society. Toward that end, James (2000) challenges W.E.B. Du Bois's concept of the Talented Tenth "as a buffer zone between white America and a restive disenfranchised Black mass" (p. 239). Instead, James calls on feminists to "maintain Combahee's integrative analysis" with "political practice that organizes in non-elite communities" (p. 243). James has specifically argued that Black feminism needs to challenge state repression, address conflictual ideologies and divergent practices within Black feminism and promote national and international solidarity with Latina, Native American, African, Asian, Middle Eastern women (p. 243).

James (2000) recalls Ella Baker's call to radically change the system by going to the root cause (p. 239), and questions the reduction of radicalism within academia to progressive liberalism. Instead, she defines radical Black feminism in the following way:

Radicalizing potential based on incisive analyses, autonomy from mainstream and bourgeois feminism, independence from masculinist or patriarchal anti-racism; a (self)critique of neoradicalism, and most importantly activism (beyond "speech acts") that connects with "grass-roots" and nonelite objectives and leadership all mark a transformative Black feminism … . [It is] to fight the authoritative body casting one off while simultaneously struggling with internal conflicts and contra-dictions. (James, 2000, pp. 249, 255)

James and other Black socialist feminist thinkers and activists, such as Angela Y. Davis and Ruth Wilson Gilmore, have indeed taken inter-sectionality forward by becoming leading abolitionist thinkers. Through abolitionism they have given deeper meaning to the interlocking of class with race and gender.

BLACK SOCIALIST FEMINIST ABOLITIONISM AS A FURTHER DEVELOPMENT OF INTERSECTIONAL THINKING

In *The Meaning of Freedom and Other Difficult Dialogues*, Davis (2012) offers a summation of her writings and activism as an abolitionist thinker. In doing so, she shows how abolitionism has elevated intersectionality to a new level.

First, Davis offers her experience as a civil rights activist and her par-ticipation within movements to free political prisoners such as George Jackson, Ericka Huggins, and other members of the Black Panther Party in the late 1960s and early 1970s. Her own experience of solitary con-finement for 15 months in 1971 gave her an understanding of the prison system as an apparatus of racist and political repression.

Second, Davis demonstrates how the expansion of the criminal justice system, the emergence of a prison-industrial complex, and a new level of demonization of Black youth and Black women on welfare starting in the late 1970s and early 1980s in the United States were connected to a period of capitalist deindustrialization and globalization:

What these processes reveal are the economic and social condi-tions that have helped to produce what we call the prison-industrial complex. Prisons catch the chaos that is intensified by de-industrialization … . Prisons and immigrant detention facilities emerge to catch those who engage in illegal acts because they are searching for better lives. And, ironically, these new prisons are represented as a secure source of employment for those who have few remaining employment opportunities. (Davis, 2012, pp. 47–8)

Third, Davis (2012) shows the humanity and resistance of prisoners challenging an inhuman carceral system. "Prisons allow this society to discard people who have social problems rather than recognize that many of them are simply hurting themselves and are in need of help" (p. 50). Furthermore, she recognizes "prisoners as human beings who have a right to participate in transformative projects" (p. 53). Thus, she calls on all activists to reach out to people inside prisons, create an "inside-outside traffic" (p. 54), and actively work on ending the carceral system.

Perhaps we can reimagine the relationship between prisoners and their allies outside as recapitulating, in part, the historical relationship between enslaved people and abolitionists … That is why many of us have suggested that we need a modern abolitionist movement. Our approach … involves the creation of new institutions that will effectively speak to the social problems that lead people to prison. (p. 52)

Davis (1998) coined the term "prison-industrial complex" in her "Masked Racism: Reflections on the Prison Industrial Complex," and explained it in the following way: "Taking into account the structural similarities and profitability of business-government linkages in the realms of military production and public punishment, the expanding penal system can now be characterized as a 'prison industrial complex.'"
This concept is what the organization Critical Resistance, co-founded by Davis, describes as "the overlapping interests of government and industry that use surveillance, policing and imprisonment as solutions to economic, social and political problems" (Critical Resistance, 2021). It has been further developed by Ruth Wilson Gilmore, feminist scholar and activist, and another co-founder of Critical Resistance.
Similar to Davis in terms of her long history of activism and scholarship, Gilmore has offered an analysis of the rise of the prison-industrial complex that takes up the connections between capitalist deindustrialization starting in the late 1970s and early 1980s in the United States, and a

rise in incarceration of Black and Latino people in the United States. In Gilmore's (2007) book, *Golden Gulag: Prisons, Surplus, Crisis, and Opposition in Globalizing California*, she further emphasizes and analyzes the role of prisons as an instrument of social control to legitimate the capitalist state, even when prisons are not a money-making entity. Gilmore (2007) demonstrates the need of the capitalist state to justify its own legitimacy and reason for existence through carceral discipline even during periods when the crime rate goes down (p. 18). In dialogue with Michel Foucault's (1979) *Discipline and Punish*, she views prisons as institutions of modernity aimed at producing stability and social control (Gilmore, 2007, p. 11).

At the same time, her analysis is rooted in Marx's capitalist crisis theory. Thus she sees a connection between the capitalist crisis of profitability since the late 1970s, the decline in the manufacturing sector, and the increase in unemployment in the West, together with a concomitant increase in state power and state prison building and policing as a means of control in the United States. Gilmore calls this phenomenon "the anti-state state" or "organized abandonment" by which she means that even as the state increases in size and social control, there is a decline in public services associated with the state (quoted in Bhandar & Ziadah, 2020, pp. 173–4).

Gilmore's (2007) book, *Golden Gulag*, began as a project for Mothers Reclaiming Our Children (Mothers ROC), a group of African American mothers in Los Angeles who had come together against police brutality and state sanctioned violence after the brutal police beating of Rodney King and the 1992 Los Angeles Rebellion. Her effort was to help find answers that could help Mothers ROC fight police and state violence on the basis of comprehensive analyses and solutions going beyond the capitalist framework.[6]

Indeed, the concern for women and opposition to violence against women and gender oppression are deeply intertwined in the work of all Black feminist abolitionist thinkers/activists. Beth E. Richie's (2012) *Arrested Justice: Black Women, Violence, and America's Prison Nation* articulates how Black feminist opposition to interpersonal violence is inseparable from opposition to state violence and the carceral system. Richie's (2012) "violence matrix" includes physical, sexual, and emotional violence, as well as a community, national, and international context (pp. 131–4). Mariame Kaba's Transformative Justice project is cognizant that "we have all so thoroughly internalized these logics of oppression that if oppression were to end tomorrow, we would be likely to reproduce previous structures." Thus, Kaba (2020) argues that "if we want to reduce or end sexual and gendered violence, putting a few perpetrators in prison does little to stop the many other perpetrators." As director of project NIA which helps incarcerated and at-risk youth, she calls for "chang[ing] a culture that makes this harm imaginable, hold[ing] the individual perpetrator accountable, support[ing] their transformation, or meet[ing] the needs of the survivors."

Romarilyn Ralston, executive director of Project Rebound in California, helps the formerly incarcerated pursue a university degree. Ralston, who was herself incarcerated at age 24 and served 23 years in prison, went on to earn both bachelor's and master's degrees in gender and feminist studies and liberal arts, and has dedicated her life to transformative justice (Ralston, 2018). This is how Ralston offers an intersectional explanation of the rise in women's and especially Black women's incarceration in the United States:

> Childhood victimization drives girls to run away from home and to use illegal drugs as a means of coping with the trauma of physical and sexual abuse. Drug selling, prostitution, and burglary often follow as a means of street survival. In a related sequence, adult women who have experienced childhood victimization resort to drugs to cope with the pain of abuse as well as other stressors in their lives such as adult intimate partner violence, sexual assault, or grief over the loss of custody of children. (quoted in Afary, 2021a)

Ralston points out that in California as in other states due to inadequate legal representation as well as racial and gender bias, mostly Black and Latinx women "are railroaded into federal and state facilities across the state to be a captive labor force for the prison regime while their children oftentimes are shuttled into a problematic and tyrannical foster care system" (quoted in Afary, 2021a).

Black women activists have also founded the Black Lives Matter Movement, which began in 2013 and led the multiracial Black Lives Matter uprising that started in the United States after the police murder of George Floyd in Minneapolis, Minnesota, in May 2020.

In her *From #BlackLivesMatter to Black Liberation*, Keeanga-Yamahtta Taylor (2016) has offered much fruitful ground for theorizing Black liberation today. She has challenged the ways in which reformist Black leaders since the 1960s have betrayed the aspirations of the Black masses by justifying the "myth of American Exceptionalism" (pp. 21–51), and the "myth of colorblindness" (pp. 51–75). Taylor specifically situates the rise of the Black Lives Matter Movement in the disappointment of Black activists with the failure of the Obama administration to challenge police brutality, mass incarceration, and the death penalty. She contrasts President Barack H. Obama to leaders such as Martin Luther King Jr. and Malcolm X, who came to the conclusion that there was no capitalism without racism. Taylor (2017) also highlights the contributions of Black socialist feminists through her publication of a new edition of the Combahee River Collective Statement.[7]

All of these women thinkers have been developing the concept of Black feminist intersectionality in creative ways. They are bringing the unique and critical standpoint of Black women to bear within the context of a movement against anti-Black racism, police brutality, state violence, and social and economic injustice.[8]

At the same time, Black feminists such as Jennifer C. Nash (2019), in *Black Feminism Reimagined: After Intersectionality*, are arguing that theorizing and practicing intersectionality should not be left only to Black women but should also be seen as the responsibility of all feminists who are serious about overcoming racism, sexism, heterosexism, and class divisions (p. 138). In that spirit, let's take a brief look at the efforts of a white socialist feminist who has tried to create a fruitful dialogue between Marxism and intersectionality.

DIALOGUE BETWEEN MARXISM AND INTERSECTIONALITY

In her *Marxism and Intersectionality: Race, Gender, Class and Sexuality under Contemporary Capitalism*, Ashley J. Bohrer (2020) criticizes some Marxist thinkers for their reduction of intersectionality to identity politics interpreted as a rejection of universality and solidarity around class struggle. Bohrer argues that although some intersectional thinkers focus on particular forms of oppression and ignore a broad class struggle, there are lessons that Marxists can learn from intersectionality to reformulate their approach to the relationship between exploitation and oppression. The main lesson that Bohrer draws is that universality and solidarity in struggle should not mean ignoring the oppressive behaviors that exist within the proletariat class itself or within any oppressed group (p. 169).

When it comes to theorizing the relationship between race, class, and gender, Bohrer argues, this means recognizing what Audre Lorde has pointed out: "The true focus of revolutionary change is never merely the oppressive situations which we seek to escape but that piece of the oppressor which is planted deep within each of us, and which knows only the oppressor's tactics, the oppressor's relationships" (Lorde, 1984, p. 123).

Furthermore, Bohrer argues that while racial, gender, and sexual oppression are intertwined with capitalist exploitation, capitalism and class can also not be reduced to exploitation alone. Bohrer instead argues for "the equiprimordiality of oppression and exploitation in both strategic and ontological senses" (pp. 204–5). This claim by Bohrer sheds light on this book's earlier discussion in Chapter 4 on Marx's concept of alienation and its relationship to gender oppression. There, we saw that in his *Ethnological Notebooks*, Marx had discerned the elements of oppression of women even in more egalitarian primitive societies, even before class distinctions in the economic sense arose (Marx & Krader, 1972). Marx, saw the oppression of women rooted in the social division of labor that created class divisions between chief and ranks, and that later developed into full-blown economic class distinctions. Thus, it can be argued that for Marx, oppression preceded exploitation in the broad historical range.

Bohrer also draws connections between Marx's Hegelian dialectics and intersectionality: "[I]ntersectionality's great contribution ... is in a deep commitment to living through contradiction, not as a death sentence but as the formation of creative possibility" (pp. 217–18). This means that "rather than simply reject them [binaries], we need to engage with them"(Bohrer, 2020, p. 215). We will further address this issue in Chapter 8 on overcoming domination.

CONCLUSION

In this chapter, I have not examined intersectionality from the oft-repeated standpoint of socialists who argue that it does not see class exploitation as primary. Instead, my examination of intersectional thinkers has aimed to shed light on their view that oppression cannot be reduced to economic exploitation. Intersectionality does not only confront race and gender discrimination within the class struggle and gender discrimination within the anti-racist struggle. It confronts the oppressive relations of domination within all of our struggles for liberation. While it does not base itself on Marx's concept of alienation, it would in my opinion greatly benefit from that concept as articulated in Chapter 4.

In the next chapter on queer theories, I will turn to the ways in which Judith Butler has used a poststructuralist analysis of power to address the issue of identity. Also examined will be socialist feminist critiques of Butler and alternative theorizations of queer identity.

6

Queer Theories

Although queer theory is mostly associated with Judith Butler and Eve Kosofsky Sedgwick, it can be argued that socialist feminist writers and thinkers such as Audre Lorde and Adrienne Rich, in the 1970s and early 1980s, also played an important early role in issuing the types of questions that initiated queer theory. In her essay, "Compulsory Heterosexuality and Lesbian Existence," Adrienne Rich (1980) called on feminists not to limit themselves to accepting lesbianism as a global and historical phenomenon, but demanded a full-blown theoretical and practical challenge to what we now call heteronormativity (p. 631).[1] Going further, Audre Lorde (1984), in her essay "Uses of the Erotic: The Erotic as Power," first delivered as a speech in 1978 at the Fourth Berkshire Conference, challenged heteronormativity, not only as a sexual phenomenon but also questioned any limited view of the erotic as heterosexual or bisexual or homosexual. Lorde called for a fundamental transformation and eroticization of all aspects of life and human relations as the basis for uprooting capitalism and creating an alternative society.

In this chapter, I will critically examine queer theories developed by three socialist feminist thinkers: Judith Butler, Rosemary Hennessy, and Holly Lewis. I will also examine critiques of Butler, posed by Allison Weir, Nancy Fraser, Hennessy, and Teresa L. Ebert. Then, I will take up the ideas of Nancy Holmstrom, Judith Grant, Maria Klotz, and Heather A. Brown on the ways in which Marx's concept of human nature can help provide fruitful ground for queer theory. I will conclude with thoughts from Sheena C. Howard's (2014) *Black Queer Identity Matrix* and further questions posed about the relationship of sexual freedom to ethical responsibility.

JUDITH BUTLER'S THEORY OF GENDER PERFORMATIVITY

When Judith Butler (2006 [1990]) published *Gender Trouble: Feminism and the Subversion of Identity*, she did not call her work "queer theory" and did not present it as one of the founding texts in this new field.

Butler challenges any fixed notion of gender or sex, and questions the very category, "woman." For her, it is impossible to speak of gender identity or the category woman as subject, because cultural and linguistic influences as well as the intersection of race, class, ethnicity do not allow these identities to be constituted coherently or consistently in different historical contexts (Butler, 2006, p. 4). Influenced by the ideas of Friedrich Wilhelm Nietzsche (1844–1900) and Michel Foucault (1926–1984), she argues that any identity is shaped by power and language.[2]

Thus, Butler (2006) emphasizes that persons become gendered through conformity with recognizable standards of gender identity. Compulsory heterosexuality requires the production of the opposition between "femininity" and "masculinity." It prohibits certain kinds of identities in which gender does not follow from sex (p. 24). It assumes that sexual desire reflects gender and that gender reflects sexual desire (p. 30). For Butler, however, it is not only gender that is culturally constructed. Sex too is constructed by power relations (pp. 10–11).

Furthermore, in Butler's (2011 [1993]) *Bodies That Matter: On the Discursive Limits of Sex*, she argues that compulsory gender identities and rules are realized through repetition of a set of norms (p. xxi).[3] This is what Butler (2006) means by gender being "performative" (p. 34). It is not as if there is an "I" which then preforms certain imposed norms that are supposed to represent a particular gender. Instead, it is the repetition of the norms themselves that creates the "I" (see also Hennessy, 2000, p. 54). To explain this idea further, Butler (2006) borrows a passage from Nietzsche's (1969) *On the Genealogy of Morals*: "There is no 'being' behind doing, effecting, becoming. The 'doer' is merely a fiction added to the deed—The deed is everything" (Nietzsche, 1969, p. 45, quoted in Butler, 2006, p. 34).

To understand how Butler arrives at this conclusion, we need to trace the main theories that have shaped her views. Here, I am greatly indebted to Allison Weir's (1996) *Sacrificial Logics: Feminist Theory and the Critique of Identity*, for illuminating the specific ways in which the ideas of Nietzsche, Foucault, Jacques Derrida (1930–2004), Sigmund Freud (1856–1939), and Simone de Beauvoir (1908–1986) have influenced Butler.

From Nietzsche and Foucault, Butler (2006) has borrowed the idea that a diffuse and historical struggle for power defines human existence. This struggle for power, in her view, creates norms and regulations that in turn create identities and gender roles. Thus, Butler (2006) quotes approvingly a passage from a commentary on Nietzsche by Michael Haar (1985): "the subject, the self, the individual are just so many false concepts ... having at the start only a linguistic reality" (Haar, quoted in Butler, 2006, p. 29).

From the French poststructuralist philosopher, Derrida, Butler has taken the idea that shared meaning or identity itself is a hegemonic concept since it is always based on the exclusion of another. In Butler's view, any concept of identity, or meaning, is repressive because it involves, in the words of Weir (1996), "a fixing or freezing of multiplicity into a unity which excludes and closes off difference and possibility" (p. 115).

From Freud and from the French psychoanalytic philosopher Jacques Lacan (1901–1981), Butler (2006, 2011) has borrowed the idea that aggression and unconscious sexual drives are the very foundation of us as humans. Based on this view, identity is thus only formed by repressing this aggression and the unconscious sexual drives in a process of sublimation.

From Beauvoir (1989), she has borrowed the idea that "[o]ne is not born, but rather becomes a woman" (p. vii). She criticizes Beauvoir, however, for implying in her formulation that there is an agent, a Cartesian cogito [I think therefore I am] (Butler, 2006, p. 11).

In essence, Butler (2006) rejects the concept of Humanism because it assumes that a subject or an agent can be potentially autonomous and use their reasoning capacity to challenge oppression and to establish solidarity with other humans to achieve emancipation (p. 195). Instead, Butler argues that Humanism leads to relations of domination because its concept of universality is a form of exclusion. Humanism, from its roots in ancient Greek philosophers such as Socrates, Plato, and Aristotle, has defined being human as having the capacity to reason and to engage in moral deliberation through dialogue and dialectical thinking. Butler correctly points out that the subject capable of reasoning has been assumed to be male. An even more important problem which she sees in Humanism is that

[i]n the philosophic tradition that begins with Plato and continues through Descartes, Husserl and Sartre, the ontological distinction between soul (consciousness, mind) and body invariably supports relations of political and psychic subordination and hierarchy. The mind

not only subjugates the body but occasionally entertains the fantasy of fleeing its embodiment altogether. (Butler, 2006, p. 17)

Thus, for Butler, reason and dialectical thinking themselves promote subordination and hierarchy by suppressing "the other."

How then are we humans to come together to challenge and to overcome oppression?

Butler (2006) believes that any effort at unity "sets up an exclusionary norm of solidarity" (p. 21). Instead, she writes, "provisional unities might emerge in the context of concrete actions that have purposes other than the articulation of identity" or meaning (p. 21). She argues that power relations need to be interrogated (p. 20). People can come together in "open coalitions" (p. 22) to accomplish immediate aims without any philosophical or normative foundations. She calls this the "anti-foundationalist approach to coalitional politics" (p. 21). Thus she hopes

for a coalition of sexual minorities that will transcend the simple cat-egories of identity, that will refuse the erasure of bisexuality ... be based on the irreducible complexity of sexuality and its implications in various dynamics of discursive and institutional power and that no one will be too quick to reduce power to hierarchy and to refuse its produc-tive political dimensions ... There is no political position purified of power. (Butler, 2006, pp. xxvii–xxviii)

For Butler (2006), the category, sex, would disappear and dissipate through the disruption and displacement of heterosexual hegemony. This does not mean that Butler replaces the masculinist subject with the lesbian subject. She criticizes the French feminist philosopher, Monique Wittig (1935–2003) for doing so (p. 27), and criticizes both Wittig and Luce Irigaray (b. 1930–) for "fail[ing] to acknowledge the ways in which power relations continue to construct sexuality for women even within the terms of a 'liberated' heterosexuality or lesbianism" (pp. 40–1). She emphasizes that the idea of "a normative sexuality that is 'before,' 'outside' or 'beyond' power is a cultural impossibility and a politically impractica-ble dream" (p. 42).

Instead, Butler (2006) calls for a "radical repudiation of a culturally constructed sexuality" (p. 42), and for "rethinking subversion within the terms of power itself (p. 42), which she argues "is not the same as to replicate uncritically relations of domination" (p. 42). She suggests doing so via cultural criticism, thereby exposing gender roles and identities that present themselves as natural, and "[s]ubverting and displacing those naturalized and reified notions of gender that support masculine hegemony and heterosexist power" (p. 46). This type of criticism is what Butler (2006) calls "agency" (pp. 195–7). Since rules promoting gender hierarchy and compulsory heterosexuality operate through repetition, Butler (2006) argues that agency is a variation on that repetition by offering "new possibilities for gender that contest rigid codes of hierarchical binarism" (p. 198), and by "practices of parody" to expose the "illusion of gender identity" (p. 200).

Butler (2006) concludes:

> The critical task for feminism is not to establish a point of view outside of constructed identities ... and hence promote itself as a global subject, a position that deploys precisely the imperialist strategies that feminism ought to criticize ... . The critical task is rather ... subversive repetition ... to affirm local possibilities of intervention. (p. 201)

Now let's critically evaluate the key concepts and presuppositions in Butler's theory of gender performativity explained above.

Socialist Feminist Critiques of Judith Butler

Weir, a Hegelian feminist philosopher, has offered one of the most profound critiques of Butler's philosophy. In her 1996 book, *Sacrificial Logics* (by which she means logics of domination), Weir writes:

> Butler ... moves from the argument that sex and gender are both constituted through discursive practices, which are regulated in part by institutions of phallogocentrism and compulsory heterosexuality, to the argument that sex and gender are products of a single, totalizing logic of language which institutes identities through the production of binary oppositions, and which thereby effects a repression of non identity ... or imposition of order on heterogeneity. (Weir, 1996, pp. 116–17, 128)

Weir (1996) emphasizes that for Butler, intelligibility always comes "at the price of violation." Intelligibility is equated to violence, universals necessarily repress particulars, identity of meaning is necessarily a form of restriction. Our capacity to speak and interact with each other is necessarily a form of violation. Weir argues that this view leads to three problems:

(1) It denies women "any capacity for reflection" (Weir, 1996, p. 124) that would provide a basis for resistance and transformation as Butler only speaks of "failure to repeat" gender norms (Weir, 1996, p. 124).
(2) It leads to action without taking responsibility for any enduring principles and ideas (Weir, 1996, p. 125).
(3) It leads to a rejection of human solidarity and the assumption that the ideal of solidarity is a repressive one.

Weir (1996) concludes that Butler's "policy of 'no commitments'" only allows for coming together around short-term goals but "evades the issues of group solidarity, the need for a sense of shared meaning and purpose, and the importance of a capacity for commitment to a future and a consciousness of a past." It also does not allow for ways of addressing differences within groups in a constructive manner that prevent disintegration and "could sustain enduring commitments to ideas and identifications with others" (p. 130).

Another socialist feminist philosopher who has offered an important critique of Butler is Nancy Fraser. In an essay titled, "False Antitheses," Fraser (1995a) asks how it would be possible to account for human critical capacities if subjectivity is always an effect of "a power/discourse/matrix." For Fraser, instead, "subjects are *both* culturally constructed *and* capable of critique" (pp. 66–7, emphasis in the original).

Fraser (1995a) believes that the purpose of feminist struggle is to: "construct practices, institutions, and forms of life in which the empowerment of some does not entail the disempowerment of others" but she does not see Butler offering any help in thinking about these issues (p. 68). That is so because of "the inadequacy of her [Butler's] conception of liberation." Butler views the very concept of identity as oppressive. Hence she "understands women's liberation as liberation *from* identity," but Fraser (1995a) finds this view "far too one-sided to meet the full needs of a liberatory politics" (p. 71). She insists that "feminists do need to make normative judgments and to offer emancipatory alternatives. We are not for 'anything goes' ... Feminists need both deconstruction *and* reconstruction, destabilization of meaning *and* projection of utopian hope" (p. 71).

A different type of critique has been offered by Rosemary Hennessy. In her book, *Profit and Pleasure: Sexual Identities in Late Capitalism*, Hennessy (2000), who belongs to the school of "materialist feminism," attempts to distinguish between Butler's concept of materiality and the historical materialist or Marxist concept of materiality.

Hennessy (2000) emphasizes that materiality for Butler is about norms and regulatory conventions: "Norms achieve this materialization of sex through their forcible reiteration ... sex is not a raw material on which gender identities are constructed, a drive, physiological configuration or bodily sensation, but rather a set of cultural conventions" (p. 56). It is the normative or power discourses that regulate the actions, behaviors, rituals, and institutions.

Hennessy's (2000) main critique of Butler is that she does not explain the relationship between sexuality, labor, and exploitation. As an alternative framework to Butler's lack, Hennessy offers the concept of "overdetermination" from the French philosopher, Louis Althusser (1918–1990), who argues that culture is relatively independent of the economic base, but in the end, the economic relations of production are the determinant (p. 61).

Hennessy also tests out Butler's critique of heterosexuality and her theory of performativity against some historical facts and statistics concerning marriage and the application of the concept of femininity. "When applied to marriage, Butler's formulation of the performativity of the law suggests that marriage functions as a performative ritual just because it has always done so, and that its reach as a social practice is simply normative" (Hennessy, 2000, p. 62). But Hennessy emphasizes that first, marriage has historically been a system for ensuring women's unpaid household labor. Second, marriage in the United States today tends to be beneficial for the middle class and the upper class who gain tax and other benefits, but not for the poor.

Furthermore, Hennessy (2000) cites the experiences of Black women in the United States and their position "outside white normative feminine gender codes" (p. 66), to show that gender is not simply a matter of performance of discursive norms. She reminds us that Black women were excluded from these norms "in order to facilitate the ruthless exploitation of their labor" (p. 66). Slaves were forbidden to marry. Norms that regulated family life among them were different from whites.

Hennessy (2000) further argues that in order to offer a radical and anti-capitalist sexual politics in the age of globalized capitalism, we need to know what social and economic forces are creating and shaping "the desiring subject and the subject of pleasure" (p. 69). We need to understand the crucial connections between local and global social structures. She concludes that Butler's theory of performativity does not offer us an adequate method. It "disparages interrogation and critical analysis" and "separates sexuality off from capitalism and class relations off from sexuality and desire" (p. 73).

Another socialist feminist thinker, Teresa L. Ebert (1995), also argues that Butler "substitute[s] linguistic determinism for a historical materialist concept of construction as determined by the forces and relations of production" (p. 208), and "reduces materiality to the materiality of the signifier" (p. 211). Ebert argues that Butler "puts forth an understanding of power as a closed, self-legitimating operation" (p. 212) instead of challenging the mode of production and the division of labor. For Ebert, the resolution of the system of power "does not come about through a linguistic resignification but through revolutionary praxis to transform the system of exploitation" (p. 215), and to break the logic of capitalism (p. 217).

Unfortunately, no possibilities for a humanist queer theory are drawn out of this critique. By criticizing Butler from the vantage point of one of the earlier crude materialist writings of Vladimir Ilyich Lenin (1870–1924) and also defending the "revolutionary role of state authority" under Mao's China, Ebert (1995) undermines some of the strong points in her critique of Butler.

Butler (2011) herself has offered a challenging response to those who accuse her of linguistic determinism at the expense of materialism. She refers us to the etymology of the word matter linked to matrix (womb) and the inseparability of materiality and signification in classical Greek philosophy. "In both Latin and Greek, matter (materia and hyla) is neither a simple brute positivity or referent, nor a blank surface or state awaiting an external signification but is always in some sense temporalized" (p. 7). Butler (2011) emphasizes that in the title of her work, *Bodies That Matter,* to matter means at once to 'materialize' and to 'mean'" (p. 7).

Furthermore, Butler (2011) cites Marx's critique of Ludwig Feuerbach and argues that for Marx, "'matter' is understood as a principle of *transformation*" (p. 7, emphasis in the original). In his early "Theses on

Feuerbach," Marx (1845) had argued that "the chief defect of all hitherto existing materialism, that of Feuerbach included" is that it views reality as either immediate knowledge or a static subject matter to be analyzed, and not as critical practical revolutionary activity or praxis. Hence, he had challenged a crude materialism and instead proposed the insepara-bility of activity and thought in shaping actuality and human experience. Butler (2011) writes that for Marx, "praxis is understood as socially trans-formative activity ... from an alienated to a non-alienated state" (p. 7). She concludes: "According to the new kind of materialism that Karl Marx proposes, the object is not only transformed but in some significant sense, the object is the transformative activity itself" (p. 7).

ROSEMARY HENNESSY'S QUEER THEORY

As a theorist of materialist feminism, Hennessy (2000) begins with "the assumption that the history of sexual identity ... has been fundamen-tally, though never simply, affected by several aspects of capitalism: Wage labor, commodity production, consumption" (p. 4). Capitalism relies on and reproduces ways of knowing and of feeling that conceal the exploita-tion of human relations. From that vantage point, Hennessy (2000) contributes to queer theory in three important ways: (1) drawing con-nections between the rise of globalized capitalism and the rise of more flexible sexual identities; (2) drawing connections between the rise of consumer capitalism in the late nineteenth century and the establishment of heteronormativity as well as the emergence of homosexual and heter-osexual identity categories; and (3) challenging economic reductionism by showing that the capitalist mode of production is not only about the extraction of surplus value but also the limiting of human potential, including sexual affective potential. Below, a brief summary of these con-tributions is offered.

Hennessy (2000) argues that the new feature of post-1980s late capital-ism is a new global division of labor: a fragmented process of production spread across continents and a transnational character (p. 6). On the one hand, "flexible production" has made resistance against capital by labor more difficult. On the other hand, globalism and the fragmentation of the labor process have created new forms of transnational identity: mul-ticulturalism, including a gender-flexible sexual identity in Europe and the United States.

Hennessy (2000) "eschew[s] the causal link between capitalism's economic arrangements and its politics and cultural forms" (p. 27). For her "cultural practices are part of a complex ensemble of social relations that includes divisions of labor, law and the state" (p. 27). Thus, she seeks to historicize or to make visible the complex mediated relationships between particular or local cultural forms and global capitalist fundamental class structures. Most importantly, she emphasizes that in the past few decades, "changes in the international sexual divisions of labor" signify that "there is no necessary relation" between accumulation of capital and "a domestic economy organized in terms of the heterosexual marital contract" (p. 66). Heterosexual marriage and the gendered division of labor remain the social arrangement. However, "a transition is under way from the private patriarchy of domestic spaces ... to a more public patriarchy that may rely less on marriage and heterosexuality" (p. 67).

In order to understand the relationship between the capitalist mode of production and sexuality, Hennessy thinks we can benefit from Georg Lukács's concept of reification. Just as Lukács built on Marx's (1976) concept of commodity fetishism in *Capital*, to show that commodity production stamps its imprints upon the whole consciousness of human beings (see Lukács, 1971, p. 83).[4]

Hennessy (2000) thinks much historical work needs to be done on the parallel emergence of commodity culture and heteronormative sexuality at the height of nineteenth-century capitalism. She argues that during the late nineteenth century, as commodity capitalism inaugurated a new culture of mass consumption, the organization of desire shifted. Along with this shift emerged new categories of identity, of permitted and outlawed human needs (p. 217).

During the eighteenth and nineteenth centuries in Europe, centers of commodity production gradually moved from the household to the market. Pleasure-seeking became a means for the creation of value. "The sensation of the body, the quality of pleasures, the nature of impressions, became fields for power" (Hennessy, 2000, p. 98). The recruitment of women into the workforce was also a critical component of these changes. The process of reification of sexual identity in the late nineteenth century "involved the formation of newly desiring subjects, forms of agency, intensities of sensation, and economies of pleasure that were consistent with the requirements of a more mobile work force and a growing consumer culture" (Hennessy, 2000, p. 99).

During the late nineteenth century, the shift to a consumer economy brought about a more widespread acceptance of pleasure, self-gratification, and personal satisfaction, which extended to the realm of sex. With this "engineered production" and "engineered desire," the erotic sensations and desires became reified and commodified (Hennessy, 2000, pp. 103–4).

Hennessy (2000) argues that it is at this point where we can single out the emergence of new identities, such as heterosexual and homosexual which had always existed throughout human history but had not been widely discussed as named and explicit categories (p. 99). She also points out that this is what George A. Chauncey calls a "major reconceptualization of the nature of human sexuality." Although the opposition between the category of femininity (sexual objectification) and the category of masculinity (active desire) remained intact, more attention was also being given to sexual object choice, man or woman (Chauncey, quoted in Hennessy, 2000, p. 100).

Another one of the important aspects of Hennessy's (2000) work is her challenge to an economic reductionist view of sexual oppression. She argues that what Marx addressed as alienated labor was not only about the workplace or the unequal distribution of surplus value. Rather, Marx was challenging the capitalist mode of production for limiting human potential which Hennessy argues includes "sex affective potential." She emphasizes that "sexual desire is only one form of sex-affective production" (p. 215; see also Marx, 1976). "We might even say affective potential is included in what Marx means by labor" (Hennessy, 2000, p. 215). Affective needs are part of the human potential for self-realization. "During the working day, labor power becomes detached from the individual's full range of human needs and potentials, and it is in this sense that capitalism is an impoverished mode of social organization" (p. 215). Marx (1976) argues that the worker's "species life" or the capacity for self-realization as social beings is taken away from them (Marx, quoted in Hennessy, 2000, p. 216).

Hennessy (2000) points out that the "alienation" of workers "from human potentials, including sex-affective potential" (p. 217) under capitalism is concomitant with what Deborah Kelsh calls the production of "outlawed need" (quoted on p. 216). Bodies and minds are abused. The "fracturing of our objective human capacities as sensuous social beings" go hand in hand with "forms of consciousness that abstract mind from the body" (pp. 217, 216). This is precisely why she insists that the fight for social justice is shaped not just by rage and anger but also by love, both collective and individual love (p. 204). Hence she asks: "What relationship would this revolutionary love have to the prevailing ways love and desire are sutured into sexual identities, and how love is practiced—and experienced—in individual terms?" (p. 208).

HOLLY LEWIS'S QUEER THEORY

Lewis's (2016) *The Politics of Everybody: Feminism, Queer Theory, and Marxism at the Intersection*, shares some similarities with Hennessy's (2000) *Profit and Pleasure*. Like Hennessy, Lewis believes that the main defect of queer theory is that its critique of heteronormativity is not rooted in a challenge to capitalism and specifically not rooted in an understanding of Marx's critique of the capitalist mode of production.

Lewis (2016) argues that the material foundation of heteronormativity can be found in capitalism's reliance on women's reproductive labor in the nuclear family for generational replacement (of workers). Citing Lise Vogel's version of Social Reproduction Theory (discussed in Chapter 3), she argues that it is not profitable for capitalism to support women when they are pregnant and raising children. Hence, capitalism attempts to put that responsibility on the shoulders of male partners and other family members.

> Economics is the origin of the "normativity" in heteronormativity: not intolerance of difference or the other, not a pure desire for power or an abstract need to control, nor a lack of sexual creativity or dullness, not a Eurocentric racial spirit .... The capitalist class benefits from this generational replacement, but it does not want to make concessions to the people who make it happen. Social gender and the management of sexuality under capitalism are shaped according to the struggle over who pays for what is necessary to socially reproduce the working class. A normative ethos is created to regulate the sexuality of those who produce children for the ruling class, a category called "woman" (which is also normative). Another category also bearing the title "woman" has

a separate normative ethos that regulates the sexuality of working-class women. (Lewis, 2016, pp. 182–3)

This view of heteronormativity as a continuing economic necessity for capitalism is a contradictory argument on Lewis's part. Elsewhere in her work, she acknowledges that according to Lise Vogel, capitalism does not necessarily need the heterosexual family or the family as such to reproduce labor power. It can rely on worker dormitories or importing immigrant labor (Lewis, 2016, p. 150). As cited earlier, Henessey (2000) too had argued that although heteronormativity has been used to satisfy the economic needs of capitalism, there is no necessary relation between accumulation of capital and the heterosexual family (p. 66).

On the question of theorizing a humanist foundation for queer theory, however, Lewis (2016) does hint at an important direction. In the course of her critique of queer theory, she offers us an intriguing general argument. She writes:

Post-Marxian thinking splits the world into binaries—humanity versus the environment, the sociopolitical versus the economic, the Idea versus the World. Such thinking reaffirms Cartesian dualism, where mind and body are separate substances that cannot be reconciled. Insofar as queer theory and other poststructuralist disciplines partake in this split by avoiding economic analysis, they actually reinforce the Cartesian thinking they claim to reject. (pp. 46–7)

Lewis's (2016) challenge to the Cartesian mind-body dualism and her promise to offer a Marxist paradigm that reconciles an "understanding of inclusivity together with gender and sexual alterity" (p. 14), however, are not adequately developed in this work. For further illumination of these ideas, let's review the work of Nancy Holmstrom, Judith Grant, and Marcia Klotz.

CAN QUEER THEORY BENEFIT FROM MARX'S CONCEPT OF HUMAN NATURE?

One of the most important contributions of queer theory is its challenge to an essentialist concept of human nature used to promote heteronormativity. As Butler (2011) argues, "the very concept of nature needs to be rethought for the concept of nature has a history … a rethinking of 'nature' as a set of dynamic interrelations suits both feminist and ecological aims" (p. xiv).

Toward that aim, Nancy Holmstrom's (1984) essay, "A Marxist Theory of Women's Nature," offers further illumination.[5] Holmstrom argues that for Marx, human needs and capacities are expressed, shaped, and created through labor (an activity of satisfying needs). Thus, it is labor, not biological determinism, that is the key to an explanation of social life and social change.

Holmstrom (1984) demonstrates that for Marx, biological differences between men and women cannot explain or justify any talk of distinct natures, because his effort is aimed at examining the nature of people as social groups not as biological groups (p. 457). Thus, "Marx is denying that there is a human nature in the traditional, transhistorical sense. On his view however, there are historically specific forms of human nature … specific to feudalism, to capitalism, to socialism and so on" (p. 459).

Furthermore, Holmstrom (1984) adds that human nature, and even biological nature, can change through sociohistorical factors and through evolution. Thus, she states that "in Marx's view, the contrast of the social with the natural and unchanging is particularly inappropriate to human beings since they are by nature social beings with a history" (p. 456). It is the social factors not the biological factors that are the primary determinants. Hence, from a Marxist standpoint, psychological differences between women and men would be related to the sorts of labor that they do and the resulting social relations.

> [T]he Marxist view is not that there is a direct causal connection between the type of labor people do and their personality structure. Rather, the type of labor people do puts them into certain social relations and those relations are institutionalized into sets of practices, institutions, cultural agencies and so on. (Holmstrom, 2002, p. 464)

It is not primarily biology, but mostly the oppressive social, economic, and historical conditions that determine the sexual/social division of labor (p. 468). Thus, even women who have non-traditional jobs and do not have a family to take care of are still influenced by dominant social and cultural institutions (p. 464–5).

Holmstrom (1984) emphasizes that while Marx did not have an essentialist view of human nature, he did believe that humans have a unique potential for free and conscious activity which can only be fully developed in a socialist society free of alienated labor (p. 471). On this basis, she argues that while there will always be some differences in men's and in women's experiences of themselves as physical beings, the meaning of those experiences will be different depending on how society develops. Furthermore, in a society not based on alienated labor, "the sexual and reproductive choices women make would not have the kind of profound social consequences for women as opposed to men that they do now" (p. 472).

In her essay, "Gender and Marx's Radical Humanism in the *Economic and Philosophic Manuscripts of 1844*," Judith Grant (2005) develops similar themes but specifically in relationship to queer liberation. Grant seeks to "unpack Marx's notion of 'species being' in order to establish Marx's idea about the historical nature of human beings" (p. 59). She emphasizes that Marx's Humanism is "radically socially constructivist yet is allied with an active political 'subject'" (p. 59). On this basis , Grant concludes that Marxian Humanism can benefit feminist and queer theories because he is "a democratic humanist and a radical constructivist who is anti-determinist" (p. 59).

Grant (2005), having established Marx's concept of the human being as socially, economically, and historically constructed and as embodying "infinite variability" (p. 59), states that the problem for Marx was "how to create a situation where those differences can be allowed to flourish according to the creative desires of humans rather than being incidental outcomes of social structures" (p. 62). She emphasizes Marx's recognition that humans are distinct from all other animals in that we alone can transcend necessity and produce freely and creatively. In other words, animals only produce that which is immediately necessary, but humans produce universally. Thus, humans can only genuinely produce as humans when they do so freely, that is, when their labor is not turned into mere "animalistic work, (i.e. coerced, divided from itself into mental and manual etc.)" (p. 62).

Based on this view, Grant (2005) argues that Marx sees the human body as "not bound by its own organic transhistorical biologically determined form." Thus, being fully human "is to be an historical 'species being' whose very nature lies in mutability" (p. 63). However, Grant

(2005) emphasizes that "this capacity to self-consciously direct change is not inevitable." Humans have a potential for "self-conscious, creative, reflective and willed activity" (p. 63), which cannot be realized so long as alienated labor is dominant in society. Simultaneously, with the abolition of capitalist alienated labor, the "denaturalization of gender relations is one of the ways in which humans ... know themselves as species beings and become constructed as a moral subject" (p. 69).

Toward those aims, Grant (2005) thinks that socialist feminism and queer theory need to reclaim Marx's Humanism as a philosophy which is anti-essentialist and takes difference into account. She notes, "From a feminist and queer point of view, a really exciting aspect of Marxian Humanism is that it includes the body, the body itself is self-consciously transformed by humans and can be self-consciously changed in a variety of directions by the fully realized species being" (p. 72).

Similar to Grant, Marcia Klotz's (2006) essay, "Alienation, Labor, and Sexuality in Marx's *1844 Manuscripts*," argues that "the kind of sex-positive politics celebrated in pro-sex feminism and queer activism is very much in keeping with a Marxist agenda" (p. 405). That is so because instead of the narrow sense of possession, Marx imagines an alternative model of sensuality which involves the "emancipation of all human senses" (p. 412). By conceptualizing a mode of existence that would allow for non-alienated, non-utilitarian, and non-possessive senses of sight, sound, touch, smell, and taste, "what Marx envisions here is nothing less than the abolition of the Cartesian mind/body split" (p. 412). In doing so, "Marx imagines a post-capitalist order in which the 'human' itself has been radically redefined" (p. 412).

Heather A. Brown's (2012) *Marx on Gender and the Family: A Critical Study* sheds further illumination on Marx's concept of nature and its relevance for socialist feminism. She argues that Marx's definition of the term "natural" in the *Economic and Philosophic Manuscripts of 1844* and in Marx and Engles's (1932), *The German Ideology*, "did not refer to a fixed biological essence but had at least two separate meanings." First, "the spontaneous unconscious organization of society" (Brown, 2012, p. 28; see also Marx, 1961; Marx & Engels, 1932), and second, "a future state in which humanity releases its full potential as a 'species being'" (Brown, 2012, p. 28). In the latter sense, Brown (2012) argues, Marx is referring to "the dialectical interdependence between humanity and nature" (p. 29), and a non-alienated society in which "the individual values the other individual as such" and not only as "means to something else" such as food, shelter, sex, and emotional support (p. 30). Brown quotes the following passage from Marx's *Economic and Philosophic Manuscripts of 1844* to show what he meant by human relations in a non-alienated society in which each individual values the others as ends in themselves and not as mere means to something else.

> Let us assume man [gender-neutral Mensch] to be man [gender-neu-tral Mensch], and his relation to the world to be a human one. Then love can only be exchanged for love, trust for trust, etc … . If you wish to influence other people you must be a person who really has a stim-ulating and encouraging effect upon others … If you love without evoking love in return, i.e., if you are not able, by the *manifestation* of yourself as a loving person, to make yourself a *beloved person*, then your love is impotent and a misfortune. (Marx, 1961, quoted in Brown, 2012, p. 30, emphasis in the original)

SHEENA C. HOWARD'S *BLACK QUEER IDENTITY MATRIX*

In *Black Queer Identity Matrix: Towards An Integrated Queer of Color Framework*, Howard (2014) raises important questions about what it means to be queer and to develop a fluid sexuality without recreat-ing relations of domination and instrumentalizing oneself or others. By raising these questions and doing so in the context of calling attention to Black women and racial oppression, she further contributes to the effort to develop a humanist queer theory.

She critiques queer theory for not being rooted in the experiences of Black lesbian women who simultaneously experience racism, patriar-chy, and homophobia. Howard's (2014) integrated model, or Black Queer Identity Matrix, also argues that there is both solidarity and "internalized sexism" in Black lesbian relationships. She demonstrates that oppressive gender roles are often recreated within Black lesbian relationships, and specifically singles out the tendency for one partner to be feminine and the other to be masculine (pp. 84–8). This issue has also been addressed by Mignon Moore (2011) in her *Invisible Families: Gay Identities, Rela-tionship, and Motherhood among Black Women*. This critique is also not limited to Black lesbians, but covers the LGBTQ spectrum and people of all races.

Howard (2014) concludes that "gender expression should remain fluid and unpoliced, however, the personification/expression of one's identity (especially an identity which is ubiquitous in one's community) should not go without critical examination (along the lines of cultural, societal and historical underpinnings) of the ways in which the gender has been constructed" (p. 91). Furthermore, Howard says there is a need to "extrapolate the often oppressive mechanisms which lead to such a performance" (p. 91).

CONCLUSION: SEXUAL FLUIDITY AND ETHICAL RESPONSIBILITY

In this chapter, I have argued that queer theory, as expressed by Butler (2006, 2011), has raised some critically important issues by challenging fixed concepts of gender and of identity. At the same time, it includes many limitations. Butler's rejection of the concepts of Humanism, universality, subject, and dialectical thinking, as well as her failure to theorize the connections between sexuality and the mode of labor, in general, and the capitalist mode of production, in particular, have limited her vision to simply exposing white male domination at the local level without offering an affirmative alternative to capitalism-imperialism.

Hennessy (2000) has attempted to historicize the rise of heteronormativity by situating it in the context of consumer capitalism and capitalism's reliance on the nuclear family, starting in the late nineteenth century. She has also drawn an association between globalization and the theorization of a fluid sexual identity known as queerness. For her, queerness does not only challenge linguistic and cultural norms but also can challenge capitalism's limiting of our human sex-affective potential if it questions alienated labor.

Lewis (2016) points out that Marx's alternative to the Cartesian mind-body dualism can open new doors to queer theory, but she does not develop this idea. Holmstrom (1984), Grant (2005), Klotz (2006), and Brown (2012) do shed light on the relevance of Marx's (1845, 1961, 1976, 1932) concept of a historical and ever-transforming human nature and his concept of free conscious activity for queer theory and the creation of ethical human relationships.

Howard (2014) challenges us to promote a concept of fluid sexuality and queerness that continues to question oppressive gender roles, even when they are recreated in the context of LGBTQ relationships. Howard's challenge further brings out the need to conceptualize and practice a sexuality that is also based on ethical responsibility. Brown (2012) helps shed illumination on what this ethical responsibility means when she discusses Marx's view of non-alienated human relationship in which we treat each other not as mere means to sex, food, shelter, and financial support, but as ends in themselves.

In Chapters 7 and 8, I will explore alternatives to capitalism and examine humanist philosophical frameworks for overcoming relations of domination. These chapters will also return to Audre Lorde's contributions and her effort to conceptualize human relations, sexual or otherwise, that go beyond domination.

7

Theorizing a Socialist Humanist and Feminist Alternative to Capitalism

In a 2016 interview with Sarah Leonard, on "capitalism's crisis of care," Nancy Fraser states:

> I call myself a democratic socialist, just as Bernie Sanders does, but we're living in a time when we have to frankly admit that we don't know exactly what that means. We know that it doesn't mean anything like the authoritarian command economy, single-party model of Communism. We know it means something deeper and more robust and egalitarian than social democracy. We know that it can't be nation-state bounded in a world where exploitation and expropriation and extraction are thoroughly transnational. We know all the things that it can't be, in other words, but we have a hard time defining the positive program. (Leonard & Fraser, 2016)

This way of posing the question is honest. It emphasizes that developing an alternative to capitalism requires articulating both what the transcendence of capitalism is and what it is not, in light of the failed experiments as well as totalitarian states that have called themselves socialist.

In this chapter, I will follow this method of affirmatively and negatively answering the question. The beginning of the chapter will briefly examine the alternatives to capitalism, posed by various socialist feminists such as Nancy Fraser, Ann Ferguson, Patricia Hill Collins, Maria Mies, Silvia Federici, and Kathi Weeks. The next section will address some of the limitations of their works and argues that re-examining Marx's concept of an alternative to capitalism can help socialist feminists develop a deeper vision aimed at transforming alienated human relations. Here I argue that grappling with Audre Lorde's vision of a non-alienated life and labor is also crucial. The final section of the chapter will examine

Raya Dunayevskaya's analyses of the former Soviet Union, or Union of Soviet Socialist Republics (USSR), and Maoist China as state capitalist societies. These analyses will show us why we cannot consider what took place in the USSR and Maoist China as examples of socialism. The conclusion will sum up and ask further questions about what theorizing a socialist humanist and feminist alternative to capitalism means in the twenty-first century.

HOW DO SOCIALIST FEMINISTS TODAY POSE THE VISION OF AN ALTERNATIVE TO CAPITALISM?

Fraser (1989) has defined her contribution as a "democratic-socialist-feminist pragmatism" (p. 6). Her concept of justice is a model based on three elements: redistribution of resources and income; recognition of cultural difference and otherness; and representation or political representation (Fraser, 1995b). However, she has also recognized that

> Affirmative remedies … associated historically with the liberal welfare state … seek to redress end-state maldistribution, while leaving intact much of the underlying political-economic structure … . Transformative remedies, in contrast, have been historically associated with socialism … . By restructuring the relations of production, these remedies would not only alter the end-state distribution of consumption shares; they would also change the social division of labor and thus the conditions of existence for everyone. (Fraser, 1995b, p. 84)

In her essay, "Socialist-Feminist Transitions and Visions," in the *Radical Philosophy Review*, Ann Ferguson (2018) tries to spell out a socialist feminist alternative by expanding on the ideas presented in sociologist, Erik Olin Wright's (2010) *Envisioning Real Utopias*. Following Wright, she defines capitalism as the private ownership of the means of production and the rule of market mechanisms in determining supply and demand. Socialism is seen as a matter of degrees. "The most fully socialist society is one whose people have social power over the economy and public policy through their democratic control over state policies and voluntary associations in civil society" (Ferguson, 2018, p. 179).

What Ferguson (2018) finds missing in Wright's vision of socialism is "feminist insights about the importance of restructuring family and sexual relations in a more democratic and egalitarian way to promote women's liberation" (pp. 180–1) She writes:

> I argue that from a feminist perspective, we need to add another variable to those by which we judge a society to be more or less social-ist: in addition to economic, political and social power, we need to add *personal power*, that is, the degree to which every individual is able to exercise their own decisions about how to live their life and negotiate their personal relations with others. (p. 181)

For this, Ferguson (2018) argues, we need to understand that it is not enough to call for abolishing the gender division of domestic labor and to call on men to do their share of housework and childcare. Rather, we need to "challeng[e] the heterosexist and sexist norms of our sexual and affective practices as well" (p. 184). Ferguson points out that "achieving property rights and wage work for women in advanced capitalist and former state-socialist countries may have created more gender equality within many families," but not in all families. "Undermining men's power as husband patriarchs" has also led to "increased domestic violence or divorces and single mother-headed families as well as more public displays of male dominance including, for example a vast increase in the production of violent, woman hating pornography, sex trafficking and tourism, and habitual sexual harassment in the workplace" (p. 185).

Thus, as socialist feminists, she argues, our vision of an alternative to capitalism must challenge the oppressive "Single-Mother Public Patri-archy" (Ferguson, 2018, p. 185), or the state patriarchy that builds on vilifying single mother-headed households and has taken the place of the oppressive "husband patriarchy based in the private sphere of the nuclear, heterosexual family" (Ferguson, 2018, p. 185). She continues to advise that we must also challenge the "reactionary Right populism of our current stage of public patriarchy in which many (not all) men would form a reactionary collective subjectivity across race and class that would seek to maintain male dominance and contain women's social equality by controlling women's sexuality and reproductive freedoms" (p. 186).

How do we create a transition to socialism that would simultane-ously address economic exploitation, racism, sexism and heterosexism? Following Wright's (2010) models of transitions to socialism, Ferguson (2018) argues that there are three approaches:

(1) The "Ruptural model" or revolutionary socialism and communism supported by the working class.

(2) The "interstitial metamorphosis" which promotes the creation of "empowering alternative spaces outside of mainstream capitalism" (Ferguson, 2018, p. 189), decentralized participatory and democratic political practices such as worker and consumer cooperatives, community-based social economy services, self-help groups, and credit unions. Ferguson further defines this model as "autonomous consciousness-raising and empowerment spaces for oppressed groups (women, LGBT, people of color), affinity groups, horizontal decision-making, and direct non-violent civil disobedience against state forces." Such practices are meant to show forth "'pre-figurative' values for creating a new society within the interstices of the old" (p. 189).[1]

(3) "Symbiotic metamorphosis" or social democracy which aims for reforms such as the creation of a welfare system, heavy taxation of corporations, imposing regulations on market capitalism within the capitalist state.

Ferguson (2018) points out that each of these approaches has limitations. However, she concludes that socialist feminists need to not exclude any of them but instead employ a combination of the three. Since what Ferguson calls the interstitial model of the transition to socialism is currently the most popular among socialist feminists, I would like to briefly discuss the views of several social feminists who, in a variety of ways, represent this model: Patricia Hill Collins, Silvia Federici, Maria Mies, and Kathi Weeks.

Patricia Hill Collins (1990), author of *Black Feminist Thought*, offers a "politics of empowerment" which she defines as "a humanist vision of community" (p. 221), or "Afrocentric models of community [which] stress connections, caring and personal accountability" (p. 223). Collins specifically speaks of Black communities in the post-Civil War period of "transition to 'free' labor" as "places of collective effort and will [which] stood in contrast to the public, market-driven exchange-based dominant political economy in which they were situated" (p. 53). She argues that an Afrocentric model of connection, caring, and personal accountability today would be synonymous with a humanist vision of self-actualization, self-definition, and self-determination. This is not separatism, but a fostering of our humanity. It views the world as a dynamic place where the goal is "not merely to survive or to fit in or cope; rather it becomes a place where we feel ownership and accountability ... while individual empowerment is key, only collective action can generate lasting social transformation of political and economic institutions" (p. 237).

Maria Mies (2014 [1986]), the author of *Patriarchy and Accumulation on a World Scale: Women in the International Division of Labour*, and a prominent ecofeminist thinker, offers us more details. Mies's (2014) thesis is that "at the beginning of history, a sexual division of labor arose whereby men specialized in the arts of violence and destruction while women specialized in activities by which life is daily and generationally produced, and in time, this consolidated into a patriarchal system" (p. x). Thus, she argues, capitalism is patriarchy's latest manifestation.

In the final chapter of Mies's (2014) *Patriarchy and Accumulation on a World Scale*, titled "Towards a Feminist Perspective of a New Society," she argues the following:

The concept which more than any other, has shaped life in capitalist patriarchy is the *concept of labour*. For a feminist perspective, the concept of labour, prevalent in *all* capitalist and socialist societies, has to be changed radically. From this changed concept will follow a change of work, of work organization, of the sexual division of labour, of the products, of the relation between work and non-work, of the division between manual and mental work, of the relation between human beings and nature, of the relation to our bodies. (p. 212)

Thus, Mies (2014) rejects both the mental/manual and the sexual division of labor, and advocates an embrace of a more rural existence with a much closer relationship to organic matter and nature, and a much larger share of the workforce in agriculture. She calls for an alternate economy based on autarky or self-sufficiency, "a movement away from employment in industries towards employment in agriculture" (p. 220), decentralization, autonomy over our bodies and lives, and responsibility by both women and men for domestic labor and childcare (p. 221).

This "feminist concept of labor," Mies (2014) argues, will mean the following: (1) the necessary labor of creating our material needs and reproduction will be viewed as both burden and pleasure and will not be alienated; (2) we will have a different concept of time in which "time is not segregated into portions of burdensome labor and portions of supposed pleasure and leisure but in which times of work and times of rest and enjoyment are alternating and interspersed ... the length of the working day is no longer very relevant" (p. 217); and (3) work as a direct interaction with nature, organic matter, and living organisms will reduce violence against women (p. 218).[2]

Mies (2014) argues that Marx's utopian vision is problematic because for Marx, "the unlimited progress of science and technology ... will be the main force to transform human society and social relations" (p. 215). This, she equates to a Brave New World scenario, "a technocratic utopia based on domination of nature, women and colonies" (p. 216).

Instead in Mies's view, a return to subsistence agriculture and a direct relationship to organic nature will be key to overcoming capitalist patriarchy, and thereby, achieving women's emancipation.

Still within the "interstitial metamorphosis" model of alternatives, Federici and Weeks offer us an autonomist perspective. In her *Revolution at Point Zero: Housework, Reproduction, and Feminist Struggle*, Silvia Federici (2012) calls for "reclaiming control over the material conditions of our production and creating new forms of cooperation around this work outside the logic of capital and the market"(p. 110). These range from "direct action (from squatting on public land to urban farming)" (p. 110), to "communal kitchens—ola communes as in Chile and Peru— thus standing in the way of a total commodification of life and beginning a process of re-appropriation and re-collectivization of reproduction that is indispensable if we are to regain control over our lives" (p. 110).

Federici (2012) also calls for reclaiming the commons, or rejecting the privatization of common property such as land, water, air, the internet, libraries, past culture, social security, and pension. She calls this concept of the commons, "a logical and historical alternative to both State and Private property" (p. 139) and concludes that

> by reclaiming land and waters, and turning them into a common, we could begin to de-link our reproduction from the commodity flows that through the world market are responsible for the dispossession of so many people in other parts of the world. We could disentangle our livelihood, not only from the world market but from the war-machine and prison system, on which the hegemony of the world market depends. (p. 144)

Thus, when Federici (2019) writes about "reenchanting the world," she means that through the growth of "communing practices" (p. 195), such as time banks, urban gardens, and community accountability structures, and "the *androgynous* models of gender identity ... and the queer rejection of gender," we can "break down the disciplinary mechanisms" of capitalism and "remold our humanity" different from and in opposition to what capitalist industrial discipline has imposed on us for centuries (p. 195, emphasis in the original). In this struggle to create an alternative to capitalism, cooperative forms of reproductive labor involving subsistence farming, education, and childrearing, will have a unique place because they involve interaction with nature and the production of people, not things, and are thus "particularly apt to generate more cooperative social relations" (p. 195).

Federici (2012) emphasizes that Marx's vision is not appropriate for care work because "he projects a world in which machines do all the work and humans only tend to them, functioning as their supervisors" (p. 121).[3] She also writes: "Marx ignores the fact that it is not work as such that is oppressive but the social relations of exploitation that sustain it" (Mies, 2014, p. xi).

While in some ways different from Federici, Kathi Weeks offers a further defined autonomist feminist alternative. In *The Problem with Work: Feminism, Marxism, Antiwork Politics, and Postwork Imaginaries*, Weeks (2011) argues that given the amount of time we as humans are expected to devote to work, examining work is an especially rich object of inquiry (p. 2), both from a quantitative and from a qualitative standpoint, and both as a source of value and as a means of disciplining and assigning a class to individuals (p. 9). She calls on socialist feminists to advocate not only for better work and less work but also for the right of "refusal of work" (p. 13). In her view the needed transformation of society does not rely on emancipating labor and making it meaningful, but on abolishing labor as such (p. 13).

Weeks (2011) questions the very idea of socialism itself because it is based on a "politics of deferment" (p. 29), one that requires a revolutionary transformation of society beginning with the mode of labor. She writes, "Today, however, it seems unlikely that socialism can serve as a persuasive signifier of a postcapitalist alternative" (p. 29). In her view, the name, socialism, itself has become obsolete, and the content of the vision is no more than "a vision of the work society perfected" (p. 30). Thus, she concludes that even Marx's concept of emancipated labor is another version of "the work society" (p. 89). Socialism, as she claims, assumes that the contours of the utopian future can be predetermined with a blueprint (p. 30). Instead, she calls for a "post-work society" with an open future to replace socialism (p. 30).

Weeks (2011) challenges the Protestant work ethic (as articulated by Max Weber) because it promotes productivism and work as an end in itself (pp. 42–3). It assumes that individual contribution to production is a prerequisite for individual consumption, and inculcates internalized voluntary submission by individuals to capitalist discipline. She also shows how capitalism simultaneously creates contradictory behaviors: rationality/irrationality, productivism/consumerism, dependency/independence, subordination/insubordination, and inclusion/exclusion (p. 42).

In agreement with Jean Baudrillard's (1975) *The Mirror of Production*, Weeks (2011) claims that Marxism romanticizes productivity and reproduces the political economy of factory labor by promoting allegiance to asceticism. In her view, Marxism subordinates spontaneity and a diversity of social practices to "an instrumental and rationalistic logic of productivity," thus "controlling nature in the service of strictly utilitarian ends" (p. 81).

In rejecting Marx's and the Marxist humanist distinction between alienated and non-alienated labor, Weeks (2011) challenges the idea that non-alienated labor—defined by Marx as not being alienated from the product of one's labor, the process of labor, other human beings, and the human potential for free and conscious activity—can be a primary means of individual self-realization and self-fulfillment. Citing the autonomist tradition's opposition to the Marxist humanist tradition, Weeks argues that although the Marxian critique of alienated labor applies to both Fordist and post-Fordist production, the problem with this critique is that "the critique of alienation becomes attached to a prior claim about the nature of the human subject" (p. 89). For Weeks (2011), such a view assumes that there is a defined human essence, and that it is the capacity for non-alienated labor.

In contrast to a humanist Marxism, which also opposes the organization and length of work under capitalism as the fundamental basis of this oppressive system, the autonomist Marxist view calls "not for a liberation of work but a liberation from work" (Weeks, 2011, p. 97). It advocates "the refusal of work" (Weeks, 2011, p. 97). While it recognizes that the necessity for work cannot be eliminated, it envisions a society in which "work does not serve as a primary force of social mediation" (p. 102), and "the link between work and income [is] severed" (p. 102). "The productive powers of cooperation, knowledge and technology are celebrated ... to reduce the time spent at work, thereby offering possibilities to pursue opportunities for pleasure and creativity outside the economic realm of production" (p. 103).

Toward those aims, Weeks (2011) proposes the immediate struggle for a shorter work day and for a universal basic income that is "paid unconditionally to individuals regardless of their family or household relationships, regardless of other incomes and regardless of their past, present or future employment status" (p. 138). She ends her book by calling for a "feminist time movement" (p. 171) that reclaims time for creativity, sensation, and affect (p. 169).

All of the socialist feminists discussed above have made attempts to articulate both what is wrong with the capitalist economic and social system under which we live and how we can begin to define an alternative that encompasses work and other aspects of life.

Both the socialist feminists who believe in the emancipation of labor, and those who believe in the abolition of labor, agree that labor, whether paid labor or unpaid reproductive labor, are critically important issues when it comes to defining an alternative to capitalism.

Autonomists and ecofeminists do not clarify how returning to subsistence farming or creating interstitial autonomous cooperatives or abolishing labor in favor of a universal basic income will overcome alienated labor and alienated human relations.[4] Mies, Federici, and Weeks offer various claims about Marx's concept of an alternative to capitalism that are in many ways inaccurate and distorted. It is important to challenge these distortions, not because socialist feminists should be uncritical supporters of Marx, but because Marx's critique of capitalist alienated labor, and his alternative concept of emancipated labor, are simply too important for the project of an alternative to capitalism and cannot be easily dismissed.[5] Let us evaluate some of Mies, Federici, and Weeks's criticisms and further explore Marx.

MARX'S IDEAS OF A NON-ALIENATED LABOR
AND LIFE AS ALTERNATIVE TO CAPITALISM

I would argue that Marx's body of ideas as a whole can give us a foundation for an alternative to capitalism that would also revolutionize human relations beginning with what Ferguson (2018) calls "affective practices" (p. 184). As argued in previous chapters, Marx critiques capitalism as a system based on alienated labor and hence value production. He does not simply call for the abolition of private property of the means of production and an end to the rule of the market. Marx's early writings in the *Economic and Philosophical Manuscripts of 1844* argue that alienated labor is not only about the alienation of the producer from their products but also from the process of labor, from their ability for free and conscious activity, and from other human beings. In those very same essays, Marx relates the issue of alienation to marriage, love, and the man-woman relationship. He argues that "in the relationship with *woman*, as the prey and the handmaid of communal lust, is expressed the infinite degradation in which man exists for himself" (Marx & Fromm, 1961, p. 126, emphasis in the original). He further emphasizes that the relationship of man to woman is the measure of how developed or undeveloped a society is, because in this relationship, in relating to another human being, one is relating to one's own sexuality. As discussed earlier, one can interpret Marx as saying that when in relating to another human being, one is also relating to one's own sexual desires, it becomes more difficult to hide feelings and attitudes that one might be able to cover over in other social interactions.

It is true that Marx's (1976, 1981) *Capital* does not theorize the relationship between women's domestic and reproductive labor and capitalist accumulation. As Federici (2019) herself has acknowledged, the phenomenon of working-class housewives did not exist until the 1890s, after Marx's death (p. 157).[6] However, Marx was very well aware of the fact that capitalism uses the unpaid domestic and reproductive labor of women to reproduce the working class. He also devoted extensive sections of *Capital* to capitalism's "pestiferous" exploitation of women, children, and the family (Marx, 1976, pp. 620–1). Marx assumed that *from the vantage point of capitalism*, women's unpaid domestic and reproductive labor does not directly contribute to the accumulation of capital because capitalism defines "value" as only labor that is sold in the market and produces surplus value.

I would argue that socialist feminists who specifically wish to theorize an alternative to capitalism that takes into account the transformation of gender relations still need Marx's body of work for various reasons:

(1) Marx's understanding of the capitalist system does not limit it to a system based on economic inequality. He identifies capitalism as a system based on alienated labor that takes the mental/manual division of labor and the separation of mind and body to the extreme. To him, the degradation and violence that women experience is a clear manifestation of this separation.

(2) Marx's affirmative alternative is not limited to reclaiming the commons and collectivizing labor or abolishing labor and simply relying on machines and technology to do the work. While in the draft of *Capital* known as the *Grundrisse*, Marx's' language in some passages may create some ambiguity about the role of technology, in *Capital* itself, which is a later work, he clearly states that technology as such is not the key to liberation.[7] He argues that technology can give us possibilities to spend less time on the work of material production of our basic daily needs. It can also help us spend less time on domestic and reproductive labor and more time on developing ourselves as multidimensional human beings with various natural and acquired talents. However, he emphasizes that technology, under capitalism, also turns human beings into cogs in a machine and denudes their work of all interest. Far from having an uncritical view of technology, Marx advocates the emancipation of human beings from alienated labor and "human self-alienation" in favor of a conscious existence, and a two-way relationship between mind and body as the key to human liberation. That is why in his early writings, he calls his philosophy a "fully developed naturalism" or "humanism" or "the return of man [Mensch] himself as a *social*, that is, really human being, a complete and conscious return which assimilates all the wealth of previous development" (Marx & Fromm, 1961, p. 127).

(3) Marx did not advocate an essentialist view of human nature and a human essence based on productivism or what Weeks (2011) calls "the work society perfected" (p. 30).[8] When in his *Critique of the Gotha Program*, Marx wrote of "a higher phase of commu-

nist society" in which "labour from a mere means of life, has itself become the prime necessity of life" (Marx, 1966, p. 10) he was referring to the flowering of the human potential for free and conscious activity. As Grant has noted, for Marx, true human essence is about constantly transforming oneself. This is what he, in the *Grundrisse*, also called "the absolute movement of becoming" (Marx & Engels, 1986, pp. 411–12).

Both Mies and Weeks advocate a feminist concept of time. Marx too was arguing for a different concept of time involved in overcoming capitalist alienated labor. At issue for him was the idea that under capitalism, the amount of time necessary for the production of a use-value is determined "behind the backs of the producers" (Marx, 1976, p. 135), and is constantly reduced to satisfy capitalism's incessant drive for the expansion of value. He argued that under capitalism, "socially necessary labor time," that is, a global social average time for the production of each use-value, dominates the process of production because producers are not allowed to determine the amount of time they need to do their work based on their abilities and their local conditions.

The capitalist concept of time, Marx demonstrated, is a manifestation of the capitalist mode of production. We cannot possibly create a free, conscious, and non-alienated existence when we are made to work faster and faster in order to keep up with capitalism's demand for a shortening of socially necessary labor time. We cannot do our work thoughtfully and have time for meaningful interpersonal relationships when we are constantly made to push ourselves to the extreme to keep up with capitalist time or what the late social theorist Moishe Postone (1993) called "the treadmill effect" (pp. 289–91).

How is it possible to overcome this capitalist push to speed up labor time? Clearly Marx did not think it could be done only by abolishing the private property of the means of production and by doing away with market mechanisms. It demanded overcoming the alienated mode of labor itself. Does this mean that socialism, as Marx envisioned it, assumes that the contours of the utopian future can be predetermined with a blueprint, and closes the door to an open future, as Weeks (2011, p. 30) argues?

Peter Hudis's (2012) *Marx's Concept of the Alternative to Capitalism* sheds light on this question. He argues that when the young Marx wrote that "Communism is the necessary form and dynamic principle of the immediate future, but communism is not itself the goal of human development—the form of human society" (Marx & Fromm, 1961, p. 140),

> Marx is here reflecting on the future on two levels: One is the idea of communism—the *immediate* principle of the future—that has as its task the elimination of private property and alienated labour. The other is a realization of the idea of freedom that is much more open-ended and harder to define or even give a name to, since it involves the return of humanity to itself as a sensuous being exhibiting a totality of manifestations of life. (Hudis, 2012, p. 75)

Hudis (2012) argues that in the *Critique of the Gotha Program*, Marx (1966) expressed a concept of an alternative to capitalism that offered both short-term and long-term goals and open-endedness. He demonstrates that what Marx called the "first phase" of communism, or communism "as it emerges from capitalist society ... still stamped with the birthmarks of the old society" (Hudis, 2012, p. 8), had the following goals.

First, alienated labor or value production would have to be abolished by ending the domination of time as an abstract standard that is determined behind the backs of the producers (Hudis, 2012, p. 191). Only then could compensation be based on actual labor time *or* energy expended (not quantitative output). Furthermore, in this very first phase of communism, compensated labor would include the kinds of work that are not valued under capitalism, such as domestic labor and childrearing. The total social product would, of course, have to be distributed after the associated producers determined what portion was to be put aside for social security, education, public health, and the reproduction of the means of production.

Second, the transcendence of value production would be possible only within the context of national and international coordination between non-state and democratic forms of self-rule by producers who include women, youth, and oppressed minorities. The Paris Commune was an example of a non-state form of democratic self-rule, which pointed beyond the state. However, it was *not*, and in its limited local form could not be, the model of national and international coordination that would be necessary to end the domination of abstract time in the process of production on a global level. For the same reason, Marx thought that workers' cooperatives, though a step forward, could not overcome value production so long as they were islands in an ocean of capitalism. There could be no socialism in one country.

Third, Marx was cognizant of the limits of the "first phase" of communism. He emphasized that although abolishing the rule of abstract time over the process of production would create transparency by allowing for compensation based on actual labor time or energy expended and not the social average time, the principle of compensation would still not go beyond the principle of bourgeois right. By that, Hudis (2012) interprets Marx to mean that in this first phase, "labor time—albeit in the radically altered form of actual and not average labor time—governs the distribution of the elements of production" (Hudis, 2012, p. 199).

That is why Hudis argues that Marx's (1966) *Critique of the Gotha Program* did not limit itself to the "first phase" of communism but envisioned what Marx called a *"higher phase"* (p. 10, emphasis is mine) *or higher phases*. This higher phase or phases presupposes an end to poverty, a great deal more leisure time and the all-round development of human beings. It embodies a life in which labor is no longer a mere means for providing one's means of subsistence or material production but the expression and development of one's natural and acquired talents, theoretical and practical.[9] This is also what Marx (1981) called "the development of human power as an end in itself" (p. 959).

Only then, Marx (1966) argued, could society practice the principle, "from each according to their ability, to each according to their needs" (p. 10). Furthermore, it can be argued that only then can humans fully go beyond utilitarian relationships and treat each other as ends in themselves.

Marx was cognizant of the fact that even if humans succeed in creating such a life form, we would not have perfectly rational human beings who would stop grappling with the conflicts between passion and reason. We would, however, live under conditions that allow us to deal with those conflicts in a peaceful and creative manner instead of killing and destroying each other.

My aim in discussing the relevance of Marx's concept of an alternative to capitalism for theorizing a socialist feminist alternative is not to be uncritical of Marx. Clearly, although he was a great visionary, he too had contradictions in his personal life and most importantly saw his philosophical project as a work in progress that needed further development.

Rather, I believe that socialist feminists who are truly serious about theorizing a vision that goes beyond private and state capitalism and all forms of oppression cannot make progress in this direction without grappling further with Marx.

We can have constructive debates as to what it means to overcome alienated labor and the capitalist concept of time, or whether it is really necessary to have what Marx envisioned as a two-phase process, to get to the point where the link between work time and income could be completely severed. However, we cannot simply skip over the issue of alienated labor and its connection to alienated human relations by advocating a return to a rural existence and subsistence farming, or by simply abolishing private property and the market and replacing them with cooperatives or a universal basic income as if these would solve the problem.

AUDRE LORDE'S VISION OF A NON-ALIENATED LABOR AND LIFE

Audre Lorde's (1984) vision of a non-alienated labor and life can help define a socialist feminist concept of an alternative to capitalism, and is in many ways similar to that of Marx. In Lorde's essay, "Uses of the Erotic: The Erotic as Power (1978)," she writes:

The principal horror of any system which defines the good in terms of profit rather than in terms of human need, or which defines human need to the exclusion of the psychic and emotional components of that need—the principal horror of such a system is that it robs our work of its erotic value, its erotic power and life appeal and fulfillment. Such a system reduces work to a travesty of necessities, a duty by which we earn bread or oblivion for ourselves and those we love. But this is tantamount to blinding a painter and then telling her to improve her work, and to enjoy the act of painting. It is not only next to impossible, it is also profoundly cruel. (Lorde, 1984, p. 55)

Lorde (1984) is not speaking of the abolition but of the *emancipation* of labor: "In the way my body stretches to music and opens into response, hearkening to its deepest rhythms, so every level upon which I sense also opens to the erotically satisfying experience, whether it is dancing, building a bookcase, writing a poem, examining an idea" (pp. 56–7). For Lorde, the key element of emancipation is a conscious existence in which mind, body, and heart are speaking to each other and are in tune with self and other, whether that other is other people or one's work. For her, emancipation is about an existence in which we are not fragmented but have the room to develop all our natural and acquired talents.

It is on the basis of such a non-alienated existence that Lorde (1984) thinks we "begin to be responsible to ourselves in the deepest sense ... we begin to give up of necessity being satisfied with suffering and self-negation and numbness which so often seems like the only alternative in our society ... . I become less willing to accept powerlessness ... resignation, despair, self-effacement, depression, self-denial" (p. 58). It is only then that we can "share the power of each other's feelings [which] is different from using another's feelings as we would use a Kleenex" (p. 58). It is only then that we can "make connections with our similarities and our differences" (p. 59).

Now, I would like to address the question of an alternative to capitalism in a different way, by posing what it is not. Let's examine the work of a Marxist feminist who argued that what existed in the former USSR and Maoist China was actually another form of capitalism.

WHAT THE ALTERNATIVE TO CAPITALISM IS NOT: RAYA DUNAYEVSKAYA'S CRITIQUE OF STATE CAPITALISM IN THE USSR AND MAOIST CHINA

Among socialist feminist thinkers, few have analyzed the specific nature of the economies of the former USSR and Maoist China. Raya Dunayevskaya offered analyses of the USSR as a state capitalist society as early as 1941 and spent a lifetime critiquing both the USSR and Maoist China as totalitarian state capitalist societies. She also reached out to and communicated with labor, feminist, and other dissident socialists within those countries. For her, state capitalism was a world stage that began in the 1930s and manifested itself in different forms, ranging from totalitarian in the USSR and Nazi Germany, to more democratic in the U.S. New Deal. Although it is not possible to do justice to her extensive writings on these topics, here I would like to single out some aspects of her analyses that can help illuminate the issue of what constitutes or does not constitute an alternative to capitalism.

Dunayevskaya[10] had been Leon Trotsky's Russian secretary in Mexico from 1937 to 1938, and broke from him in 1939 over his continued defense of the Soviet Union as a "degenerated workers' state" (Trotsky, 1937, pp. 245–7; and see J. Afary, 1985). In 1939, Joseph Stalin (1878–1953) had formed an alliance with Adolf Hitler (1889–1945) that was simply unacceptable to Dunayevskaya. In face of the 1939 Molotov-Ribbentrop Pact, also known as the Hitler-Stalin Pact, she refused to accept the designation of the nature of the USSR as any form of a workers' state. She followed her break with a study of Russia's Five Year Plans (1928–40), a deeper study of Marx's *Capital* and discovery of Marx's *Economic and Philosophical Manuscripts of 1844*. She also joined forces with Trinidadian Marxist, C.L.R. James, and Chinese American Marxist, Grace Lee Chin (later Grace Lee Boggs), with both of whom she went on to form the Johnson-Forest Tendency,[11] within the U.S. Workers' Party in 1940. That tendency advocated a state capitalist analysis of the USSR, which Dunayevskaya and James had each independently arrived at prior to their collaboration.

In February 1941, she published an essay titled "The Union of Soviet Socialist Republics is a Capitalist Society," which was published by the Workers' Party under her pen name, Freddie James. In this essay, she challenged Leon Trotsky's view that nationalization of property made the USSR a workers' state. Instead, she argued that the determinant for identifying a society as socialist was not whether the means of production were nationalized, but whether the means of production were no longer capital, that is, not used as a means for the extraction and expansion of value. Dunayevskaya pointed out that the development of productive forces in the Soviet Union had not raised the workers' standard of living. Instead, they had reproduced capitalist relations of production through the production of value and surplus value. Later in 1942, in an essay titled "Labor and Society," which was written as the introduction to her study of the USSR's economy, she reclaimed Marx's critique of alienated labor in his *Economic and Philosophical Manuscripts of 1844* and argued that "for Marx, the abolition of private property was not an end in itself but a means toward the abolition of the alienated mode of labor" (Dunayevskaya, 1992, p. 23).

Her study of the USSR's three Five Year Plans (1928–40), which covered the period before Nazi Germany invaded the USSR, pointed out that the USSR's economy had moved in the direction of the preponderance of the production of the means of production over the production of the means of consumption.[12] This reality, and the huge gap between the increase in the rate of productivity and the low increase in the rate of wages (or rather a 50 percent decrease in real wages compared with 1928), were, from her Marxist standpoint, one of the determinants signifying the capitalist nature of the USSR. In addition, the state provided some chosen workers with exceptional equipment, asked them to increase the intensity of their work during show events, and used them as models for other workers to emulate. These workers, named after Alexei Grigorievich Stakhanov (1906–1977), became known as Stakhanovites, and were used to pressure other workers to produce at the same level, regardless of their physical ability or age. The state turned to piecework, the Stakhanovist speed up, and the turnover tax (similar to the value-added tax or consumption tax) on basic food items, as means of extracting additional surplus value from the working class. In Dunayevskaya's view, the Stakhanovist technical intelligentsia along with the state administrators and the army leadership represented the new ruling class (Dunayevskaya, 1992, p. 76, see also pp. 25–83; see also Dunayevskaya, 2000, pp. 212–39).[13]

Dunayevskaya (1992) also emphasized that the USSR's reliance on a mode of labor based on the extraction of value and surplus value, and the domination of dead labor in the form of machines over living labor, was codified in the 1936 constitution proposed by Stalin. This constitution's stated principle for labor was "from each according to his ability, to each according to his work" (Stalin, 1936). She argued that it demonstrated an economy based on piecework which was best suited for capitalism by extracting the maximum amount of work from each, and paying based on the quantity and monetary value of output (Dunayevskaya, 1992, pp. 75–6).

The 1936 constitution was followed by the 1936 to 1938 Moscow Trials, through which Stalin accused the general staff of the Bolshevik Revolution of "treason" and conspiring with Western powers, and then eliminated them through a series of executions. What followed was also repression and mass executions of workers and citizens who resisted the Stalinist state, whether in forced labor camps or outside of them (see Stalin, 1936). About these developments, Dunayevskaya (1992) argued,

The Counter-Revolution is the legitimate offspring of the "new" mode of production, out of Stalinism and fired by the imperialist world economy. It is this method of production, and not the legal enactments, that needs, above all, to be investigated. In this investigation we will find that, as in any capitalist economy, the two major contending forces are capital and labor. (p. 76)

She pointed out that the slogan of the first Five Year Plan (1928–32) remained the aim of all the Five Year Plans (see Souvarine, 1930), and Russia's future development: "To Catch Up with and Overtake the Capitalist Lands" at the expense of working the USSR masses to death or killing them through executions, forced labor camps, and other forms of repression. This slogan promoted Stalin's lie of "socialism in one country."

In 1943, Dunayevskaya translated and analyzed an article titled "Teaching of Economics in the Soviet Union" that had been published in a prominent USSR state-sponsored economics journal, *Pod Znamenem Marxizma*. The authors of the article were assumed to be the journal's editors. They admitted that the law of value functioned in the USSR. Dunayevskaya (1944) published her translation along with her commentary in the prominent U.S. journal, *American Economic Review*, and engaged in a debate about it with other U.S. economists such as Paul Baran, Leo Rogin, and Oscar Lange.

The original article had claimed that since commodity production, exchange, and the use of money preceded the appearance of capitalist production, these phenomena could function under socialism as well. Furthermore, it claimed that what Marx called "the dual character of labor" (Marx, 1976, p. 131) under capitalism could also exist under socialism. However, it argued that the planned character of the USSR's economy removed the harmful and capitalistic aspects of these phenomena because the surplus produced was not privately accumulated and went to the state which claimed to represent the working class (Baran, 1944, p. 867).

In her commentary about the *Pod Znamenem Marxizma* article, which Dunayevskaya entitled "A New Revision of Marxian Economics," she argued that "*In its Marxian interpretation … the law of value entails the use of the concept of alienated or exploited labor, and, as a consequence, the concept of surplus value*" (Dunayevskaya, 1944, p. 533, emphasis in the original). What she sought to emphasize was that although money, and production for exchange had historically existed before the rise of capitalism, they were not dominant. Under capitalism, commodity production in the sense of a mode of production based on the dual character of labor and the law of value, hence money and price, became dominant.

The existence of such a mode of production and its consequences could not be justified in a socialist society. "To Marx, value is not a quantitative relationship but a qualitative relationship, that is a class relationship" (Dunayevskaya, 1945, p. 663).

Furthermore, she argued that when Marx's (1966) *Critique of the Gotha Program* addressed what he called the "first phase" of communism emerging from capitalist society, he was suggesting that producers would be compensated in means of consumption and services (not money) and based on actual labor time. He was not referring to a global social average time (socially necessary labor time) determined behind the backs of the producers (Dunayevskaya, 1945, p. 663).

This question of the concept of labor time under socialism, and how it differed from the concept of labor time under capitalism, remained a preoccupation for Dunayevskaya because it was a key manifestation of whether producers controlled the process of production or whether, as in capitalism, the process of production controlled them.

Dunayevskaya (1985) was also deeply concerned about the ways in which women's struggles and achievements after the Russian Revolution were stifled by the Stalinist state capitalist counter-revolution, and she emphasized that "the retrogression was seen most actively in the abolition of the Zhenotdel," the Working and Peasant Women's Department of the Communist Party (p. 97; see also Stites, 1978, pp. 317–416).

In the case of Maoist China, Dunayevskaya's analysis examined what was different about state capitalism in China, and in Mao's thought in particular. The Chinese Revolution of 1949 embodied an alliance of the Communist Party and the Chinese national bourgeoisie. It was not a revolution with the working class in leadership (Meisner, 1999, p. 56). The "Report on the Draft Constitution of the People's Republic of China" stated the following on September 15, 1954: "The transitional form for the socialist transformation of industry and commerce is state capitalism …. State capitalism under the control of a state led by the working class is different in nature from state capitalism under bourgeois rule."[14]

In Mao's own words:

We must by no means allow a recurrence of such ultra-left, erroneous policies as were adopted toward the petty and middle bourgeoisie by our party in the period from 1931 to 1934 (the advocating of uneconomically high standards in working conditions, excessively high income tax rates ... the shortsighted, one-sided view of the so-called "welfare of the toiler" instead of making our objective the development of production, the prosperity of our economy, the taking into account of both public and private interests and benefits of both labor and capital). (Mao, quoted in Kautsky, 1956; cited in Dunayevskaya, 2000, p. 303)

In line with Stalin's policies, Mao's concept of "the bloc of four classes" also defined the urban petit-bourgeoisie and the national bourgeoisie as allies of the working class.[15] In 1952 and 1953, full state ownership of industry was implemented in China. With the First Five Year Plan (1953–57), former capitalist owners became managers and were promised higher pay. Strikes were banned and workers were told to produce more and more. Trade unions became organs of disciplining workers. Forced labor became a regular feature. Soon afterward, the "One Hundred Flowers Campaign," in 1956, was crushed and more youth and dissident intellectuals were killed.

In the words of China scholar, Maurice Meisner (1999), the Chinese state plan established in 1952

emphasized to an even greater degree than had been the case in the Soviet Union, the development of such heavy industries as steel, machine building, fuel, electric power, metallurgy, and basic chemicals. Only 11.2 percent of state capital investments in industry was to go to light industry (consumer production), while 88.8 percent went to heavy industry. (p. 112)

In her book, *Marxism and Freedom* which was originally published in 1958 and then expanded in new editions, Dunayevskaya's (2000) discussion of the specificity of state capitalism in China focused on the Great Leap Forward and the experience of the Cultural Revolution. In the case of the Great Leap Forward (1958–62), she singled out the following distinct features in what she viewed as a process of accumulation of capital:

(1) Mao's goal was for China to achieve in ten years, the type of industrialization that it had taken the USSR 40 years to achieve.
(2) The militarization of labor (men and women) was called mass mobilization or "the mass line."

(3) Under miserable working conditions with no personal freedoms, the Chinese masses were forced to build irrigation projects and other means of industrial growth. They were to make up for China's industrial underdevelopment with bare hands and sheer *voluntarism* or willpower (Dunayevskaya, 2000, pp. 312–15).

(4) Marxist language about ending the division between mental and manual labor was used to promote this campaign.

In reality, however, the Great Leap Forward led to a famine that killed more than 30 million people in China (Meisner, 1999, pp. 257–8).

In Dunayevskaya's (2000) view, Chinese state capitalism differed from Russian state capitalism and included a concept of "thought reform." "Mao has raised the concept of 'thought reform' both to a philosophic category and a veritable way of life" (p. 314). What she specifically had in mind was Mao's view that the class struggle would continue for decades or even several centuries under socialism, and that political and cultural reforms would become the principal and decisive factors (see Mao Zedong, 1937, 1957). In her *Philosophy and Revolution* originally published in 1973, Dunayevskaya (2003) wrote:

What is central to the thought of Mao and distinguishes him from Stalin is his concept of the peasantry as revolutionary and his belief in "rectification." The latter is seen not only as a purge from above but as if a remolding of thought could actually be achieved without any relationship to a historical materialist base. (p. 161)

Thus she argued that Mao "*has totally denuded the Marxian theory of its class nature and its historicity*" (p. 164, emphasis in the original).

This Maoist effort downplayed the continuation of exploitative class relations in China and placed the focus instead on a cultural revolution. Mao claimed that it was possible to have a genuine cultural revolution while objective material economic exploitation and a class society continued. This revision of Marxism was, in Dunayevskaya's view, most clearly expressed in the Cultural Revolution (1966–76), which Mao initiated. Indeed the slogan of the Cultural Revolution was "Grasp the Revolution and Increase Production" (Dunayevskaya, 2003, p. 160; see also Kraus, 2012, pp. 63–84). Another slogan was "politics in command," by which Mao meant *voluntarism* or pushing oneself to work harder on the basis of sheer willpower, regardless of physical bodily and objective material limitations (Kraus, 2012, p. 24).

However, Dunayevskaya (2003) points out that "though set in motion from above, the masses broke through the boundaries set by Mao and designed workers' control of production" (p. 160). She specifically singles out Sheng-Wu-Lien (Hunan Provincial Proletarian Revolutionary Great Alliance Committee), a genuine proletarian and youth socialist revolutionary struggle in Hunan province, which likened itself to the Paris Commune of 1871, and called for the overthrow of the Chinese leadership as the "Red Capitalist Class," at which point they were brutally crushed by government forces.[16]

Dunayevskaya (2003) also points out that Mao called the demands of Sheng-Wu-Lien and those of other genuine revolutionaries in the Cultural Revolution, "economism" and opposed the movement from below as "ultra leftist," "anarchist," and "irresponsible." He also unleashed the Chinese army, led by Lin Biao, against the grassroots revolts (p. 160).

During the years of the Cultural Revolution (1966–76), over 400,000 were killed. Millions were arrested and sent to forced labor camps (Meisner, 1999, p. 354). Production was militarized and became more efficient. The GDP increased 6 percent per year. With the exception of some improvements in rural health care and primary school education, however, the standard of living of Chinese peasants and workers did not increase. Similar to the USSR, heavy industry grew at the expense of light industry (Kraus, 2012, pp. 81–2).

In Dunayevskaya's (2003) view, what motivated Mao was a nationalist and state capitalist ambition for overtaking first, the USSR, and then the West, thereby making China a global power expressing "*single* world mastery" (p. 185, emphasis in the original). It is this drive that she saw as the root of the Sino-Soviet conflict, emerging in the early 1960s, since the USSR too aimed to overtake the West and become a global superpower.

As against U.S. feminist Roxane Witke, who glorified the role of Mao's wife, Jiang Jing in the Cultural Revolution, Dunayevskaya (1985) denounced Jiang Jing for her uncritical following of Mao, her role in promoting murders and horrors during the Cultural Revolution, and for acting as a "Chinese Stakhanovite" (p. 153). Instead, Dunayevskaya singled out and praised Chinese Marxist feminist Ding Ling (1904–1986), who was purged from the party after the 1957 Hundred Flowers Campaign for criticizing the views of the party on marriage and love, and for her earlier essay, "Thoughts on March 8," which exposed the cruel ways in which the wives of party leaders were used (Ding Ling, 1989, pp. 316–21).

CONCLUSION: MOVING TOWARD THEORIZING A SOCIALIST HUMANIST AND FEMINIST ALTERNATIVE TO CAPITALISM

In this chapter, I began by reviewing conceptions of alternatives to capitalism posed by Nancy Fraser, Ann Ferguson, Patricia Hill Collins, Maria Mies, Silvia Federici, and Kathi Weeks. I argued that socialist feminist demands for reforms or creating autonomous zones and cooperatives are progressive, but are not enough to overcome capitalism, sexism, and racism, heterosexism and alienation.

It is entirely possible for socialist feminists to reclaim the commons, create communes, establish a universal basic income, or go back to subsistence agriculture, change the legal system of distribution and representation, but still have alienation, exploitation, oppression, and not go beyond a state capitalist society. Methods such as opposing privatization of the means of production, calling for collectivization of domestic and reproductive labor, or focusing on agricultural production and more egalitarian distribution, would not necessarily address the issue of capitalist alienation.

Audre Lorde's (1984) essay, "Uses of the Erotic: The Erotic As Power (1978)," provides us with a glimpse of what non-alienated labor and existence might be like. It helps us broaden our vision of an affirmative alternative to capitalism. It is not only focused on relations of distribution but also on reconceptualizing the relationship of mind to body and heart, ending the fragmentation of the human being and creating a thoughtful and creative existence in which human relations are not utilitarian.

I have argued that a return to and a deeper examination of Marx's concept of an alternative to capitalism is necessary to realize this goal. Marx shows us that the capitalist mode of production is based on alienated labor which in turn leads to the production of value and the creation of a system in which the expansion of value becomes an end in itself. Capitalism does not just lead to income inequality but also commodifies and thingifies all human relations, dehumanizes us, and alienates us from each other. It takes the mental/manual division of labor characteristic of all class societies to the extreme.

Marx's concepts and analyses help us see the limitations of simply arguing for communal ownership and income redistribution. They address the ways in which the capitalist mode of labor creates not only inequality but also an impersonal system of domination and calculating relationships, whether in romantic love or the family and other social relations.

Marx's idea of ending the domination of abstract time over the process of production is promising and gives more content to the socialist aim of workers' control of production. On the one hand, abstract time or socially necessary labor time, or a social average time as the measure of labor, is the consequence of alienated labor itself which reduces labor to simple average labor. On the other hand, alienated labor cannot be overcome so long as abstract time, or a social average time determined behind the backs of the producers, governs the process of production.

Money or value, which is an expression of alienated labor, would only be abolished if alienated labor, and hence a social average time as the measure of labor, are also abolished. In that case, compensation would only be through means of consumption, not through money or means of consumption acting like money.

There are many questions about problems that would arise during what Marx called "the first phase" of communism. Some types of labor are more onerous and exhausting than others, and would require greater compensation or would count as more actual time. Furthermore, people with different levels of skill and education would not easily accept the idea that all should be entitled to equal compensation for an equal number of hours worked. At the same time, the idea of creating an extensive system of classification of labor compensation based on skill levels would be capitalistic and would take us back to the failed models that called themselves socialist.

A normal work week would have to be much shorter than 40 hours, and every effort would have to be made to create more leisure time. At the same time, the idea of simply abolishing the connection between time worked and compensation received for healthy people within the normal work age would most likely not be immediately accepted by humanity as a whole, given the hundreds of years of existence of capitalism. Marx's proposed "first phase" might, in some ways, look like a system based on a universal basic income in the sense that people would get compensated with means of consumption on the basis of actual work time and not on a socially average time. In other words, one person's hour will not be entitled to more compensation than another's unless it involves onerous work or work that takes up a great deal more energy, such as working at a childcare center or teaching elementary school or working in an emergency room.

In a socialist society, reproductive labor for one's own family would have to count as work time but not as a permanent full-time job or a job for one gender only. Time spent on higher education or continuing education would also have to be counted as work time. Health care and education for all would be free in the sense that those services would be made possible by shares taken out of each healthy adult person's contribution to the total social product, and would not have to be paid for by individuals upon receiving a service.

Experimenting with various forms of love and various forms of family would have to be part and parcel of socialism from the very beginning. There can be no fundamental transformation in the mode of production if family and love relationships are not also transformed. However, the Maoist idea of a cultural revolution without transforming the mode of production, and without the abolition of alienated labor, would be unacceptable. We cannot possibly accept the idea that it would take a century to abolish class society and separate the changes in culture and in family relations from transformations in labor.

At the same time, we must oppose the Maoist distortion of the Marxian concept of ending the mental/manual division of labor. In the name of this concept, Mao forced people to work themselves to death to promote production for the sake of production. In a socialist society, ending the mental/manual division of labor would certainly have to mean that no one would do only mind work or only physical work. We would need what Michael Albert (2003) has called "balanced job complexes" (p. 103, also see pp. 103–11), to allow people to perform a variety of tasks and learn new skills, and also what Frigga Haug (2020b) calls "Four-in-One-Perspective" (p. 38).[17] What is considered "menial work" would also have to be shared. However, ending the mental/manual division of labor is about much more than this. It is about making our work *thoughtful* and creating a purposeful and meaningful existence in which we humans move toward developing all our natural and acquired talents. It is not about voluntarism or forced labor, nor is it about nationalist competition in the name of socialism.

The experiences of the USSR and Maoist China, which Raya Dunayevskaya has analyzed as state capitalism, show that socialism cannot be realized in one country alone. Socialism, in the sense of abolition of both the private and state ownership of the means of production and the abolition of alienated labor, would have to be a locally and globally coordinated effort, or there will be no socialism. Since capitalism is a global system, a socialist alternative to it cannot be established in one country alone. Ending capitalism requires a global movement to overcome alienated labor, capitalism's system of value production, and its concept of time. The global coordination would also involve reparations for historically colonized and enslaved populations, and open borders. The challenge of creating new human relationships also demands reconceptualizing the relationship of self to other, and exploring what it means to overcome domination. It is to this topic that we turn in the next chapter.

8

Overcoming Domination: Reconceptualizing the Self-Other Relationship

Drama makes more visible what each of us does when we pass over in our deepest, most immersive forms of reading. We welcome the Other as a guest within ourselves, and sometimes we become Other. For a moment in time we leave ourselves; and when we return, sometimes expanded and strengthened, we are changed both intellectually and emotionally.

—Maryanne Wolf (2018), *Reader, Come Home*[1]

In the previous chapter, we examined the topic of alternatives to capitalism from a socioeconomic point of view. In this chapter, we will examine this topic from a philosophical point of view. Does the dynamic of *self-other* always have to be about domination? How have socialist feminists analyzed this issue and sought to offer alternatives? This chapter will discuss the ideas of Simone de Beauvoir and Jessica Benjamin on the roots of domination. It will then examine the ideas of Allison Weir, Raya Dunayevskaya, Georg Wilhelm Friedrich Hegel, Frantz Fanon, and Audre Lorde on overcoming domination.

SIMONE DE BEAUVOIR AND JESSICA BENJAMIN ON THE ROOTS OF DOMINATION

Simone de Beauvoir (1949) begins *The Second Sex* by asking why women throughout history have been considered the "Other," the object, the inessential, the particular, the immanent, the dependent, while men are considered the subject, the essential, the universal, the transcendent, the independent, the Absolute (Beauvoir, 1989). She blames women for accepting their role and failing to bring about change. In contrast to proletarians and African Americans who identify as a WE and fight for their rights, women, she claims, do not see themselves as subjects. They do not seek freedom, which begins with transcending oneself (Beauvoir, 1989, p. xxxv).

Clearly, the claim that women have accepted their role and do not see themselves as subjects was not entirely true, even in 1949, and is certainly not valid in the third decade in the twenty-first century, when women have been in the forefront of uprisings and revolts. Beauvoir's discussion of woman as "Other," however, is still quite relevant to the focus of this chapter on overcoming relations of domination.

Beauvoir's analysis of the relationship of self to other presupposes the model presented by Hegel (1985) in the section titled "Lordship and Bondage" in his *Phenomenology of Mind* (1807). Here, Hegel begins by arguing that consciousness of the self is only possible when the self is acknowledged or "recognized" by another self-consciousness. He demonstrates the process of arriving at this recognition by beginning with the bare level of life. At this stage, each individual consciousness views the other as an unessential object. Each aims at the destruction and death of the other and risks his life in a life and death struggle, in order to gain certainty of being for self. Killing the other, however, would end the possibility for the self to gain certainty of itself and recognition from the other. Therefore, the other must not be killed, but rather reduced to a position of submission. Hence, this life and death struggle results on one side in a dominant independent consciousness, whose essential nature is to be for itself, and a dependent subordinated consciousness whose essence is existence for another. The former becomes the master, the latter becomes the bondsman. This form of recognition is one-sided and unequal. Hegel then proceeds to demonstrate the process of tran-scendence of this unequal relationship: the slave, who is supposed to represent the inferior consciousness, gradually gains an independent consciousness that is higher than the master's because she shapes and fashions things through her activity of laboring, and is engaged in a more genuine overcoming of externality. Furthermore, for Hegel, this is not the end. In order to achieve liberation, self-consciousness will have to develop further to reach the stages of Reason and Absolute Knowledge in the *Phenomenology of Mind* (Hegel, 1985 [1949], pp. 228–40). We will come back to the Hegelian concept of transcendence later in this chapter.[2]

In Beauvoir's (1989) analysis, woman does not gain a mind of her own through struggle.

> Proletarians say "We." Negroes also. Regarding themselves as subjects, they transform the bourgeois, the whites into "others." But Women do not say "We" ... They do not authentically assume a subjective attitude. ... They have gained only what men have been willing to grant. (p. xxv)

Hence, Beauvoir's emphasis in most of *The Second Sex* is on the circumstances that have prevented women from experiencing transcendence.

These barriers to transcendence, Beauvoir (1989) argues, cannot be adequately explained by biological determinism. First, she emphasizes that the division of the species into two sexes is not clear-cut because "every biological fact implies transcendence" (p. 10). By this she might mean that biology itself involves evolution and change. Second, she argues that while biological considerations are "extremely important," they do not establish "a fixed and inevitable destiny" (p. 32). A person's identity and future also depend upon the economic and the social circumstances.

Beauvoir also believes that the psychoanalytic Freudian point of view does not adequately explain the barriers to women's experiencing transcendence of domination. While "an advance" over biological determinism, Freudian psychoanalysis does not distinguish between emotions and sexuality. For Freud, all human behavior seems to be the outcome of desire. He thus ignores the role of motives, purpose, or projects. In sum, Freudian psychoanalysis "reject[s] the idea of choice and the correlated concept of values" (Beauvoir, 1989, p. 45). Thus, Freud's framework, too, does not explain why woman is the "Other."

In historical materialism by which Beauvoir means Marxism, she justifiably challenges Friedrich Engels's (1977) *The Origin of the Family, Private Property and the State* by arguing that the rise of private property cannot explain what Engels called "the world historical defeat of the female sex" (p. 57). Engels's "project is still not enough to explain why she [woman] was oppressed, for the division of labor between the sexes could have meant a friendly association" (Beauvoir, 1989, p. 57). Furthermore, Beauvoir (1989) argues, Engels does not explain how the passage from the regime of community ownership to that of private property came about and why private property necessarily involved the enslavement of women. He does not explain how friendly relations between men changed into enslavement (p. 57).

Beauvoir (1989) instead uses an existentialist framework to explain what she considers to be the origins of domination in general, and of the domination of women by men in particular. She argues that

> for it [the concept of personal possession] to appear, there must have been at first an inclination in the subject to think of himself as basically individual, to assert the autonomy and separateness of his existence. ... The discovery of bronze enabled man, in the experience of hard and productive labor, to discover himself as creator; dominating nature, he was no longer afraid of it, and in the fact of obstacles overcome he found courage to see himself as an autonomous active force, to achieve self-fulfillment as an individual. (p. 56)

Hence, in Beauvoir's (1989) view, the phenomenon of enslavement of man by man or of woman by man

> is a result of the imperialism of the human consciousness, seeking always to exercise its sovereignty in objective fashion. If the human consciousness had not included the original category of the other, and an original aspiration to dominate the other, the invention of the bronze tool could not have caused the oppression of woman. (p. 58)

Here we see Beauvoir asserting that there is a desire for domination of others at the core of the human psyche. This "imperialism of the human consciousness" is the root of oppression. She goes on to argue that what is different about the oppression of women, however, is that it is internalized and accepted as *natural* by women.

For further illumination on Beauvoir's views on this issue, we can turn to Jean-Paul Sartre's (1993 [1943]) *Being and Nothingness*, the foundational work of Existentialism, which he wrote in dialogue with Beauvoir and which also became the philosophical foundation for *The Second Sex*.

Sartre's (2001) discussion of a manner of being called "being-for-others" is based on Hegel's master-slave dialectic. However, unlike Hegel, for Sartre, the power struggle for domination cannot be transcended. One party always dominates the other. Since "I" gain my self-consciousness by being recognized by the other, Sartre concludes that the other "holds the secret of my being" (p. 226). Thus "the profound meaning of my being is outside of me. ... The Other has the advantage over me" (p. 226). I can either "transcend the Other's transcendence or, on the contrary, to incorporate that transcendence within me" (p. 226). However, since Sartre considers these attitudes as fundamentally opposed to each other, he concludes that we cannot do both. "There is no dialectic for my relation toward the Other but rather a circle. ... We can never get outside the circle" (p. 227). "The Other holds a secret—the secret of what I am. ... Thus my project of recovering myself is fundamentally a project of absorbing the Other" (pp. 227–8). He continues, "[s]ince the Other is the foundation of my being, he could not be dissolved in me" (p. 228). Hence, a never-ending conflict ensues.

Sartre's (2001) discussion of "being-for-others" can also illuminate why Beauvoir emphasizes women's acceptance of their status as inferior. Sartre argues that although in the master-slave dialectic, the master wants to be the center of attention for the slave, there is no claim to freedom in the relationship. In a love relationship, moreover, the person who is loved, the beloved, wants to be the freely chosen center of attention. Hence, the beloved is held captive not necessarily by brute force but by the promotion of ideal love and exclusivity. "It is the one who wants to be loved who by the mere fact of wanting someone to love him alienates his freedom" (p. 239). Sartre calls this a "masochistic attitude" (p. 241).

Beauvoir (1947) elaborates on this further in her *Ethics of Ambiguity*, which is her effort at theoretically articulating the existentialist frame-work. In critiquing Hegelian dialectics as it relates to human relations, she writes:

> The essential moment of Hegelian ethics is the moment when con-sciousnesses recognize one another; in this operation the other is recognized as identical with me, which means that in myself, it is the universal truth of myself which alone is recognized; so individuality is denied ... moral salvation will lie in my surpassing toward that other who is equal to myself and who in turn will surpass himself toward another. (p. 112)

In contrast, she argues, "After Descartes, how can we ignore the fact that subjectivity radically signifies separation?" (p. 113). Thus, she speaks of an existentialist ethics of ambiguity as an effort to articulate "permanent tension" (p. 144) between self and Other, individual and universal. She believes that human consciousness is always characterized by conflict between self and Other, and the desire to dominate the Other.

Furthermore, she questions Hegel for assuming that in the master-slave dialectic, the slave comes to reject their own oppressive situation and gains a mind of their own. Beauvoir argues that:

> there are cases where the slave does not know his servitude and where it is necessary to bring the seed of his liberation to him from the outside. … The slave is submissive when one has succeeded in mystifying him in such a way that his situation does not seem to him to be imposed by men but to be immediately given by nature … He cannot even dream of any other [condition]. … What must be done is to furnish the ignorant slave with the means of transcending his situation by means of revolt, to put an end to his ignorance. (Beauvoir, 1947, pp. 91–2)

These foundational existentialist views can help us better understand why Beauvoir thinks that the relationship of Self to other will always be characterized by domination. They also reveal why from her standpoint, women always see themselves as the Other.[3]

How then will women liberate themselves from this otherness? In the penultimate chapter of *The Second Sex*, Beauvoir (1989) argues that for women to liberate themselves, they need to gain "the sense of the universal," to reason, revolt, imagine, and create. Women's liberation must be collective (pp. 616–27). Women need economic independence through meaningful work. They also need to freely express their sexuality "not [as] a mere matter of satisfying erotic desire but of maintaining their dignity as human beings while obtaining satisfaction" (p. 688), because love is not about victory or defeat but about "a free exchange" (p. 692).

The most critical aspect of achieving transcendence for Beauvoir (1989) is for woman to "go forward with her eyes fixed straight ahead on a goal" (p. 699), and to "passionately lose herself in her project" (p. 702). Women need to explore and "discover meanings" (p. 710), ask questions and expose contradictions (p. 711), "take the weight of the world upon their shoulders" (p. 713), "regard the universe as one's own, to consider oneself to blame for its faults and glory in its progress" (p. 713). This is what Beauvoir thinks a historical character like Rosa Luxemburg

(1871–1919), a Polish-German Marxist revolutionary theoretician was able to demonstrate.

In the penultimate paragraph of *The Second Sex*, Beauvoir (1989) cites the passage from Karl Marx's (1961) *Economic and Philosophical Manuscripts of 1844* on the relationship of man to woman with which we are familiar now:

> The nature of this relation determines to what point man himself is to be considered as a generic being, as human kind ... to what point the natural behavior of man has become human or to what point the human being has become his natural being; to what point his human nature has become his nature. (Marx, 1961, p. 126, quoted in Beauvoir, 1989, pp. 731–2)

As I stated earlier in Chapter 4, this passage from Marx is proposing a concept of human nature based on the potential for free and conscious activity. He is arguing that the relationship of man to woman, especially when sexuality is involved, can reveal whether man is moving in the direction of achieving the human potential for free and conscious activity or sinking deeper and deeper into alienation.[4]

In contrast to Marx, however, Beauvoir (1989) concludes: "It is for man to establish the reign of liberty in the midst of the world of the given" (p. 732). This conclusion seems to flow from her earlier view that slaves do not necessarily revolt against their servitude when their situation is presented to them as a "natural" condition.

In her later writings, Beauvoir becomes a feminist and an active participant in the women's liberation movement after 1970 (see Beauvoir, 2014; Schwarzer, 1984). At that point, she no longer argues that it is up to men to establish the reign of liberty for women. She instead becomes a strong supporter of autonomous women's organizations while she continues to advocate socialist revolutionary transformations.

Now, let us turn to Jessica Benjamin, a Freudian psychoanalyst and relational feminist who has been deeply influenced by Beauvoir, but who has also attempted to modify Beauvoir's explanation of relations of domination in interpersonal and gender relations.

Benjamin's (1988) *The Bonds of Love: Psychoanalysis, Feminism, and the Problem of Domination*, like Beauvoir, argues that domination is not simply exercised through repression. Rather, it can involve voluntary submission, idealization, and love of the dominator. Benjamin traces this phenomenon back to a complex process of psychic development starting from boys' and girls' different relationships to their mother and father. Her effort is to "retell Freud's story of domination" (p. 10), and to offer a way of coping with the contradiction between self and other.

Benjamin's argument is based on two different understandings of the relationship of self to other. The Hegelian master-slave dialectic in contrast to the concept of recognition offered by Donald Winnicott (1896–1971), British pediatrician and neo-Freudian psychoanalyst. In the Hegelian master-slave dialectic, according to Benjamin (1988), "Hegel posits a self that has no intrinsic need for the other, but uses the other only as a vehicle for self-certainty" (p. 33). This "monadic, self-interested ego" (p. 33), she argues, is also present in classical Freudian psychoanalytic theory. In ego psychology or "internalization theory" (p. 43), where development occurs through separation and identification, she emphasizes that the self is "omnipotent" (p. 67). Everything is an extension of the self and its power. The isolated subject engages in an "internalization of what is outside to develop what is inside" (p. 43). The other is "consumed, incorporated, digested by the subject self" (p. 43). The other "seems more and more like a cocoon or a husk that must gradually be shed—one has got what one needs, and now goodbye" (p. 43). Benjamin rejects this "instrumental relationship" (p. 43) because it is about "obliterating difference" (p. 48).

In contrast, Benjamin (1988) argues, in Winnicott's theory of recognition, which she considers to be an "intersubjective theory" (p. 45) or an intersubjective view of differentiation and development, there is a "paradoxical balance" (p. 46) of tension "between recognition of the other and assertion of self" (p. 46), between sameness and difference of two interacting subjects, each of whom contributes without being incorporated by the other. The other always remains external and other. Benjamin's main thesis is that when this tension and this "paradoxical balance" (p. 46) is not maintained, the relation of self to other leads to various forms of domination (p. 50).

Similar to Beauvoir, Benjamin (1988) dismisses the idea that in the Hegelian master-slave dialectic, the slave gains a mind of their own and challenges the master. Instead, Benjamin equates Hegel and Freud's views on the relationship of self to other, and claims that they implicitly explain why the oppressed submit to domination (p. 54). Both thinkers, she argues, "assume the inevitable human aspiration to omnipotence and they begin and end in the no-exit of domination, in the closed system of opposites, doer and done to, master and slave" (p. 62). In Hegelian dialectics, she claims, "the slave fears that the master will abandon her to aloneness" (p. 65). In Freud's theory of instincts, she argues, the "death drive that impels us toward the complete absence of tension" explains domination (p. 66).

In contrast, the intersubjective theory of Winnicott, Benjamin (1988) argues, offers an alternative to domination by experiencing the other "as external reality" (p. 68). In Winnicott's proposed "experience of attunement" (p. 74), separate individuals can share the same feeling.

How is it that "the subjugation of women takes hold in the psyche and shapes the pattern of domination?" (Benjamin, 1988, p. 74). Basing her philosophy on the work of Nancy Chodorow, an American psychoanalytic sociologist, Benjamin (1988) argues that male children, who initially identify with the mother who is their primary caregiver, eventually come to the realization that they are not women, and that to achieve their masculinity, they must deny their original identity or oneness with their mothers. Hence, masculine identity formation becomes a rejection of the mother. Benjamin writes, "She is not seen as an independent person (another subject) but as something other—as nature, as an instrument or object, as less than human (p. 76).

Benjamin then takes Chodorow's argument further. Benjamin (1988) explains that around the age of two years, toddlers begin to identify with an adult who represents the outside world and independence. If the environment and society is such that women represent dependence and the home, and men represent independence and the outside world, toddlers identify with and idealize the father or other male characters (p. 100). The child in turn needs to be recognized by the very person they idealize. If that character is the father, for the boy, idealization of the father does not lead to submission because the father accepts him as "you are like me" (p. 107). However, for the girl, the idealization of the father as independent does not lead to the father's acceptance of her as a member of the same gender. Therefore, the girl always feels unrecognized and unacknowledged. She thus develops a tendency to form her identity by being in gender relationships in which she is not recognized as an equal (p. 107).

Benjamin (1988) interprets Freud's "penis envy" as evidence that little girls, like little boys, wish to identify with and gain recognition from a father who represents independence and the outside world (pp. 108–9). Since fathers do not recognize their daughters as equals, little girls develop a sense of inferiority. They "are left with a lifelong admiration for an omnipotent individual" who does not validate their desire for recognition. Hence, as they grow older and become involved in relationships with men, they succumb to overt or unconscious submission. They grow to idealize the man who has what they can never possess—power and desire (pp. 108–9). The rejection of an early "identificatory love" from a figure who represents independence damages a child's sense of self, "in particular sense of sexual agency" and leads to relationships in which women play a passive or subordinate role (p. 115). Thus, women can lose their sense of self, submit to powerful men, and even to self-denial and masochism (p. 116).

In this "process of alienation," in which a woman's desire for recognition is transformed into submission and the adoration of a male figure, the relationship of self to other is transformed "from the concrete inter-subjective mode to symbolic phallic mode in which recognition is not of subject to subject" but of active and passive, subject and object, woman and idealized man (Benjamin, 1988, p. 131).

On one level, the solution to this problem of domination, Benjamin (1988) argues, is the reorganization of parenting. Both parents need to take on roles that represent the concepts of separation and attachment for their children. Parents would also have to make it possible for their children to experience the continuous tension between self-assertion and mutual recognition. They would need to create an "environment of controlled abandon" in which they allow their children to creatively express themselves without being judged (p. 120). Benjamin (1988) also notes that little girls should not be told to be "good girls." They should not be prevented from being selfish or greedy (p. 121).

On another level, Benjamin (1988) argues, the root of the problem of domination is the Western concept of the autonomous rational individual itself. Western philosophy, she argues, identifies rationality with separation, independence, masculinity, and counterposes it to dependence, emotional attunement, nurturance, irrationality, and femininity (p. 171). Hence, domination from its inception is also gendered.

In speaking of rationality, Benjamin (1988) specifically takes up Max Weber's (1864–1920) idea of "instrumental rationality" or a capitalist "rationality that reduces the social world to objects of exchange, calculation and control" (p. 184). She argues that, similar to Max Weber's concept of rationalization, "male domination ... works through the hegemony of impersonal organization: of formal rules ... of instrumental knowledge ... of the accumulation of profit. It is this protean impersonality that makes it so elusive" (p. 216).

Hence, Benjamin (1988) calls on feminists to offer a critique of the capitalist concept of the autonomous individual that "parallels the Marxian critique of the bourgeois individual" (p. 187). She sees her project as part of a challenge to the concept of autonomy and individuality under capitalism that pits one against the other and does not allow for the creation of close nurturing relations.

Benjamin (1988) concludes that overcoming domination requires not only formal equality between men and women at work and at home, but also more day care and alterations in work organization to allow mothers to develop themselves as independently existing subjects. It also requires "dealing with the contradictory tendencies within the self" (p. 222), "a play of power" that is not hardened into domination (p. 223). Here the goal is "to sustain the tension between universal commonality and specific differences" (p. 195), and the "reconstruction of the vital tension between recognition and assertion, between dependency and freedom" (p. 177).

ALLISON WEIR, RAYA DUNAYEVSKAYA, AND FRANTZ FANON ON OVERCOMING DOMINATION

Allison Weir (1996), a social and political philosopher and co-founder of the Institute for Social Justice in Sydney, Australia, argues in her *Sacrificial Logics: Feminist Theory and the Critique of Identity* that for feminist theory, too often identity is viewed as the repression of difference, "as the product of sacrificial logic, a logic of domination" (p. 3). In her opinion, Beauvoir's (1949) *The Second Sex* is the origin of the feminist critique which equates the logic of identity and universality with a logic of domination. Weir (1996) specifically argues that Beauvoir, drawing on Alexander Kojève's (1902–1968) reading of Hegel (Kojève, 1980), and Claude Levi Strauss's (1908–2009) structuralist theory of human culture, views individual and collective identities as always opposed to each other. That standpoint in turn means that for Beauvoir,

> one's identity as a subject is established only through the constant (and constantly failing) attempt to negate the otherness of other subjects and of one's own body ... [I]dentity is necessarily a negation and exclusion of the object by the subject; and therefore women will be able to affirm their collective and individual identities only through opposing themselves to an object/other. (p. 4)

Weir (1996) finds Beauvoir's analysis problematic because it assumes a model of identity that is "universal and transhistorical" (pp. 14–15). She points out that, on the contrary, the concept of the self as defined in opposition to an other is a phenomenon that has emerged concomitant with the rise of capitalism.

Weir (1996) challenges Beauvoir's "misrecognition of Hegel" concerning the master-slave dialectic in the *Phenomenology of Mind*. Hegel's master-slave dialectic, Weir argues, is really an explication of "Hegel's critique of the Enlightenment's conception of the subject as an atomistic individual. Thus, the struggle for recognition represents only one stage in the historical development of human 'self-consciousness'" (p. 20). It is not an expression of a permanent state of human existence. It is in fact an effort on the part of Hegel to show that self and other cannot remain opposed to each other because they are interdependent.

Furthermore, Weir (1996) argues that Kojève's "dualist ontology" (p. 18) offers a static relationship of self to other that remains at the level of "abstract negation" (p. 20), or undifferentiated negation, and not a Hegelian dialectical or determinate negation. Weir thus concludes that "Beauvoir's opposition of transcendence and immanence, her repudiation of the body as 'mere being' is based on the same logic of domination and subordination, the same logic of the negation of the other, which underlies the subordination of women" (pp. 23–4). In other words, it is based on the idea that the other is always a barrier to one's transcendence or freedom.

Weir (1996) acknowledges feminists such as Jean Grimshaw (1986), Mary O'Brien (1981), and Genevieve Lloyd who have criticized Beauvoir for promoting a masculine self as model. However, Weir challenges feminists for not taking the critique of Beauvoir far enough and for not questioning Beauvoir's "fundamental assumption" (p. 24) that self-identity is based on the negation of the other.

Weir also challenges Benjamin's assumption that there is, and will always be, a fundamental tension between self-assertion and mutual recognition. She argues that for Benjamin, the self is paradoxical (Benjamin, 1988, p. 221), or always oscillating between self-assertion and mutual recognition, because Benjamin is unable to conceptualize "a form of individual autonomy that can mediate between self and other, between self and society, without domination" (Weir, 1996, p. 72). Benjamin, like Beauvoir, she argues, universalizes Hegel's master-slave dialectic, instead of seeing how Hegelian dialectics transcends that stage and offers concepts for overcoming the false opposition of self and other.

In contrast to Beauvoir and Benjamin, and in an effort to create the vision of "a social self," Weir (1996) draws out several concepts from Hegelian philosophy that she thinks can help feminists theorize a relationship of self to other that can transcend domination (p. 70). Specifically, the concepts that she singles out are *mediation, internalization,* and *subjectivity.*

Whereas for Benjamin, recognition or intersubjectivity involves shared feeling, emotional attunement, and direct and immediate grasping of the needs and feelings of others, for Weir, recognition based on mediation and internalization involves a cognitive process. It is a mediated process in which autonomous subjects use their capacity for critical thinking and reflection to express themselves and communicate with each other. Mediation is defined as "a capacity to interpret, abstract from and reflect upon particularities through an appeal to universal principles—which includes, therefore, a capacity for critique … the capacity to participate in a social world" (Weir, 1996, p. 82).

Whereas for Benjamin, internalization is critiqued and equated to instrumentalization of the other, for Weir, internalization from a Hegelian standpoint is about a socially mediated development of the self, based on critical reflection. Also for Benjamin, subjectivity involves merely self-assertion and requiring acknowledgment of one's self-assertion, but for Weir (1996), "subjectivity is not a primary affective experience but a cognitive achievement" (p. 89). It is a cognitive process in which critical reflection is needed for us to express ourselves as autonomous subjects and to recognize others as autonomous subjects. Weir (1996) thus concludes:

Once autonomy is conceived as separation/objectification/domination, and intersubjectivity as shared feeling, we are left with no choice but to sustain an absolute, eternal paradox. But once autonomy is conceived as a capacity for full participation in a social context—and thus entails the internalization of social roles and norms and the capacity to relate particulars to universals, and hence to appeal to principles for critical reflection—then the paradox of the self begins to look much less eternal. (Weir, 1996, p. 89)

Like Weir, the Marxist-Humanist philosopher, Raya Dunayevskaya has argued that socialist feminism can greatly benefit from the Hegelian concept of mediation in order to conceptualize a relationship of self to other that transcends domination. She has pointed out that the key lesson to be drawn from Hegel's master-slave dialectic is not even that the slave gains "a mind of his own" (Hegel, 1985, p. 239), but that merely staying at the level of a mind of one's own is insufficient (Dunayevskaya, 2003, p. 36). As Hegel (1985) describes it,

having a "mind of its own" (der eigene Sinn) is simply stubbornness (Eigensinn), a type of freedom which does not get beyond the attitude of bondage ... it is rather a piece of cleverness which has mastery within a certain range, but not over the universal power nor over the entire objective reality. (p. 240)

That is why he continues the journey of the struggle for freedom through the stages that he calls Reason, Spirit, and Absolute Knowledge.

In her book *Philosophy and Revolution: From Hegel to Sartre, and from Marx to Mao*, Dunayevskaya (2003) places a great deal of emphasis on Hegel's concept of the Absolute. The Absolute, she argues, is not a closed ontology or absolutism, but Hegel's effort at reviewing and comprehending the whole process of development of his history of philosophy as the basis for new beginnings in thought. Hegel (1976) rejects formal logic and any reduction of method to an application or an instrument, but instead calls for "second negation" (p. 835), which involves constantly reviewing the whole process of development and addressing internal contradictions in order to move the idea and struggle for emancipation forward. This never-ending process which Dunayevskaya (2003) calls "absolute negativity as new beginning: the ceaseless movement of ideas and of history" is what she considers essential for challenging domination as well as dogmatism (pp. 3–46).

In Dunayevskaya's view, the key to the Hegelian concept of mediation is to not get stuck at the level of the individual or the particular or the universal but to develop the movement from the individual to the particular and the universal or the reverse, from the universal to the particular to the individual, through the process of determinate negation. This is key for developing a type of individuality that is not narrow and does not seek to dominate others but is both unique and an expression of an expanding human universality and solidarity.

Dunayevskaya also calls on feminists, social justice activists, and revolutionaries to explore Hegel's discussion of the "attitudes of thought to objectivity" in his *Encyclopedia Logic* (1978). She specifically points out Hegel's discussion of the "Third Attitude of Thought to Objectivity: Immediate or Intuitive Knowledge" where he critiques the reduction of truth to immediate knowledge. Hegel writes of this attitude:

> Since the criterion of truth is found, not in the nature of the content, but in the mere fact of consciousness, every alleged truth has no other basis than subjective certitude and the assertion that we discover a certain fact in our consciousness. What I discover in my consciousness is thus exaggerated into a fact of the consciousness of all, and even passed off for the very nature of consciousness. (1978, p. 105)

This attitude, Hegel argues, reduces truth to mere unscrutinized assertions, and leads to dogmatism (1978, p. 111).

For Dunayevskaya (2003), "such an attitude of thought to objectivity would always recur *when* in the process of battling contradiction, the Subject becomes impatient with the seemingly endless stages of negation it must suffer through, and therefore, instead slides backward into Intuition" (p. 20, pp. xlii–xliv). This backward slide is a move away from mediation or determinate negation, toward immediate knowledge and "reducing Truth itself from something arising from the 'nature of the content' to pure subjectivism" (p. 21).

Both Weir and Dunayevskaya stress the importance of Hegel's concept of mediation and determinate negation for working out a relationship of self to other that transcends domination. Both also view the master-slave dialectic in Hegel's *Phenomenology of Mind* as only one step in the long process in the journey of consciousness to overcome barriers to its liberation. Both see identity, transcendence, and freedom as the working out of the relationship between individuality, particularity, and universality through critical reflection. Dunayevskaya emphasizes that this process cannot take place without a revolutionary transformation of capitalist alienated labor, racism, and sexism.

Dunayevskaya also reaches out to Frantz Fanon's effort to articulate a liberatory relationship between individuality, particularity, and universality in his *Black Skin, White Masks* and his *Wretched of the Earth*. Indeed, Frantz Fanon articulates his concept of a "new humanism" (Fanon, 1963, p. 246) through an encounter with Hegel's master-slave dialectic. In Fanon's (1967) *Black Skin, White Masks*, he argues that "at the foundation of Hegelian dialectics, there is an absolute reciprocity which must be emphasized" (p. 217). We are only human to the extent that we are recognized by other humans. The only way for us to break the vicious cycle of master and slave is for both sides to recognize each other's humanity. This, he argues, requires working toward "a supreme good that is the transformation of subjective certainty of my own worth into a universally valid objective truth for the creation of a human world—that is, of a world of reciprocal recognitions" (p. 218).

However, Fanon (1967) emphasizes that not only is the humanity of the Black enslaved person not recognized by the master, but also the reality of the struggle for Black people is that even when whites claim that they are not racist and that "there is no difference between us" (p. 221), they show nothing but indifference and paternalistic curiosity toward Black people. That is why Fanon emphasizes that the struggle for recognition has to go much deeper. It has to express pride in Blackness, a deep understanding of Black struggles and achievements, and also call on people of all colors to engage with the universal achievements of humanity. "What I have to recapture is the whole past of the world. Every time a man has contributed to the victory of the dignity of the spirit, every time a man has said no to an attempt to subjugate his fellows, I have felt solidarity with his act" (Fanon, 1967, p. 226). Thus, "Practical solidarity" can only be realized through a joint struggle and commitment to the principle that "never again would a people on the earth be subjugated" (Fanon, 1967, p. 227).

For Fanon (1967), the preconditions for overcoming subjugation are: "That the tool never possess the man. That the enslavement of man by man cease forever. That is, of one by another. That it be possible for me to discover and love man, wherever he may be" (p. 231). In order for "authentic communication" to be possible, all humans must "turn their backs on the inhuman voices which were those of their respective ancestors" (p. 231). Thus, freedom requires an effort at "disalienation." It is an "attempt to touch the other, to feel the other, to explain the other to myself" (p. 231). This, he emphasizes, requires a consistently critical and self-critical attitude: "O my body, make of me always a man who questions" (p. 231).[5]

The efforts of Weir, Dunayevskaya, and Fanon to relate Hegelian ideas to the conceptualization of emancipatory human relationships do not mean that Hegel as a person or his philosophy were free of contradictions. Rather, they show that despite these contradictions, Hegel's philosophical contributions have much to offer us. Now, I would like to argue that we can also benefit from putting together the ideas of Hegel and Audre Lorde on the relationship of self to other, identity to difference, and individuality to particularity and universality.

CAN HEGEL AND AUDRE LORDE SPEAK TO EACH OTHER ON IDENTITY AND DIFFERENCE?

In the years 1993 through 1996, I was involved in activities in solidarity with the people of Bosnia-Herzegovina in their struggle against Serbia's genocidal war, rape camps, and ethnic cleansing. My effort to draw lessons from this solidarity work led to writing an essay that sought to capture what was philosophically unique about the popular resistance to the siege of Sarajevo (1992–96). The Bosnian feminists that I was working with insisted that they were defending not just pluralism but an identity which could not be compartmentalized or separated into Muslim, Christian, or European but embodied all these traditions and represented something new and unique. At the time, I started to explore Hegel's discussion of diversity and his critique of its limitations because it seemed that Hegel's critique of the limitations of diversity could illuminate contemporary critiques of the limitations of pluralism and help articulate what the Bosnian feminists were reaching for. Years later, when I started my study of a series of essays by Audre Lorde and learned more about her views on identity and difference, I was struck by how her views could also shed light on the statements of the Bosnian feminists. Indeed, there were similarities between Lorde's views on identity and difference and Hegel's critiques of the limitations of diversity. Both Hegel and Lorde provide concepts to overcome the problem of indifference in the relationship of self to other. Both argue that it is not enough for self and other to simply tolerate each other or coexist. Rather, self and other need to hear each other and comprehend each other's differences as the basis for developing new enriched concepts and identities.

In his *Science of Logic*, Hegel (1976 [1969]) argues that "truth is complete only in the unity of identity with difference" (p. 414). That is why he is critical of the inadequacy of the category of "diversity" because in it, the moments of identity and difference are "indifferent to one another" rather than in dialogue with each other (p. 419). This relationship of "mutual indifference" (p. 420) is at the same time, in his view, a transition from diversity to "polar opposition" (Hegel, 1976, p. 424), and finally to "contradiction" (p. 431), which Hegel considers to be "the root of all movement and vitality" (p. 439).

According to the noted Hegel scholar J.N. Findlay (1976 [1958]),

Hegel's real motive in passing from mere Diversity to Polar Opposition lies in his dissatisfaction with connections that do not delve deep into the nature of their terms, which depend upon arbitrary, external points of view, which are not, in the last resort, real connections at all. ... Against this, the aim of philosophy is to banish indifference and to recognize the necessity of things. (p. 192)

That is why Hegel's (1976 [1969]) treatment of identity, difference, and otherness, in the final chapter of his *Science of Logic*, the "Absolute Idea," emphasizes that in dialectics, the other is not just the negation of the first term of which it is an other. It includes the first term and is a further development of it. Furthermore, he emphasizes that the contradiction between the first term and the other is not transcended through a synthesis in which the contradictory determinations lie side by side. In contrast to "formal thinking [which] makes identity its law, and allows the contradictory content before it to sink into ordinary conception, into space and time, in which the contradictions are held *asunder* in juxtaposition and temporal succession and so come before consciousness without reciprocal contact" (p. 835), in dialectical cognition, we think through the contradictions.

Hegel's emphasis here is on the concept of "absolute negativity," a deeper development of the idea of freedom through its confrontation with contradiction, otherness, difference, and the creation of a newer, deeper and more differentiated idea of freedom. He is not advocating using the other as simply a vehicle or instrument for self-affirmation.

I would argue that such a humanist vision, in which one affirms the humanity of the other through comprehending and having empathy with the other, can also be seen in the profound words of Lorde (1984). In a letter addressed to the organizers of a conference on the lives of American women, she wrote:

Difference must be not merely tolerated but seen as a fund of necessary polarities between which our creativity can spark like a dialectic. ... Within the interdependence of mutual [nondominant] differences lies that security which enables us to descend into the chaos of knowledge and return with true visions of our future, along with the concomitant power to effect those changes which can bring that future into being. Difference is that raw and powerful connection from which our personal power is forged. (Lorde, 1984, pp. 111–12)

Furthermore, in her essay, "Scratching the Surface: Some Notes on Barriers to Women and Loving," Lorde (1984) wrote that racism, sexism, heterosexism, and homophobia are akin to forms of blindness, all with the same root:

an inability to recognize the notion of difference as a dynamic human force, one which is enriching rather than threatening to the defined self, when there are shared goals, ... For it is through the coming together of self-actualized individuals, female and male, that any real advances can be made. The old sexual power relationships based on a dominant/subordinate model between unequals have not served us as a people nor as individuals. (Lorde, 1984, pp. 45–6)

Lorde (1984) challenges the distorted view of relationships that leads from disagreement to destruction. "This jugular vein psychology is based on the fallacy that your assertion or affirmation of self is an attack upon my self—or that my defining myself will somehow prevent or retard your self-definition." Instead, she envisions, "moving together as self-defined persons toward a common goal" (p. 51).

Here we see both Lorde and Hegel calling for a type of relationship of self to other in which both sides are autonomous beings and critical thinkers who share a commitment to human liberation, to shared universal concepts. Both sides acknowledge and argue out differences with the aim of arriving at a deeper conception of being human, more enriched universal concepts, and as a result, move forward individually and conceptually enriched, as they encounter more differences.

CONCLUSION

In this chapter we have evaluated two fundamentally different ways in which socialist feminists, ever since Beauvoir, have conceptualized the relationship between self and other, and between identity and difference. For Beauvoir, the self and other are always opposed. Identity is always formed at the expense of difference. Influenced by existentialist philosophy of which she herself was a founding theoretician, and also influenced by Friedrich Wilhelm Nietzsche's (2000) concept of will to power, Beauvoir sees individuality as always opposed to universality. She also emphasizes that women accept their status as the other because their repression by men is often couched in the form of love.

Beauvoir's alternative is to ask women to take on a masculine role and aggressively promote themselves as autonomous beings. Although she ends *The Second Sex* by calling for egalitarian relations between women and men and the brotherhood of humanity, she does not offer a conceptual framework that goes beyond relations of domination.

Benjamin fundamentally agrees with Beauvoir's views about the permanent state of tension and opposition between self and other. From a Freudian standpoint, she adds the influence of the Oedipus and Electra complexes to the picture and argues that girls learn to identify love with subservience because they do not get recognition from their fathers at the stage of identificatory love.

Instead of accepting Beauvoir's call for women to take on masculine roles and exert their autonomy in the form of domination, Benjamin (1988) abandons the concept of an autonomous self. Instead, she offers interdependency and "emotional attunement" in relationships as an alternative conceptual framework. This interdependency does not transcend the tension between self and other, but tries "to sustain the tension between universal commonality and specific differences" (p. 195), as "a play of power" (p. 223). In the immediate sense, Benjamin calls for women and men to take equal responsibility for parenting and to break with traditional roles. In the broader philosophical sense, she rejects the Western concepts of Reason and the autonomous self as the sources of domination.

For Weir, Dunayevskaya, Fanon, and Lorde, it is possible to create relationships in which autonomous selves develop their ability for critical reasoning to comprehend and to learn from each other's differences, to become enriched by the process, and to transcend domination. Weir, Dunayevskaya, and Fanon all use a Hegelian and humanist framework to conceptualize these relationships. Lorde identifies herself as a dialectical thinker and considers herself a humanist. For Weir, Dunayevskaya, Fanon, and Lorde, identity is not formed through the rejection of difference or of being indifferent to difference. Rather, there is a dialectical relationship between individuality, particularity, and universality that needs to be forever recreated.

In 2022, we face capitalist authoritarianism's open and brutal use of the self-other dynamic as a dynamic of hate, and in opposition, the growing visibility of a global Black Lives Matter uprising. The humanist critiques of Existentialism or Freudian psychology discussed in this chapter might resonate with a new generation of feminists.

Weir's direct critiques of Beauvoir's existentialist framework and Benjamin's Freudian framework also challenge the very assumption that most feminist theory, since the 1980s, has taken for granted: the Nietzschean and Foucauldian power or domination model of the relationship of self to other.[6] Weir argues that this model should not be viewed as transhistorical since it was specific to the rise of capitalism. Dunayevskaya, Fanon, and Lorde are of the mind that if we change the material and the social conditions of human existence, we could create the possibility for relations based on overcoming domination and comprehending differences.

Benjamin views Hegel's dialectic of self and other as a model in which the other is simply the masked "I," to be used in an instrumental manner. However, Weir and Dunayevskaya think differently. Instead of remaining at the level of the master-slave dialectic, they have both taken up Hegel's further development of the self-other dialectic and have singled out the

Hegelian concepts of mediation and determinate negation, as concepts that can help socialist feminists theorize a humanist relationship of self to other. They see Hegel as offering a dialectic of self-other and of identity-difference that seeks to comprehend the Other or difference, and develops a richer and more inclusive concept of liberation in a continuing process.

Fanon shows that Hegel's dialectic of reciprocity in the master-slave dialectic is not true in a racist society where Black people are not recognized as human beings. However, he also thinks that Hegel's concept of the relationship between universality and particularity allows us to develop human solidarity around universal concepts and toward the transcendence of capitalism, racism, and sexism without erasing or negating the unique contributions of marginalized peoples and cultures. As mentioned, this is what Fanon (1963) calls "a new humanism" (p. 246).

Both Lorde's critique of the limitations of pluralism and Hegel's critique of the limitations of diversity offer us a concept of democracy, identity, and human development that is based on comprehending differences and not simply tolerating or ignoring them.

Today, we live in a world where, on the one hand, capitalist authoritarianism, racism, misogyny, and homophobia are growing. On the other hand, we have had the emergence of Black Lives Matter Movement in the United States, #MeToo Movement against gender and sexual violence, and global struggles against authoritarianism. Given capitalism's open and brutal use of the self-other dynamic as a dynamic of hate, it is urgent for socialist feminists to offer a humanist concept of the relation of self to other as an alternative. Socialist feminists around the world also need to reach out to each other, engage with the content of each other's struggles, and connect them.

Conclusion: Socialist Feminist Revolutionary Organizing in the Twenty-First Century

In this work, I started by arguing that the global feminist movement has entered a new stage with the rise of the #MeToo Movement, the Black Lives Matter uprising, as well as global uprisings against authoritarianism, imperialist invasion/war, and ecological protests for saving the planet. All of these movements offer tremendous questions, opportunities, and challenges for socialist feminist organizing.

At the same time, the terrifying reality of growing fascistic grabs for power and imperialist war reveal the immensity of the challenges we face. Vladimir Putin's genocidal invasion of Ukraine, the white supremacist January 6, 2021 coup attempt, and the legalization of vigilante assaults on abortion rights in the United States, as well as the return to power of the misogynist and racist Taliban in Afghanistan after a withdrawal deal with the U.S. imperialist occupier (Afary, 2022a) portend what might be the future for all humans in the twenty-first century. A global imperialist war seems imminent.

In this context, this book's effort to rethink socialist feminism for the twenty-first century can help address these challenges by getting to the heart of the problem that faces us: transcending capitalism, racism, sexism, heterosexism both at the structural and the personal level, transforming human relations, and developing thoughtful relationships among humans, between mind and body and between humanity and nature. Each socialist feminist conceptual framework taken up in this book has been a pathway to asking questions about how to develop a humanist alternative to capitalism, racism, sexism, and heterosexism.

Theories of social reproduction, by tracing gender oppression to the devaluation of women's reproductive labor, raise critically important questions about women's reproductive work in the family and in society at large, and how we can rethink and reorganize it. However, I argue that valuing reproductive labor or socializing or collectivizing it is not enough to overcome gender oppression. Authoritarian capitalism in the twenty-first century can do away with the family as the place for reproducing labor power, only to turn society into one large labor camp. It might even be able to use ectogenesis to turn the process of reproduction into an industrial one, with terrifying consequences. Thus, theories of social reproduction give us only part of the picture of gender oppression under capitalism.

Marx's critique of alienated labor, and its relation to gender oppression, both as articulated by Marx and by various socialist feminists who have tried to theorize the relationship between alienated labor and alienated human relations under capitalism pinpoint the extreme alienation of mind from body. I argue that this theorization is more adequate for explaining gender oppression under capitalism and can also speak to the new questions posed by the #MeToo Movement which has challenged sexual harassment and gender violence in all spheres, and especially among cultured and educated men.

At the same time, the ideas and efforts of Black feminist intersectional thinkers who challenge the erasure of Black women, and oppose both external oppressors and oppressive attitudes within the movement are critically important for developing a humanist alternative to capitalism. For Black feminists, the unity of theory and practice is not a slogan but a reality, as seen in the creative ways in which intersectional thinking has expressed itself in abolitionism and in Black Lives Matter.

Queer theory and its challenge to fixed concepts of gender and identity, if in the context of advocating a reappropriation of humanist concepts of universality, subjectivity, solidarity, and ethical responsibility, can also greatly expand the emancipatory vision of socialist feminism. I have argued that in contrast to Judith Butler's ahistorical approach to gender and identity, the efforts of various socialist feminists to draw on Marx's concept of a historical and ever-transforming human nature are more adequate. Rosemary Hennessy's effort to connect alienated labor to capitalism's limiting of our human sexual-affective potential, and Sheena Howard's refusal to accept the recreation of oppressive gender roles within LGBTQ relationships were singled out as urgently needed for the project of developing an alternative to capitalism.

Ecofeminist thinkers, Maria Mies and Ariel Salleh as well as other autonomist feminists such as Silvia Federici and Kathi Weeks pose important demands such as reclaiming the commons, creating cooperatives, and establishing a universal basic income. However, they still do not address the question of how to overcome alienated labor.

Audre Lorde's posing of the question of labor and life in her "The Uses of the Erotic," however, can offer us a glimpse of a non-alienated existence. In that spirit, I have returned to Marx's concept of an alternative to capitalism and his view of ending the domination of abstract time over the process of production in what he calls the "first phase" of a complete break with capitalism. I have also examined Raya Dunayevskaya's analyses of state capitalism in the USSR and Maoist China because they can also help us develop an alternative that does not re-establish state capitalism.

The questions of reconceptualizing the self-other relationship and of overcoming models based on domination are also integral parts of developing an alternative to capitalism, sexism, and racism. After exploring the existentialist and Nietzschean model of Simone de Beauvoir, and the Freudian and alternative relational models of Jessica Benjamin, which are more familiar to students of feminism in the twenty-first century, I have argued that it is the dialectical and humanist frameworks developed by Allison Weir, Raya Dunayevskaya, Frantz Fanon, and Audre Lorde which can help us conceptualize relationships that overcome domination.

Developing a coherent socialist feminist emancipatory vision for the twenty-first century, however, is both a theoretical/analytical and a practical and organizational question. It demands grappling with what is new in the twenty-first century and reaching out internationally to global women's struggles against capitalist imperialism, racism, sexism, and heterosexism.

Here, I would like to share some thoughts about what this book's re-examination and rethinking of socialist feminism can mean for international organizing now.

Socialist feminism is deeply intertwined with opposition to war, militarism, and capitalism-imperialism (Archer, 2008). However, in a multi-polar world, that opposition to militarism cannot be limited to one pole of capitalism-imperialism—U.S. and Western powers and their allies Israel, Saudi Arabia, and Turkey—while ignoring Chinese and Russian imperialisms and their regional allies, such as Iran and Syria. (See Reimann and Zuur, 2018, Heller, 2022). In my own organizing experiences over the years, I have observed that the failure to take a principled stand against all capitalist-imperialist powers has been a major barrier to solidarity work. During the years prior to the collapse of the USSR in 1991, when a large part of the Left had sided with totalitarian states such as the Soviet Union or Maoist China, leftist apologists used the false claim that these states were "socialist." In the twenty-first century, however, when both Russia and China are openly rapacious capitalist-imperialist states, and when China competes with the United States in mass incarceration and military might, and also engages in genocidal levels of ethnic cleansing of Uyghur Muslims, it is astonishing to see how some leftists still side with Russia or support China as "progressive" or "socialist" (Hioe, 2021). For many within the Left, the only guiding standard is that "the enemy of my enemy is my friend." As the world faces the strong possibility of an openly declared and direct shooting war between the United States and Europe on one side and Russia and China on the other, it is incumbent upon socialist feminists to challenge this madness, take a principled stand against both poles of capital, and reach out to feminist, labor, and oppressed minority struggles in each country.

At the same time opposition to capitalism/imperialism and militarism does not mean negating the right of the people of a country such as Ukraine under invasion by Russia, to take arms to defend themselves against a brutal imperialist power that is annihilating them.

This book has argued that socialist feminists need to strengthen the global #MeToo Movement and center it on challenging capitalism's alienation, dehumanization, and commodification of women and children. Toward this aim, engaging with the work of Tarana Burke, Black feminist abolitionist and founder of the #MeToo Movement is critical. Her goal is "real structural change," transformative justice, and the creation of an environment that allows for the healing of both the survivors and the perpetrators (Adetiba, 2017; Burke, 2021). Burke's abolitionist feminism challenges both gender and state violence as connected phenomena. In doing so, she can help us expand abolitionist feminism to include struggles against gender violence in countries such as Afghanistan, South Africa, Russia, and China. Her work also opens the way for discussing a needed humanist socialist feminism.

While many socialist feminists would agree that we need to connect Black Lives Matter and abolitionism to the global struggles against authoritarianism, my organizing experiences with socialist activists have shown me that this aim often remains at the level of sloganeering. Creating such a connection demands seriously engaging with and comprehending the rich contributions and achievements of African American struggles/thought, of Black Lives Matter/abolitionism as we try to respond to global struggles against state violence and mass incarceration. These include opposition to the mass incarceration of Uyghur Muslims by the Chinese government in Xinjiang province; state violence and mass incarceration in Syria, Iran, Egypt, and Turkey; Israel's colonization, murder, and imprisonment of Palestinians; various Middle Eastern states' assaults on the Kurdish struggle for self-determination; the ethnic cleansing of Rohingya Muslims by the Myanmar government; anti-Black violence in Sudan; and the murder and imprisonment of democratic activists around the world, from Hong Kong to Russia, Belarus, and from Nigeria, Congo, and Tigray to Brazil, Venezuela, and Nicaragua (Afary, 2021b, 2021c).

The awarding of the 2020 Right Livelihood or Alternative Nobel Award to U.S. abolitionist attorney, Bryan Stevenson, imprisoned Iranian feminist human rights lawyer, Nasrin Sotoudeh, Nicaraguan environmentalist activist and indigenous human rights lawyer, Lottie Cunningham Wren, and Belarusian democracy and human rights activist, Ales Bialiatski, shows the *inseparability* of these struggles (Democracy Now, 2020). Another proof of the inseparability of our struggles is the profound act of Black Women for Wellness, an organization of reproductive justice activists in Los Angeles which organized a discussion to bring together the plight of women in Afghanistan and Haiti (Black Women for Wellness, 2021).

The misogynist and anti-life anti-abortion campaign in the United States and globally has for many years called itself "pro-life" and has been able to hold onto that designation. Socialist feminism can learn from the Reproductive Justice Movement and make an important effort to reclaim the designation "pro-life," and give it new meaning. Being "pro-living," from a socialist feminist perspective, means not only supporting women's right to self-determination and their right to choose if and when they wish to have children, but also creating the kind of life, labor, resources, education, and assistance that allows women to meet their own needs and the needs of their children, so that both may flourish. Reclaiming the designation "pro-living" is urgently needed to fight the anti-abortion and anti-woman onslaught.

Among socialist feminists there are differences about what it means to have a queer and sex-positive movement that opposes all forms of sexual exploitation, all oppressive gender norms, and all forms of instrumentalization of ourselves or others (Goldberg, 2021; Srinivasan, 2021). Some advocate the full legalization and normalization of sex work and argue that it can be "creative" or "satisfying" (Smith & Mac, 2020; Vitale, 2017). Others, who also defend the rights of sex workers and their efforts to self-organize for safety, view sex work as a practice of commodification and instrumentalization of one's body and feelings. While they support the decriminalization of sex workers, they emphasize that sex work in addition to being exploitative and abusive does terrible long-term physical and psychological damage to those who perform it, whether they are forced to do it or do it "voluntarily" (Holmstrom, 2014).[1] I agree with this view and argue that rather than channeling our organizing efforts into legalizing sex work, it would be best if we help expand the message of the #MeToo Movement to challenge the normalization of sexual abuse and assault in all spheres of life (Boussedra, 2017; Dustdar, 2015; Fonseca, 2021; Lang, 2019; Mock, 2014, Spector, 2006; Williams, 2019). The facts indicate that extending the legalization of sex work to pimps and clients facilitates further exploitation of women and children, and increases sex trafficking (Harvard Law School, 2014). Adding sex work to the list of normal service sector jobs also means that unemployed women who receive assistance from the state would not be able to refuse sex work as employment. Normalizing sex work means that more and more young women, men, and trans people would consider sex work as a full-time or side job to make money. Is this the future that socialist feminists want to promote?

This book has sought to offer alternate ways of thinking about ecofeminism in order to work out solutions to the worsening environmental destruction caused by the capitalist mode of production. I have argued that we need an ecofeminism that offers an alternative to capitalist alienated labor, whether in private or state form. Simply returning to subsistence farming and reproductive work in cooperatives does not abolish capitalist alienated labor and its logic of using humanity and nature as mere means for the expansion of value. Marx's critique of alienated labor and his concept of a humanist alternative can offer us much ground for developing a "metabolic interaction" between humanity and nature (Saito, 2017).[2]

Socialist feminism is inextricably bound with the issue of universal health care. However, it can offer the possibility of a universal health care movement that opposes not only for-profit health care, but also challenges the capitalist fragmentation of the human being. The problem with the existing medical system is not only that it is mostly unaffordable and discriminates based on class, race, and gender. The capitalist medical system fragments human beings into body parts and does not see the whole human being—body and mind (Cruise et al., 2018). It also does not allow enough time to address the specific needs of each individual. Instead of addressing root causes of problems, it primarily addresses symptoms of illnesses through the use of medication and surgical options. The COVID-19 pandemic, which has caused the death of over 25 million people around the world as of May 2022 (Economist, 2021e, 2022) and has infected many more (Worldometer, 2021), has alarmingly laid bare the massive problems of the global health care system with more urgency and forcefulness. While vaccines are needed, the fact that the coronavirus is constantly mutating shows that no vaccine is the ultimate solution. We need to end capitalism's destruction of and massive encroachment into nature, which is allowing deadly viruses from wildlife to enter the human body. We also need a holistic approach to human health that strengthens the immune system and allows it to resist new viruses.

Socialist feminists have a responsibility to offer specific ideas about a post-capitalist educational system that can help develop reflective human beings and critical thinkers. Challenging capitalist authoritarianism, populist disinformation and "post-truth" demands reclaiming the concepts of truth, objectivity, dialectical reason, and critical reflection. This does not mean giving in to the capitalist concept of a so-called objectivity which ignores or marginalizes the experiences of the oppressed, or accepting the capitalist interpretation of rationality as utilitarianism and calculation of narrow self-interest. However, it does mean heeding Maryanne Wolf's call for ending the overreliance on fast online reading, and instead promoting an education which is rich in the humanities and social sciences and inculcates a global view of human development. Such an education can offer people, young and old, an understanding of conceptual frameworks that they need to engage in "deep reading" so that they can in turn read inquisitively and develop new ideas and concepts that further advance what it means to be human.

In the United States the most immediate focus needed for educators is to confront the book bans and the white supremacist assault on Critical Race Theory, a concept which shows the connections between white supremacy, slavery, and the U.S. legal system. There can be no critical thinking in the United States without an educational system that challenges white supremacy and the system of slavery that was at the foundation of the United States. True education whether in the United States or any other country begins with teaching young and old, true history that cuts through the dehumanization of people of color and women.

Finally, the concept of democratic socialist organization itself is desperately in need of discussion and clarification. Decentralized forms of organization are important but they can only be truly meaningful and effective if they offer emancipatory ideas and concepts, the vision of a humanist alternative to capitalism, racism, sexism, heterosexism, and develop members who become rooted in history, theory, political economy and thus act as critical, ethical, and independent thinkers. Otherwise, socialist organizing will simply limit itself to sloganeering about anti-capitalism. I would argue that simply focusing on a decentralized form of organization and proceduralism, at the expense of developing the philosophical content, historical/economic understanding and vision of the organization, actually leads to pure voluntarism and more arbitrariness. This problem has opened up the Left to populism, meaning that most leftists are only against the system and offer simplistic answers without comprehending the core causes of oppression or offering a genuine alternative. I have personally experienced this problem in various organizations. I have also seen how efforts at international coalition building have collapsed when people come together around a commitment to certain agreed upon principles and responsibilities, but in practice, turn away from these principles, and reject any call for responsibility and accountability.

The principles and vision of the democracy that we as socialists advocate need to be articulated. How does it help people to become ethical human beings who do not abuse themselves or each other? How do we deal with differences in ways that move us forward? What standards do we have for truth, accountability, and fairness? In this book, I have drawn on the contributions of thinkers whose visions of working out the relationship between self and other, identity and difference, universality, particularity, and individuality, speak to a type of organization that is not dogmatic, but one that also offers an affirmative philosophical content, deeply rooted in history and can deal with conflicts in a democratic manner, one that leads to growth for all parties involved.

It is my hope that this book has helped readers find fruitful ground for a rethinking of socialist feminism that can truly meet the challenges of the twenty-first century and beyond, in theory and in practice.

Notes

Introduction. Rethinking Socialist Feminism to Find a Pathway Out of Authoritarian Capitalism and Develop a Humanist Alternative

1. See *Venezuelan Voices* for an independent socialist opposition to Chavismo, Nicolas Maduro and Juan Guaido, https://venezuelanvoices.org/.
2. See Timothy Snyder on the genocidal character of Russia's 2022 invasion of Ukraine (Snyder, 2022).

Chapter 1. The Pandemic, the #MeToo Movement, and Contradictory Developments in Gender Relations

1. See Räthzel, Mulinari, and Tollefsen (2020) whose study of women factory workers in Mexico, South Africa, and Sweden shows that women workers with children got only three to four hours of sleep per night (p. 192) even before the COVID-19 pandemic started.
2. Between March 17 and June 17, 2020, there were over 100 rebellions in U.S. prisons and jails over lack of safety and health measures related to COVID-19. There have been prisoner hunger strikes inside U.S. Immigration and Customs detention centers, in Iran, Turkey, and elsewhere, as well as prison breakouts in Spain, Brazil, Iran, and elsewhere (Cuffe, 2020; Romero, 2020; Sepehri Far, 2020).
3. As of October 2021, only seven out of 198 nations around the world allowed for elective abortion on demand after the 20th week of pregnancy. These were Canada, China, the Netherlands, North Korea, Singapore, United States, Vietnam. Seventy five percent of all nations do not permit abortion after 12 weeks of pregnancy except (in most instances) to save the life and physical health of the mother (Lee, 2017; Liptak, 2021).
4. In Venezuela, despite all the claims of Hugo Chavez that his "Bolivarian Revolution" represented "Twenty-First Century socialism," abortion was not legalized (see Marquina, 2021).
5. Since 1981, more than 70 million people around the world have died of AIDS or HIV-related complications (Avert, 2020; Ayar, 2018). Recently, the U.S. Food and Drug Administration approved a new HIV prevention drug, but not for women, because Gilead, the drug company that made it, had only tested it on men (Mandavilli, 2019).

Chapter 2. Distinctive Features of Authoritarian Capitalism/Imperialism Today and the New Challenges of Black Lives Matter and Global Uprisings

1. Karl Marx (1976) concludes that

In any given branch of industry, centralization would reach its extreme limit if all the individual capitals invested there were fused into a single capital. In a given society this limit would be reached only when the entire social capital was united in the hands of either a single capitalist or a single capitalist company. (p. 779)

2. Various U.S. technology companies are aggressively courting business from U.S. government agencies and the military. Their collaborative projects include the development of highly advanced weaponized drones (see Metz, 2021).

3. In fact the negotiations with the Taliban started under President Obama when the Obama administration supported the opening of a Taliban office in Qatar in 2013 (Tankel, 2018; Whitlock, 2021). The Trump administration took these negotiations to a new level in 2020 when Trump met directly with Taliban representatives and promised the release of 5,000 imprisoned Taliban fighters and a May 2021 U.S. withdrawal date. The Biden administration continued Trump's policy and simply delayed the withdrawal date by a few months.

4. See also Smith and Lin (2020).

5. Shamefully, on December 15, 2020, the International Criminal Court announced that it had decided not to pursue an investigation into China's mass detention of the Muslim population of Xinjiang. It has argued that since the abuses described "have been committed solely by nationals of China within the territory of China," an investigation of this case is not within its jurisdiction (Hernández, 2020).

6. Also see Anton Mukhamedov's (2021) interview with Lokman Slim and Monica Borgmann, co-founders of the MENA Prison Forum and producers of the documentary film, *Tadmor*, about the notorious prison of the Assad regime in Palmyra, Syria. Slim was assassinated in Lebanon on February 4, 2021. www.aljumhuriya.net/en/content/%E2%80%9Ci-don%E2%80%99t-talking-about-fear%E2%80%9D (last accessed March 8, 2021).

7. Feminist abolitionist scholar Joy James has created the expression "Captive Maternals" to describe women and men who have dedicated their lives to the struggle against slavery and anti-Black racism. She writes the following about Erica Garner, daughter of Eric Garner who was murdered by a New York City police officer in 2014:

> Erica Garner advocated fiercely for justice following her father's 2014 death. She died several years later from poor health and stress at the age of 27, leaving two young children behind. Advocates for justice, such as Erica Garner, who suffer negative health amplified by the stress of losing a loved one and mobilizing against an imperial and indifferent or hostile state become even more vulnerable to negative health outcomes that increase impoverishment and limit resources and mobility. This transpires internationally, from favelas, townships and urban centres to rural sites and reservations. Disease and mortality rates among mothers and Captive Maternals who try and fend and protect or bring dignity to the

needs of their slain children, and family and community members can lead to stroke, heart disease, hypertension, etcetera. (James, 2021)

8. According to Iraqi feminist activist, Huda Samir:

    Technically, Iraq still uses law number 188 issued in 1959 concerning women's rights. However, since the law is not enforced, there are systemic violations of the law 188. In fact what is going [on] on the ground is the opposite of what is stated in the law. In addition, article number 41 of the constitution states that in personal life, the religious teachings of each sect could be used when it comes to family affairs. Other laws violating human rights for women are still in place. Law 111 allows men to punish women. It also allows men who rape women to be forgiven if they marry their victim. (Samir, 2021, personal correspondence with author). Also see Ali (2018, 2020a, 2020b)

Chapter 3. Women, Reproductive Labor, and Capital Accumulation: Theories of Social Reproduction

1. Also see Nancy Holmstrom's (1981) response to Sheila Rowbotham and John Harrison on whether housework constitutes a mode of production.
2. Karl Marx (1976) in *Capital. Volume 1. A Critique of Political Economy*, trans. Ben Fowles (New York: Vintage). See not only part 8, "So-Called Primitive Accumulation," but also Marx's discussion of capitalism's reliance on slavery in chapter 10, "The Working Day," which begins with a section titled "The Voracious Appetite for Surplus Labor" (pp. 344–5). Also see Marx (1981), *Capital. Volume 3. A Critique of Political Economy*, intro. Ernest Mandel, trans. David Fernbach (London: Penguin Classics), part 3, "The Law of the Tendential Fall in the Rate of Profit," and his discussion of "countervailing factors" such as "the reduction of wages below their value" and the use of slave labor (pp. 342, 345).

Chapter 4. Alienated Labor and How It Relates to Gender Oppression

1. According to the Marxist feminist philosopher, Raya Dunayevskaya, all of Marx's work can be seen as a further development of the essays in the *Economic and Philosophical Manuscripts of 1844* (Marx & Fromm, 1961; Dunayevskaya, 2002, p. 3).
2. Also see Nancy Holmstrom (2013a) on the meaning of the word "conscious."

    Now what does "conscious" mean in this context? How could alienated labor not be conscious? Aren't humans—unlike machines— always conscious of their labor? Yes, or usually, in the sense of "aware," but this is not the sense that Marx identifies as distinctive of human labor. In *Capital*, he says "We presuppose labor in a form that stamps it as exclusively human…. What distinguishes the worst architect from the best of bees is this, that the architect raises his structure in imagination before he erects it in reality." And this purpose then directs his/her actions. So "conscious" here has the specific sense of the labor being the carrying out, or the execution, of an idea or purpose of the worker him/herself, the agent. Alienated labor is not conscious in this sense. Instead, it is the capitalist's ideas and purposes that the worker is executing, just as a machine does. Indeed if the labor is not conscious in this sense, it may require more consciousness in the sense of attention. A machine is designed to carry out a task set by the owner; if it does not, it is replaced. The same is true of workers in capitalism. Thus since free, conscious activity is the distinctive character of the human species, its human nature, alienated labor also means alienation from this human nature.

3. Dunayevskaya's (1958) translation is, in my view, slightly clearer:

> The infinite degradation in which man exists for himself is seen in relationship to the woman as the spoils and handmaid of communal lust. For the secret of the relationship of man to man finds its *unambiguous*, definitive, *open*, obvious expression in the relationship of man to *woman* ... . From this relationship, the human being's whole level of development can be assessed. It follows from the character of this relationship how far *the human being* has become, and has understood himself as, a *species-being, a human being* ... to what degree *another* human being is needed as a human being. (p. 292, emphasis in the original)

4. The original Persian can be found in Narges Imani (2020). The English translation has been provided in Afary (2020a).

Chapter 5. Black Feminism and Intersectionality

1. Bohrer (2020, p. 121).
2. Maria W. Stewart, born Maria Miller, was the author of the pamphlet, *Religion and the Pure Principles of Morality*, and one of the first women to speak in public in the United States. See Maria Miller Stewart (1831/1995).
3. See this short video clip from Angela Davis (2018) which situates her work in the context of intersectional feminism: www.youtube.com/watch?v=9GDjT3Fw_6w
4. Also see Roxane Gay's introduction to her new selection of the works of Audre Lorde in Lorde (2020).
5. Also see Christian (2000).
6. On Mothers ROC, also see Kamran Afary (2009, pp. 121–60).
7. This 2017 new edition includes editor Keeanga-Yamahtt Taylor's introduction and new interviews with the Combahee River Statement co-authors, as well as Alicia Garza and comments by Barbara Ransby.
8. Also see Jones (2019).

Chapter 6. Queer Theories

1. Also see Barbara Smith (1995).
2. Also see Weir (1996, p. 113).
3. For example, for a view of the evolution of the norms of sexuality in modern Iran, see Janet Afary (2009).

4. Also see Drucker (2015) and Floyd (2009).
5. Also see Holmstrom (1994, 2013b).

Chapter 7. Theorizing a Socialist Humanist and Feminist Alternative to Capitalism

1. See also Julie Graham and Cathy Gibson (Gibson-Graham, 2003; 2006).
2. German socialist feminist, Frigga Haug (2020a) also proposes an alternative organization of society in which each person has time for labor that involves producing the means of life, labor of reproductive care, artistic work, and political work. She calls this the "Four-in-One Perspective." "Four-in-One means that all individuals should be able to have the time to develop all four kinds of practices" (pp. 37–8).
3. Also see Federici (2021).
4. Ariel Salleh (2020), an ecofeminist thinker, argues that reproductive labor and subsistence farming are inherently non-alienating because "reproductive labor is a metabolic bridging of human and natural cycles" (p. 46). See also Plumwood (1994, 2001).
5. Nancy Holmstrom (2014) agrees. She writes:

   So in Marx's view labor (work) is not inherently oppressive. In fact, when it is determined by an individual's wants, needs, passions, it is free in the fullest possible sense. When on the other hand, the work is required by the facts of nature (i.e. what satisfies our physical needs requires work to get it), it can still be free in a more limited sense, if it is we who decide how to do it.

6. In *Re-enchanting the World*, Silvia Federici (2019) writes:

   When Marx was writing *Capital*, very little housework was performed in the working-class family (as Marx himself recognized) for women were employed side by side with men in the factories from dawn to sunset ... . Only in the second part of the nineteenth century after two decades of working-class revolts in which the specter of communism haunted Europe, did the capitalist class begin to invest in the reproduction of labor power. (p. 157)

7. In her *Re-enchanting the World*, Federici (2019) begins to acknowledge this: "It is also agreed that there are important differences between his two major works, Capital and the Grundrisse" (p. 152).
8. In the *Economic and Philosophical Manuscripts of 1844*, we saw the ways in which Marx (1961) contrasted alienated labor to the human potential for free, conscious activity. In *Capital*, Marx contrasts *abstract* or alienated or value-producing labor to *concrete* labor. In the first chapter of *Capital*, where he discusses what he calls the "dual character of labor under capitalism" (Marx, 1976, p. 131), he writes: "Labor, then, as the creator of use-values, as useful labor, is a condition of human existence which is independent of all forms of society; it is an eternal natural necessity which mediates the metabolism between man and nature, and therefore human life itself" (p. 133). Under capitalism, however, labor becomes "simple average labor" (p. 135). It is

denuded of its particularity and specificity. Labor under capitalism becomes something mechanical.

Furthermore, for Marx, labor as "an exclusively human characteristic" is not an instinctive but a purposeful process in which an ideal developed in the mind is realized in the labor process. Hence,

what distinguishes the worst architect from the best of bees is that the architect builds the cell in his mind before he constructs it in wax. At the end of every labor process, a result emerges which had already been conceived by the worker at the beginning, hence already existed ideally. (Marx, 1976, p. 284)

But "[t]he less he is attracted by the nature of the work and the way in which it has to be accomplished, and the less, therefore, he enjoys it as the free play of his own physical and mental powers, the closer his attention is forced to be" (p. 284). In sum

The labor process as we have just presented it is purposeful activity aimed at the production of use values ... . It is the universal condition for the metabolic interaction between humans and nature, the everlasting nature-imposed condition of human existence and it is therefore independent of every form of that existence , or rather it is common to all forms of society in which human beings live. (Marx, 1976, p. 290)

In contrast to this labor process, he presents "the valorization process" which is characteristic of the capitalist mode of production. In this process "use-values are produced by capitalists only because and in so far as they form the material substratum of exchange-value, the bearers of exchange-value" (Marx, 1976, p. 293). Labor is considered only in so far as it creates value. One type of labor differs in no respect from another. "We are no longer concerned with the quality, the character and the content of the labor, but merely with its quantity" (p. 296).

From the standpoint of the valorization process, the means of production consume the human being as a means for the expansion of value as an end in itself (Marx, 1976, p. 425). "[T]his inversion, indeed this distortion which is peculiar to and characteristic of capitalist production, of the relation between dead labor and living labor ... is mirrored in the consciousness of the capitalist" (p. 425). This inversion or what Marx calls the domination of dead over living labor becomes the basis for capitalism's constant revolutionizing of the technical basis of production.

Thus, capitalism seeks to extract more and more value from less living labor by increasing the productivity of labor. In doing so it takes the mental/ manual division of labor characteristic of all class societies to an extreme, and fragments and alienates the human being more and more.

9. Also see Afary (2014).

10. Raya Dunayevskaya was born in 1910 in Ukraine, pre-revolutionary Russia in an impoverished orthodox Jewish family and had experienced anti-Semitism and pogroms as a child. In 1922, her family left Russia and migrated to the United States, where they settled in a working-class neighborhood

on Chicago's West Side where she attended primary and secondary school. In 1937–38, she moved to Mexico to work with Leon Trotsky, a Bolshevik leader who was by then a member of the Left Opposition fleeing Stalin's persecution and living in exile in Mexico with his wife Natalia. Trotsky was murdered by an agent of Stalin in 1940.

11. J.R. Johnson was the pseudonym for C.L.R. James, and Freddie Forest was the pseudonym for Raya Dunayevskaya.

12. In *Capital*, Marx divides the total social product of society into "means of production" and "means of consumption" and argues that under capitalism, the production of the first predominates over the production of the second. "Means of production" are "commodities that possess a form in which they either have to enter productive consumption [production of value] or at least can enter this" (Marx, 1978, p. 471). "Means of consumption" are "commodities that possess a form in which they enter the individual consumption of the capitalist and working classes" (Marx, 1978, p. 471). We can broadly think of means of production as machines, tools, buildings, roads. We can also think of means of consumption as food, clothing, books, and services such as health care and education, etc. Marx argues that the capitalist mode of production leads to a system of expanded reproduction in which an increasing portion of the surplus produced is invested in the direction of acquiring means of production at the expense of wages. This direction, he argues, emanates from capitalism's need to have more means of production to extract more value from living labor in order to expand value as an end in itself. Thus, capitalism also leads to the preponderance of the production of means of production over the means of consumption (see Marx, 1976, pp. 726–39).

13. Nancy Holmstrom writes the following about the nature of labor in the former USSR:

> In the Soviet system although workers did not sell, i.e. alienate their labor power, but instead worked for the state, it does not follow, as Soviet "Marxists" claimed, that alienation is ruled out by definition. Property was nationalized but this is a property form, a juridical form, not a relation of production. Workers did not control the state, hence they did not decide what to produce or how to do it and hence their labor was not the unity of conception and execution of un-alienated labor. Moreover, their products did not belong to them. (Holmstrom, 2013a, p. 25)

14. From *Documents of the First Session of the First National People's Congress of the People's Republic of China* (Beijing: Foreign Language Press, 1965, p. 95, cited in Dunayevskaya, 2003, p. 165).

15. For more on Mao's concept of the "Bloc of Four Classes," see *Encyclopedia of Marxism*, s.v. "Glossary of Terms: B1," www.marxists.org/glossary/terms/b/l.htm (last accessed February 24, 2021).

16. For the statement of Sheng-Wu-Lien (1969), see "Whither China?" *International Socialism*, 1st series, 37:24–7. www.marxists.org/history/etol/newspape/isj/1969/no037/shengwulien.htm (last accessed February 24, 2021).

17. Also see Frigga Haug's (2020b), "Thirteen Theses of Marxism-Feminism."

Chapter 8. Overcoming Domination: Reconceptualizing the Self-Other Relationship

1. Wolf (2018, p. 44); Maryanne Wolf is Professor of Education, and a children's advocate at the UCLA Graduate School of Education and Information Studies.
2. Simone de Beauvoir's understanding of overcoming the master-slave relationship seems to be more influenced by Friedrich Wilhelm Nietzsche's (2000 with 1967 and 1995 copyright) *On the Genealogy of Morals*. I am referring to the concept of "the sovereign *individual* ... liberated again from morality of custom, autonomous and supramoral (for 'autonomous' and 'moral' are mutually exclusive)" in his *On the Genealogy of Morals* (p. 495, emphasis in the original), and his concept of "will to power" as "a subduing, a *becoming* master ... an adaptation through which any previous 'meaning' and 'purpose' are necessarily obscured or even obliterated" (p. 513, emphasis in the original). For Nietzsche, "the essence of life, its *will to power* is ... the essential priority of the spontaneous, aggressive, expansive, form-giving forces that give new interpretations and directions" (p. 515, emphasis in the original). It counters civilization's repression of our animal instincts and drives (pp. 520–3).
3. In the course of the unfolding of *The Second Sex*, these views also lead to a major contradiction. Although one of the core concept of Existentialism is opposition to Essentialism ("one is not born a woman, one becomes a woman"), Simone de Beauvoir's (1989) views concerning the "imperialism of human consciousness" and domination as inherent to the human psyche can be interpreted as expressing an essentialist view of human nature.
4. Earlier in *The Second Sex*, Simone de Beauvoir (1989) had expressed the revealing character of sexuality and intimate relations when she wrote about the way a cultured man can sink to his "lower nature" in his behavior toward women:

> His relations with women, then, lie in a contingent region, where morality no longer applies, where conduct is a matter of indifference. With other men, he has relations in which values are involved; he is a free agent confronting other free agents under laws recognized fully by all; but with woman—she was invented for this purpose—he casts off the responsibility of existence, he abandons himself to the mirage of his en sui, or fixed lower nature; he puts himself on the plane of inauthenticity. He shows himself tyrannical, sadistic, violent, or puerile, masochistic, querulous; he tries to satisfy his obsessions and whims; he is "at ease," he "relaxes" in view of the rights acquired in his public life. (Beauvoir, 1989, p. 613)

5. See Peter Hudis's (2015) discussion of Fanon's concept of "disalienation" in *Frantz Fanon: Philosopher of the Barricades* (pp. 47–54).
6. For various feminist discussions of Foucault, see Diamond and Quinby (1988), J. Afary and Anderson (2005).

Conclusion. Socialist Feminist Revolutionary Organizing in the Twenty-First Century

1. See Nancy Holmstrom's (2014) explanation of why sex work is not like other types of service work:

> The client is buying the right to use a woman's body as he wishes, without any desire on her part. Once she has contracted to provide a particular service—assuming she has this power to set limits—she has to allow him to enter into her body, her vagina, her mouth, her anus, to put his hands all over her body, and she must do whatever she has contracted to do to his body with her hands and mouth. This is domination at a most intimate level, whether or not he plays the dominating role in the interaction; it may be he who wants to be penetrated or spanked. It is the client's power to determine that and how he gets sexual satisfaction from a prostitute that makes male domination central to prostitution, not a male desire to dominate. And, except at the lowest end of the business where there is no pretense, she must pretend to be enjoying it; the interaction, therefore, is always a charade, a performance on the prostitute's part. Thus what the client is buying (renting) is not only her body, but the (appearance of) her emotions. If she just lies there and looks at her watch, he will not be satisfied; an important part of what he is buying is the appearance of her pleasure. His motivation may be to dominate a woman, to affirm his masculinity to himself or others, to have (particular kinds of) sexual experiences because he cannot get them without paying for them, or he may be looking for bodily/emotional connection (kissing costs more too), or to have a "girlfriend experience" without responsibilities. Whichever it is, the prostitute is selling him the right to use her body in this way. This indicates an important difference from the employment contract, as Pateman has pointed out. What the capitalist is paying workers for is to use their bodies to make products, and workers' bodies can be replaced by machines. Not so in prostitution … It is because human sexual experiences are highly intimate and both physical and emotional that they can range from ecstatic to horrific and everything in between. Only with great effort of dissociation is sex ever purely physical, Even when conscious memory is gone, the body retains experiences, e.g. of abuse, which is why abusers were usually abused as children. That's why we tell children that they should decide if they want to be touched and how. Thus selling sexual services is not like selling other services. Selling intimate bodily experiences is a kind of ultimate alienation (which has degrees, as discussed above). … The challenge for socialist feminists therefore is how to support women working as prostitutes without giving up our critique of the work and the institution of prostitution. But support for the women in the business must always be conjoined with struggles to change the political economic conditions that push so many into it. We should fight for jobs with living wages, affordable housing and childcare, substance abuse programs, help with immigration problems and whatever else sex workers say they need. (Holmstrom, 2014)

2. In *Capital*, Karl Marx (1976) writes:

    Capitalist production ... disturbs the metabolic interaction between man and the earth, i.e. it prevents the return to the soil of its constituent elements consumed by man in the form of food and clothing; hence it hinders the operation of the eternal natural conditions for the lasting fertility of the soil. Thus it destroys at the same time the physical health of the urban worker and the intellectual life of the rural worker. (pp. 637–8)

Bibliography

100 Faces of the Syrian Revolution. (2020) *Omar Alshogre Reflects on Brotherhood in Assad's Prisons Under Torture*. (Video). June 26. www.facebook.com/watch/?v=268450564418369 (last accessed February 18, 2021).

Abbas, Reem. (2020) "Sudan: Women Led the Revolution and Continue to Push for Change." *Elephant*. September 23. www.theelephant.info/videos/2020/09/23/sudan-women-led-the-revolution-and-continue-to-push-for-change/?fbclid=IwAR3Sy4tq_zADbbHND2p9humjgv3Gp1qgbuDWh-qLjcctFqVcOSjoxr5oTvM (last accessed February 14, 2021).

Abramsky, Sasha. (2020) "Ever-Growing Millions of Americans Face Eviction and Hunger." *Truthout*. November 21. https://truthout.org/articles/ever-growing-millions-of-americans-face-eviction-and-hunger-will-congress-act/ (last accessed February 14, 2021).

Achcar, Gilbert. 2021. "Who's Buried in the Graveyard of Empires?" New Politics. August 22.

Adetiba, Elizabeth. (2017) "Tarana Burke Says #MeToo Should Center Marginalized Communities." *Nation*. November 17. www.thenation.com/article/archive/tarana-burke-says-metoo-isnt-just-for-white-people/ (last accessed February 14, 2021).

Afary, Frieda. (2014) "From the Transcendence of Capitalism to the Realization of Human Power as an End in Itself: Reading Marx's Corpus as a Whole." *Radical Philosophy Review*, 17(1):263–7. https://doi.org/10.5840/radphilrev20141712.

—— (2016) "Critique of Thomas Piketty's *Capital in the 21 Century*." *Alliance of MENA Socialists*. April 3. https://allianceofmesocialists.org/critique-of-thomas-pikettys-capital-in-the-21st-century/ (last accessed February 17, 2021).

—— (2017) "How Did We Go from Arab Spring and the Occupy Movement to the Destruction of the Syrian Revolution and the Global Rise of Racist Authoritarianism?" *New Politics*. August 15. https://newpol.org/how-did-we-go-arab-spring-and-occupy-movement-destruction-syrian-revolution-and-global-rise/ (last accessed February 17, 2021).

—— (2018) "On Capitalism, Authoritarianism and What Is New about Trumpism." *Alliance of MENA Socialists*. April 11. https://allianceofmesocialists.org/on-capitalism-authoritarianism-and-what-is-new-about-trumpism/ (last accessed February 17, 2021).

—— (2020a) "The Me Too Movement in Iran: What Is New about It? What Can It Learn from Abolitionist Feminism in U.S." *New Politics*. September 23. https://newpol.org/the-me-too-movement-in-iran-what-is-new-about-it-what-can-it-learn-from-abolitionist-feminism-in-u-s/ (last accessed February 14, 2021).

—— (2020b) "Report on Dialogue between Iraqi, Palestinian-Lebanese, Chilean and Iranian Socialist Feminists." *Akhbar Rooz*. February 20. https://akhbar-rooz.com/?p=19505 (last accessed May 27, 2022).

—— (2020c) "What is New about State Capitalism in the 21st Century?" *New Politics.* February 12. https://newpol.org/?s=What+is+New+About+State+Capitalism&post_types=post,issue_post,review,issue,symposium (last accessed February 14, 2021).

——(2020d) "The Iranian Uprising of 2019–2020." In *A Region in Revolt: Mapping the Recent Uprisings in North Africa and West Asia,* edited by Jade Saab, pp. 135–62. Ottawa, ON: Daraja Press.

—— (2021a) "U.S. & Iranian Formerly Imprisoned Women Talk Abolitionism." *Captured Words, Free Thoughts,* 17(Winter):53–5. https://clas.ucdenver.edu/communication/sites/default/files/attached-files/cwft_17_winter_2021.pdf (last accessed February 22, 2021).

——(2021b) "Conversation with Palestinian Socialist Feminist Journalist, Budour Hassan." *Iranian Progressives in Translation.* May 22. https://iranianprogressives.org/conversation-with-palestinian-socialist-feminist-journalist-budour-hassan/ (last accessed October 12, 2021).

——(2021c) "Pathways to Solidarity: Struggles Against Police Brutality in the U.S., Myanmar and Iran." *New Politics.* June 15. https://newpol.org/pathways-to-solidarity-struggles-against-police-brutality-in-the-u-s-myanmar-and-iran/ (last accessed October 12, 2021).

—— (2022a) "Afghanistan and Its Challenge to Feminism." *New Politics.* Winter. https://newpol.org/afghanistan-and-its-challenge-to-feminism/ (last accessed May 27, 2022).

—— (2022b) "Interview with a Russian Anti-War Feminist." *Iranian Progressives in Translation.* March 22. https://iranianprogressives.org/interview-with-a-russian-anti-war-feminist-about-putins-invasion-of-ukraine/ (last accessed May 27, 2022).

—— (2022c) "Interview with a Ukrainian Socialist Feminist." *Iranian Progressives in Translation.* March 19. https://iranianprogressives.org/interview-with-a-ukrainian-socialist-feminist/ (last accessed May 27, 2022).

Afary, Frieda, and Lara Al-Kateb. (2020) "What Is Holding Back the Formation of a Global Prison Abolitionist Movement to Fight COVID-19 and Capitalism?" *Spectre Journal.* April 3. https://spectrejournal.com/what-is-holding-back-the-formation-of-a-global-prison-abolitionist-movement-to-fight-covid-19-and-capitalism/ (last accessed February 14, 2021).

Afary, Janet. (1985) "Marxist-Humanism: An Interview with Raya Dunayevskaya." *Chicago Literary Review,* 94(41):16–19.

—— (2009) *Sexual Politics in Modern Iran.* Cambridge: Cambridge University Press.

Afary, Janet, and Kevin B. Anderson. (2005) *Foucault and the Iranian Revolution: Gender and the Seductions of Islamism.* Chicago, IL: University of Chicago Press.

Afary, Janet, and Jesilyn Faust, eds. (2021) *Iranian Romance in the Digital Age: From Arranged Marriage to White Marriage.* London: I.B. Tauris/Bloomsbury.

Afary, Kamran. (2009) *Performance and Activism: Grassroots Discourse after the Los Angeles Rebellion of 1992.* Lanham, MD: Lexington Books.

Akram-Boshar, Shireen. (2020) "The Lebanese Uprising Continues: Interview with Rima Majed." *Jacobin.* February 17. https://jacobinmag.com/2020/02/lebanon-uprising-protests-banks-sectarianism-hezbollah (last accessed February 14, 2021).

Albert, Michael. (2003) *Parecon: Life after Capitalism.* London: Verso.

Alexander, Michelle. (2020) *The New Jim Crow: Mass Incarceration in the Age of Colorblindness.* New York: New Press.

Alfa, Ismail, and Mike Ives. (2021) "Captors Free Hundreds of Schoolgirls in Nigeria." *New York Times.* March 3. www.nytimes.com/2021/03/02/world/africa/nigeria-kidnapped-students.html?searchResultPosition=1 (last accessed May 27, 2022).

Alghoul, Diana. (2018) "'Stop Protecting Sexual Abusers' Demand Algerian Women." *New Arab.* June 4. https://english.alaraby.co.uk/english/blog/2018/6/4/stop-protecting-sexual-abusers-demand-algerian-women (last accessed February 14, 2021).

Ali, Zahra. (2018) *Women and Gender in Iraq.* Cambridge: Cambridge University Press.

—— (2020a) "Women and the Iraqi Revolution." *Al Saffir Al Arabi.* March 9. http://assafirarabi.com/en/29572/2020/03/09/women-and-the-iraqi-revolution/ (last accessed February 17, 2021).

—— (2020b) "The Civic and the Popular: Reflections on the Iraqi Uprising." *Immanent Frame.* April 29. https://tif.ssrc.org/2020/04/29/the-civic-and-the-popular/ (last accessed February 17, 2021).

Alliance of MENA Socialists. (2019) "Campaign in Solidarity with Feminist Political Prisoners in the Middle East and North America." *Alliance of MENA Socialists.* July 2. https://allianceofmesocialists.org/campaign-in-solidarity-with-feminist-political-prisoners-in-the-middle-east-and-north-africa/ (last accessed February 14, 2021).

—— (2020) "Dialogue between Socialist Feminists from China, Russia, Turkey." *Alliance of MENA Socialists.* March 1. https://allianceofmesocialists.org/dialogue-between-socialist-feminists-from-china-russia-turkey/ (last accessed May 27, 2022).

Amadeo, Kimberly. (2020) "Who Owns the US National Debt?" *Balance.* October 14. www.thebalance.com/who-owns-the-u-s-national-debt-3306124 (last accessed February 27, 2021).

Amnesty Internation (2016) "Syria: Reports of Extrajudicial Killings in Aleppo Point to War Crimes." Amensty International. December 16. www.amnesty.org/en/latest/news/2016/12/syria-reports-of-execution-style-killings-in-aleppo-point-to-war-crimes/ (last accessed May 26, 2022).

—— (2020a) "Iraq: Protest Death Toll Surges as Security Forces Resume Brutal Repression." *Amnesty International.* January 23. www.amnesty.org/en/latest/news/2020/01/iraq-protest-death-toll-surges-as-security-forces-resume-brutal-repression/ (last accessed February 17, 2021).

—— (2020b) "COVID-19 Makes Gulf Countries Abuse of Migrant Workers Impossible to Ignore." *Amnesty International.* April 30. www.amnesty.org/en/latest/campaigns/2020/04/covid19-makes-gulf-countries-abuse-of-migrant-workers-impossible-to-ignore/ (last accessed October 12, 2021).

Amos, Deborah. (2020) "Nasrin Documentary Spotlights Life and Work of Jailed Iranian Human Rights Lawyer." *National Public Radio (NPR).* October 30. www.

npr.org/2020/10/30/928341366/nasrin-documentary-spotlights-life-and-work-of-jailed-iranian-human-rights-lawye (last accessed February 14, 2021).

Anderson, Kevin B. (2008) *Marx at the Margins*. Chicago, IL: University of Chicago Press.

—— (2020a) "Indonesia: Mass Strikes Show Intersection of Class, Gender, and Ecology." *New Politics*. October 22. https://newpol.org/indonesia-mass-strikes-show-intersection-of-class-gender-and-ecology/ (last accessed February 17, 2021).

—— (2020b) *Class, Gender, Race and Colonialism: The "Intersectionality" of Marx*. Ottawa, ON: Daraja Press.

Anderson, Kristin J. (2014) *Modern Misogyny: Anti-Feminism in a Post-Feminist Era*. Oxford: Oxford University Press.

APM Research Lab. (2020) "COVID-19 Deaths by Race and Ethnicity in the U.S." *APM Research Lab*. www.apmresearchlab.org/covid/deaths-by-race (last accessed February 14, 2021).

Arab Reform Initiative. (2020) "Our Revolution Is Feminist: Meeting with Women Activists in Lebanon." *Arab Reform Initiative*. January 17. www.arab-reform.net/video/our-revolution-is-feminist-meeting-with-women-activists-in-lebanon/ (last accessed February 17, 2021).

Archer, Susan A. (2008) "Feminism and Imperialism, 1890–1920: Our Anti-Imperialist Sisters—Missing in Action from American Feminist Sociology." *Sociological Inquiry*, 78(4):461–79. https://doi.org/10.1111/j.1475-682X.2008.00257.x.

Avent, Ryan. (2016) *The Wealth of Humans: Work, Power, and Status in the Twenty-First Century*. New York: St. Martin Press.

Avert. (2020) "History of HIV and AIDS Overview." *Avert: Global Education and Information on HIV and AIDS*. www.avert.org/professionals/history-hiv-aids/overview (last accessed February 14, 2021).

Ayar, Avat. (2018) "Attention to Vulnerable Groups at the International AIDS Conference in Amsterdam." *Zamaneh*. July 26. radiozamaneh.com/404924.

Banks, Nina. (2020) "Black Women in the United States and Unpaid Collective Work: Theorizing the Community as a Site of Production." *Review of Black Political Economy*, 47(4):343–62. https://doi.org/10.1177/0034644620962811.

Baran, Paul A. (1944) "New Trends in Russian Economic Thinking?" *American Economic Review*, 34(4):862–71. www.jstor.org/stable/1807403.

Barnard, Anne. (2019) "Inside Syria's Secret Torture Prisons: How Bashar al-Assad Crushed Dissent." *New York Times*. May 11. www.nytimes.com/2019/05/11/world/middleeast/syria-torture-prisons.html (last accessed February 17, 2021).

Barrett, Michele. (1980/2014) *Women's Oppression Today: The Marxist-Feminist Encounter*. Reprint. London: Verso.

Baudrillard, Jean. (1975) *The Mirror of Production (Le Miroir de la production)*. Translated by Mark Poster. New York: Telos Press.

Beauvoir, Simone de. (1947) *The Ethics of Ambiguity*. Translated by Bernard Frechtman. New York: Open Road.

—— (1989 [1949]) *The Second Sex*. Translated and edited by H.M. Parshley. New York: Vintage.

—— (2014) "10 Key Quotes." *Guardian*. January 9. www.theguardian.com/books/2014/jan/09/simone-de-beauvoir-google-doodle-quotes (last accessed February 26, 2021).

Beech, Hannah. (2021) "'She Is a Hero': In Myanmar's Protests Women Are on the Frontlines." *New York Times*. March 4. www.nytimes.com/2021/03/04/world/asia/myanmar-protests-women.html (last accessed March 8, 2021).

Beech, Hannah, and Muktita Suhartono. (2020) "Young Women Take a Frontline Role in Thailand's Protests." *New York Times*. September 25, p. A8. www.nytimes.com/2020/09/24/world/asia/thailand-protests-women.html (last accessed February 17, 2021).

Benhabib, Seyla, Judith Butler, Drucilla Cornell, and Nancy Fraser. (1995) *Feminist Contentions: A Philosophical Exchange*. Introduction by Linda Nicholson. Leiden: Routledge.

Benjamin, Jessica. (1988) *The Bonds of Love: Psychoanalysis, Feminism, and the Problem of Domincation*. New York: Pantheon.

Benston, Margaret. (1969) "The Political Economy of Women's Liberation." *Monthly Review Press*, 21(4):13–27. https://doi.org/10.14452/MR-021-04-1969-08_2.

Bhandar, Brenna, and Rafeef Ziadah, eds. (2020) *Revolutionary Feminisms: Conversations on Collective Action and Radical Thought*. London: Verso.

Bhattacharya, Tithi, ed. (2017) *Social Reproduction Theory: Remapping Class, Recentering Oppression*. London: Pluto Press.

—— (2020) "Liberating Women from 'Political Economy': Margaret Benston's Marxism and a Social-Reproduction Approach to Gender Oppression." *Monthly Review*. January 1. https://monthlyreview.org/2020/01/01/liberating-women-from-political-economy/ (last accessed February 20, 2021).

Bhowmick, Nilanjana. (2021) "Carrying the Revolution: Women Are on the Front Lines for India's Farmer Protests—and Making Themselves Heard." *Time*. March 15.

Bitar, Lara, and Miriam Younes. (2019) "New Ways of Relating to Each Other." *Rosa Luxemburg Stiftung*. November 12. www.rosalux.de/en/news/id/41305/new-ways-of-relating-to-each-other/ (last accessed February 14, 2021).

Black Women for Wellness. (2021) "Reflecting on Haiti and Afghanistan." September 10. www.facebook.com/BlackWomenForWellness/videos/404871651239194 (last accessed May 27, 2022).

Blakeley, Grace. (2020) *The Corona Crash: How the Pandemic Will Change Capitalism*. London: Verso.

Bloom, Mia, and Sophia Moskalenko. (2022) "Ukraine's Women Fighters Reflect a Cultural Tradition of Feminist Independence." *The Conversation*. March 21. https://theconversation.com/ukraines-women-fighters-reflect-a-cultural-tradition-of-feminist-independence-179529 (last accessed May 27, 2022).

Bohrer, Ashley J. (2020) *Marxism and Intersectionality: Race, Gender, Class and Sexuality under Contemporary Capitalism*. Bielefeld, Germany: Transcript-Verlag.

Bonnefol, Pascale, and Ernesto Londono. (2021) "Chile Legalizes Same Sex Marriage at Fraught Political Moment." *New York Times*. December 7. www.

nytimes.com/2021/12/07/world/americas/chile-gay-marriage.html?search
ResultPosition=1 (last accessed May 27, 2022).

Boniol, Mathieu, Michelle McIsaac, Lihui Xu, Tana Wuliji, Khassoum Diallo, and Jim Campbell. (2019) "Gender Equity in the Health Workforce: Analysis of 104 Countries." *World Health Organization.* March. https://apps.who.int/iris/bitstream/handle/10665/311314/WHO-HIS-HWF-Gender-WP1-2019.1-eng.pdf (last accessed February 14, 2021).

Bosman, Julie. (2020) "When Staying Home, or Trying to Leave, Carries Its Own Risk." *New York Times.* May 17, p. A10. www.nytimes.com/2020/05/15/us/domestic-violence-coronavirus.html (last accessed February 14, 2021).

Bouie, Jamelle. (2020) "Facebook Is a Disaster For the World." *New York Times.* September 21, p. A25. www.nytimes.com/2020/09/18/opinion/facebook-democracy.html (last accessed February 17, 2021).

Boussedra, Saliha. (2017) "Marx and Prostitution." *Resources Prostitution.* February 13. https://ressourcesprostitution.wordpress.com/2017/02/13/marx-and-prostitution/ (last accessed May 27, 2022).

Brooks, Kim. (2018) "Mothers Are Dying. Does Anyone Care?" *New York Times.* November 18, p. SR1. www.nytimes.com/2018/11/16/opinion/sunday/maternal-mortality-rates.html (last accessed February 14, 2021).

Brown, Heather A. (2012) *Marx on Gender and the Family: A Critical Study.* Leiden and New York: Brill.

Brown, Jenny. (2019) *Without Apology: The Abortion Struggle Now.* London: Verso.

Brynjolfsson, Erik, and Andrew McAfee. (2016) *The Second Machine Age: Work, Progress, and Prosperity in a Time of Brilliant Technologies.* New York: W.W. Norton.

Buckley, Chris, and Steven Lee Meyers. (2021) "China Military Taunts Taiwan, Testing the U.S." *New York Times.* October 10.

Buckley, Chris, and Austin Ramzy. (2019) "China's Push to Turn Its Muslims into Loyal Army of Cheap Labor." *New York Times.* December 31, p. A1. www.nytimes.com/2019/12/30/world/asia/china-xinjiang-muslims-labor.html (last accessed February 17, 2021).

—— (2020) "Night Images Show China Has Added Detention Sites in Mostly Muslim Xinjiang." *New York Times.* September 24, p. A9. www.nytimes.com/2020/09/24/world/asia/china-muslims-xinjiang-detention.html (last accessed February 17, 2021).

Burke, Tarana. (2021) *Unbound: My Story of Liberation and the Birth of the Me Too Movement.* New York: Flatiron Books.

Butler, Judith. (2006 [1990]) *Gender Trouble: Feminism and the Subversion of Identity.* New York: Routledge.

—— (2011 [1993]) *Bodies That Matter: On the Discursive Limits of Sex.* New York: Routledge.

—— (2021) "Why Is the Idea of 'Gender' Provoking Backlash the World Over?" *Guardian.* October 23. www.theguardian.com/us-news/commentisfree/2021/oct/23/judith-butler-gender-ideology-backlash (last accessed May 27, 2022).

Castillo, Andrea. (2020) "How Two Black Women in LA Helped Build Black Lives Matter from Hashtag to Global Movement." *Los Angeles Times.* June 21. www.

latimes.com/california/story/2020-06-21/black-lives-matter-los-angeles-patrisse-cullors-melina-abdullah (last accessed February 18, 2021).

Cave, Damien, Emma Bubola, and Choe Sang-Han. (2021). "World Is Facing First Long Slide in Its Population." *New York Times*. May 23. www.nytimes.com/2021/05/22/world/global-population-shrinking.html (last accessed October 12, 2021).

Chalabi, Mona. (2017) "Equal Pay Day: A Wage Gap Fact Check." *Guardian*. April 4. www.theguardian.com/us-news/datablog/2017/apr/04/equal-pay-day-us-wage-gap-gender-race-ethnicity (last accessed February 14, 2021).

Charmes, Jacques. (2019) "Unpaid Care Work and the Labor Market. An Analysis of Time Use Data Based on the Latest World Compilation of Time-Use Surveys." *International Labour Organization*. Geneva, Switzerland. www.ilo.org/wcmsp5/groups/public/---dgreports/---gender/documents/publication/wcms_732791.pdf (last accessed February 20, 2021).

Chen, Elsie and Sui-Lee Wee (2021) "China Tried to Slow Divorces by Making Couples Wait. Instead They Rushed." *New York Times*. February 28. www.nytimes.com/2021/02/26/business/china-slowing-divorces.html?searchResultPosition=1 (last accessed May 27, 2022).

Chi Leung, Lam. (2019) "Hong Kong Protests Defend Political Freedoms." *Socialist Resurgence*. November 24. https://socialistresurgence.org/2019/11/24/hong-kong-protests-defend-political-freedoms/ (last accessed February 18, 2021).

—— (2020) "Hong Kong Mass Movement Challenges China's National Security Law." Interview by Ernie Gotta. *Socialist Resurgence*. May 29. https://socialistresurgence.org/2020/05/29/hong-kong-mass-movement-challenges-chinas-national-security-law/ (last accessed February 18, 2021).

—— (2022) "Interview: After the Hong Kong Rebellion." *International Socialism*. January 10.

Choi, Susanne Y.P. (2020) "When Protests and Daily Life Converge: The Spaces and People of Hong Kong's Anti-Extradition Movement." *Critique of Anthropology*. March 4. https://journals.sagepub.com/doi/10.1177/0308275X20908322 (last accessed May 26, 2022).

Cohen, I. Glenn. (2017) "Artificial Wombs Are Coming. They Could Completely Change the Debate over Abortion." *Vox*. August 23. www.vox.com/the-big-idea/2017/8/23/16186468/artificial-wombs-radically-transform-abortion-debate (last accessed February 20, 2021).

Cohen, Patricia. (2020) "Recession's Toll on Women Points to a Lasting Setback." *New York Times*. November 18, p. A1. www.nytimes.com/2020/11/17/business/economy/women-jobs-economy-recession.html (last accessed February 14, 2021).

Cohen, Patricia, and Tiffany Hsu. (2020) "Economic Strain Grows, Hitting Working Mothers." *New York Times*, June 5, p. B1. Updated June 30, 2020. www.nytimes.com/2020/06/03/business/economy/coronavirus-working-women.html (last accessed February 14, 2021).

Cole, Juan. 2021. "Taliban 'Islam' Versus the Islam of the Prophet Muhammad and Qur'an." *Informed Comment*. August 18.

Collins, Patricia Hill. (1990) *Black Feminist Thought: Knowledge, Consciousness, and the Politics of Empowerment*. Abingdon, UK: Routledge.

—— (2000) "The Social Construction of Black Feminist Thought." In *The Black Feminist Reader*, edited by Joy James and T. Denean Sharpley-Whiting, pp. 183–207. Malden, MA: Wiley-Blackwell.

—— (2012) *On Intellectual Activism*. Philadelphia, PA: Temple University Press.

Collins, Patricia Hill, and Sirma Bilge. (2016) *Intersectionality*. Malden, MA: Polity Press.

Christian, Barbara. (2000) "The Race for Theory." In *The Black Feminist Reader*, edited by Joy James and T. Denean Sharpley-Whiting, pp. 11–23. Malden, MA: Wiley-Blackwell.

Conger, Kate, and David Sanger. (2021) "Pentagon Cancels Deal It Awarded to Microsoft." *New York Times*. July 7.

Conger, Kate, David E. Sanger, and Scott Shane. (2019) "Microsoft Wins Pentagon Deal over Amazon." *New York Times*. October 26, p. A1. www.nytimes.com/2019/10/25/technology/dod-jedi-contract.html (last accessed February 18, 2021).

Conron, Kerith J., Kathryn K. O'Neill, Luis A.,Vasqueze, and Christy Mallory. (2022) "Prohibiting Gender-Affirming Care for Transgender Youth." *UCLA School of Law Williams Institute*. March. https://williamsinstitute.law.ucla.edu/publications/bans-trans-youth-health-care/ (last accessed May 27, 2022).

Coontz, Stephanie. 2006. *Marriage, a History: How Love Conquered Marriage*. New York: Penguin Books.

Coyle, Diane. (2021) "A Crisis for Women of Color." *New York Times*. January 15, p.A23.www.nytimes.com/2021/01/14/opinion/minority-women-unemployment-covid.html (last accessed February 14, 2021).

Crenshaw, Kimberlé. (2000) "Demarginalizing the Intersection of Race and Sex: A Black Feminist Critique of Antidiscrimination Doctrine, Feminist Theory and Antiracist Politics." In *The Black Feminist Reader*, edited by Joy James and T. Denean Sharpley-Whiting, pp. 208–38. Malden, MA: Wiley-Blackwell.

—— (2002) "Background Paper for the Expert Meeting on the Gender-Related Aspects of Race Discrimination." *Revista Estudos Feministas*, 10(1):171–88. www.researchgate.net/publication/262736590_Background_Paper_for_the_Expert_Meeting_on_the_Gender-Related_Aspects_of_Race_Discrimination (last accessed February 22, 2021).

Critical Resistance. (2021) "What Is the PIC? What Is Abolition? The Prison Industrial Complex." *Critical Resistance*. http://criticalresistance.org/about/not-so-common-language/ (last accessed February 22, 2021).

Cruise, Maureen, Ignacio Guerrero, Omar Abbas, Frieda Afary, and Clinic Health Car Worker. (2018) "Symposium on Health Care and Alternatives to Capitalism." *Alliance of MENA Socialists*. November 9. https://allianceofmesocialists.org/symposium-on-health-care-and-alternatives-to-capitalism/ (last accessed February 27, 2021).

Cudd, Ann, and Nancy Holmstrom. (2011). *Capitalism: For and Against*. Cambridge: Cambridge University Press.

Cuffe, Sandra. (2020) "Feminist Groups Hold Mass Women's Day Marches across Chile." *Aljazeera*. March 8. www.aljazeera.com/news/2020/3/8/feminist-groups-hold-mass-womens-day-marches-across-chile (last accessed February 14, 2021).

Daher, Joseph. (2019) *Syria after the Uprising: The Political Economy of State Resilience.* Chicago, IL: Haymarket Books.

Dahir, Abdi Latif, Ruth McLean, and Lynsey Chutel. (2020) "Floyd's Killing Prompts Africans to Seek Police Reform in Their Countries." *New York Times.* July 5, p. A11. www.nytimes.com/2020/07/03/world/africa/george-floyd-protests-police-africa.html (last accessed February 18, 2021).

Dalla Costa, Mariarosa, and Selma James. (1971) *The Power of Woman and the Subversion of the Community* (pamphlet). December 29. www.e-flux.com/wp-content/uploads/2013/05/2.-Dalla-Costa-and-James-Women-and-the-Subversion-of-the-Community.pdf?b8c429 (last accessed February 22, 2021).

Davis, Angela Y. (1983) *Women, Race & Class.* New York: Vintage.

—— (1998) "Masked Racism: Reflections on the Prison Industrial Complex." *Journal of ColorLines.* (Online). September 10. www.colorlines.com/articles/masked-racism-reflections-prison-industrial-complex (last accessed February 18, 2021).

—— (2000) "Women and Capitalism: Dialectics of Oppression and Liberation." In *The Black Feminist Reader,* edited by Joy James and T. Denean Sharpley-Whiting, pp. 146–82. Malden, MA: Wiley-Blackwell.

—— (2012) *The Meaning of Freedom and Other Difficult Dialogues.* San Francisco. CA: City Lights Publishers.

—— (2018) "Davis on Intersectional Feminism." *Youtube.* April 19. www.youtube.com/watch?v=9GDjT3Fw_6w (last accessed May 27, 2018).

Delmore, Erin. (2020) "This Is How Women Voters Decided the 2020 Election." *NBC News.* November 13. www.nbcnews.com/know-your-value/feature/how-women-voters-decided-2020-election-ncna1247746 (last accessed February 14, 2021).

Democracy Now. (2020) *Watch: 2020 Right Livelihood Award Ceremony* (Online video; 1:14:01). December 2. www.democracynow.org/live/watch_2020_right_livelihood_award_ceremony (last accessed February 27, 2021).

Deutsche Welle. (2019) "Marriage Rate in Iran Has Decreased by 40% in One Decade." *Deutsche Welle.* November 11. www.dw.com/fa-ir/a-51340679 (last accessed February 14, 2021).

Diamond, Irene, and Lee Quinby, eds. (1988) *Feminism and Foucault: Reflections on Resistance.* Boston, MA: Northeastern University Press.

Dickerson, Caitlin, Seth Freed Wessler, and Miriam Jordan. (2020) "Immigrants Say They Were Pressured into Unneeded Surgeries." *New York Times.* September 29. www.nytimes.com/2020/09/29/us/ice-hysterectomies-surgeries-georgia.html (last accessed March 8, 2021).

Ding Ling. (1989) *I Myself Am a Woman: Selected Writings of Ding Ling.* Boston, MA: Beacon Press.

Dockterman, Eliana. (2021) "Love or Money" in "Special Report: Women and the Pandemic." *Time.* March 15.

Do Something. (2020) "11 Facts about Human Trafficking." *Do Something.* www.dosomething.org/us/facts/11-facts-about-human-trafficking (last accessed February 14, 2021).

Dolan, Mara. (2020) "COVID-19 Could Set Back Women's Economic Progress for Decades." *Truthout.* August 30. https://truthout.org/articles/covid-19-could-set-back-womens-economic-progress-for-decades/ (last accessed February 14, 2021).

Drucker, Peter. (2015) *Warped: Gay Normality and Queer Anti-Capitalism*. Leiden: Brill.

Dunayevskaya, Raya. (1944) "A New Revision of Marxian Economics." *American Economic Review*, 34(3):531–7. www.jstor.org/stable/1810242.

—— (1945) "Revision of Reaffirmation of Marxism? A Rejoinder." *American Economic Review*, 35(4):660–4. www.jstor.org/stable/1809387.

——(1958) *Marxism and Freedom: From 1776 until Today*. New York, NY: Bookman Associates.

—— (1979) "Iran: Unfoldment of and Contradictions in Revolution." Raya Dunayevskaya Collection. March 25. https://rayadunayevskaya.org/category/vol10/ (last accessed May 27, 2022)

____ (1981) *Iran: Revolution and Counter-Revolution*. Raya Dunayevskaya Collection. https://rayadunayevskaya.org/raya/ArchivePDFs/7219.pdf (last accessed May 27, 2022).

—— (1985) *Women's Liberation and the Dialectics of Revolution: Reaching for the Future, a 35-Year Collection of Essays, Historic, Philosophic, Global*. London: Humanities Press.

—— (1991) *Rosa Luxemburg, Women's Liberation, and Marx's Philosophy of Revolution*. 2nd edn. Urbana, IL: University of Illinois Press.

——(1992) *The Marxist-Humanist Theory of State-Capitalism*. Chicago, IL: News and Letters Committees.

——(2000) *Marxism and Freedom: From 1776 until Today*. Amherst, NY: Humanity Books.

——(2002) *The Power of Negativity: Selected Writings on the Dialectic in Hegel and Marx*. Edited and introduction by Peter Hudis and Kevin B. Anderson. Lanham, MD: Lexington Books.

—— (2003) *Philosophy and Revolution: From Hegel to Sartre, and from Marx to Mao*. London: Lexington Books.

Dunn, Bill. (2017) "Against Neoliberalism as a Concept." *Capital & Class*, 41(3):435–54. https://doi.org/10.1177/0309816816678583.

Dustdar, Naima. (2015) "Sex Work: Compulsion or Choice?" *Zamaneh*. August 15. www.radiozamaneh.com/232552/ (last accessed May 27, 2022).

DuVernay, Ava. (2016) *13th*. Directed by Ava DuVernay (Online film). Los Gatos: Netflix. www.netflix.com/title/80091741 (last accessed February 18, 2021).

Eavis, Peter, and Steve Lohr. (2020) "Big Tech Firms Tighten Grip on Flailing Economy." *New York Times*. August 20, p. A23. www.nytimes.com/2020/08/19/technology/big-tech-business-domination.html (last accessed February 18, 2021).

Ebert, Teresa L. (1995) *Ludic Feminism and After: Postmodernism, Desire, and Labor in Late Capitalism*. Ann Arbor, MI: University of Michigan Press.

The Economist. (2012) "State Capitalism's Global Reach: New Masters of the Universe." *The Economist*. January 21. www.economist.com/special-report/2012/01/21/new-masters-of-the-universe (last accessed February 18, 2021).

——(2015) "Pornography: A Users' Manual." *The Economist*. September 26. www. economist.com/international/2015/09/26/a-users-manual (last accessed February 14, 2021).

——(2016) "A Giant Problem: The Rise of the Corporate Colossus Threatens Both Competition and the Legitimacy of Business." *The Economist*. September 17. www.economist.com/leaders/2016/09/17/a-giant-problem (last accessed February 18, 2021).

—— (2017a) "China: In Search of Women." *The Economist*. November 23. www. economist.com/special-report/2017/11/23/a-distorted-sex-ratio-is-playing-havoc-with-marriage-in-china (last accessed February 14, 2021).

—— (2017b) "A Looser Knot: The State of Marriage as an Institution." *The Economist*. November 23. www.economist.com/special-report/2017/11/23/the-state-of-marriage-as-an-institution (last accessed February 14, 2021).

—— (2017c) "Special Report on Marriage: The West, For Richer." *The Economist*. November 23. www.economist.com/special-report/2017/11/23/marriage-in-the-west (last accessed February 14, 2021).

—— (2017d) "The Triumph of Love: Marriage in India Is Becoming Less Traditional." *The Economist*. November 23. www.economist.com/special-report/2017/11/23/marriage-in-india-is-becoming-less-traditional (last accessed February 14, 2021).

—— (2018a) "Behind Closed Doors: American Business and #MeToo." *The Economist*. September 27. www.economist.com/business/2018/09/27/american-business-and-metoo (last accessed February 14, 2021).

—— (2018b) "Sex and Power: #MeToo, One Year On." *The Economist*. September 29. www.economist.com/leaders/2018/09/27/metoo-one-year-on (last accessed February 14, 2021).

—— (2019a) "Slowbalisation: The Steam Has Gone Out of Globalisation." *Economist*. January 24. www.economist.com/leaders/2019/01/24/the-steam-has-gone-out-of-globalisation (last accessed February 18, 2021).

—— (2019b) "We All Want to Change the World: Economics, Demography and Social Media." *The Economist*. November 14. www.economist.com/international/2019/11/14/economics-demography-and-social-media-only-partly-explain-the-protests-roiling-so-many-countries-today (last accessed February 18, 2021).

——(2020a) "COVID-19 and Poverty: Failing the Poor." *The Economist*. September 26. www.economist.com/leaders/2020/09/26/covid-19-has-reversed-years-of-gains-in-the-war-on-poverty (last accessed February 14, 2021).

——(2020b) "Feminism in Egypt: Speaking Up about Sex Crimes." *The Economist*. November 12. www.economist.com/middle-east-and-africa/2020/11/14/egyptian-women-speak-up-about-sex-crimes (last accessed February 14, 2021).

——(2020c) "Grim Tallies: One Million and Counting." *The Economist*. September 26. www.economist.com/briefing/2020/09/26/the-covid-19-pandemic-is-worse-than-official-figures-show (last accessed February 14, 2021).

——(2020d) "Xinjiang: Orphaned by the State." *The Economist*. October 17. www. economist.com/china/2020/10/17/how-xinjiangs-gulag-tears-families-apart (last accessed February 14, 2021).

—— (2020e) "Black Lives Matter: The George Floyd Effect." *The Economist*. December 12. www.economist.com/united-states/2020/12/10/six-months-after-mass-protests-began-what-is-the-future-of-blm (last accessed February 18, 2021).

—— (2020f) "China Wants to Put Itself Back at the Centre of the World: The Belt and Road Initiative Revives Memories of China's Imperial Tributary System." *The Economist*. February 6. www.economist.com/special-report/2020/02/06/china-wants-to-put-itself-back-at-the-centre-of-the-world (last accessed February 27, 2021).

—— (2020g) "Goodbye Globalisation: The Dangerous Lure of Self-Sufficiency." *The Economist*. May 16. www.economist.com/weeklyedition/2020-05-16 (last accessed February 18, 2021).

—— (2020h) "Orphaned by the State: How Xinjiang's Gulag Tears Families Apart." *The Economist*. October 17. www.economist.com/china/2020/10/17/how-xinjiangs-gulag-tears-families-apart (last accessed February 18, 2021).

—— (2020i) "Migrant Workers in Cramped Gulf Dorms Fear Infection." *The Economist*. April 25. www.economist.com/middle-east-and-africa/2020/04/23/migrant-workers-in-cramped-gulf-dorms-fear-infection (last accessed October 12, 2021).

—— (2021a) "Homophobia in Africa: Out and Preyed on." *The Economist*, March 6.

—— (2021b) "Special Report: Chinese Youth." *The Economist*. January 23. www.economist.com/special-report/2021/01/21/young-chinese-are-both-patriotic-and-socially-progressive (last accessed February 14, 2021).

—— (2021c) "Working Parents and COVID-19: Take Your Child to Work (Every) Day." *The Economist*, May 22.

—— (2021d) "America, China and the Moon: The Eagle and the Rabbit." *The Economist*, July 17.

—— (2021e) "Counting the Dead." *The Economist*, May 15.

—— (2022) "The Pandemic's True Death Toll." *The Economist*, April 12. www.economist.com/graphic-detail/coronavirus-excess-deaths-estimates (last accessed May 26, 2022).

Eisenstein, Zillah. (2019) *Abolitionist Socialist Feminism: Radicalizing the Next Revolution*. New York: Monthly Review Press.

Elson, Diane. (1994) "Micro, Meso, Macro: Gender and Economic Analysis in the Context of Policy Reform." In The Strategic Silences: Gender and Economic Policy, edited by Isabella Bakker, pp. 33–45. London: Zed Books.

Encyclopedia of Marxism. s.v. "Glossary of Terms: B1." www.marxists.org/glossary/terms/b/l.htm (last accessed February 24, 2021).

Engelbrecht, Cora, and Sharif Hassan. 2021. "At Afghan Universities, Increasing Fear That Women Will Never Be Allowed Back." *New York Times*. September 27, updated September 30.

Engels, Friedrich. (1972) *Origin of the Family, Private Property and the State*. Introduction by Evelyn Reed. Atlanta, GA: Pathfinder Press.

—— (1977). *The Origin of the Family, Private Property and the State*. Moscow: Progress Publishers.

Fakier, Khayaat, Diana Mulinari, and Nora Räthzel, eds. (2020) *Marxist-Feminist Theories and Struggles Today: Essential Writings on Intersectionality, Postcolonialism and Ecofeminism*. London: Zed Books.

Faludi, Susan. (2000) *Stiffed: The Betrayal of the American Man*. New York: William Morrow.

—— (2006) *Backlash: The Undeclared War Against American Women*. New York: Three Rivers Press.

—— (2020) "'Believe All Women' Is a Right-Wing Trap." *New York Times*. May 18. www.nytimes.com/2020/05/18/opinion/tara-reade-believe-all-women.html (last accessed February 14, 2021).

Fallon, Katy, Antonia Cundy, and Rosabel Crean (2022) "Vigilantes Stalk Ukraine Border as Sex Traffickers Target Fleeing Women and Children." *Guardian*, March 24.

Fanon, Frantz. (1963) *The Wretched of the Earth*. Translated by Constance Farrington. New York: Grove Press.

—— (1967) *Black Skin, White Masks*. Translated by Charles Lam Markman. New York: Grove Press.

Fassler, Ella. (2020) "Report Finds over 100 Rebellions in Jails and Prisons over COVID Conditions." *Truthout*. November 13. https://truthout.org/articles/report-finds-over-100-rebellions-in-jails-and-prisons-over-covid-conditions/ (last accessed February 14, 2021).

Federici, Silvia. (2004) *Caliban and the Witch: Women, the Body and Primitive Accumulation*. New York: Autonomedia.

—— (2012) *Revolution at Point Zero: Housework, Reproduction, and Feminist Struggle*. Oakland, CA: PM Press.

—— (2019) *Re-enchanting the World: Feminism and the Politics of Commons*. Introduction by Peter Linebaugh. Oakland, CA: PM Press.

—— (2021) *Patriarchy of the Wage: Notes on Marx, Gender and Feminism*. Oakland, CA: PM Press.

Federici, Silvia, George Souvlis, and Ankica Čakardić. (2017) "Feminism and Social Reproduction: An Interview with Silvia Federici." *Salvage*. January 19. https://salvage.zone/online-exclusive/feminism-and-social-reproduction-an-interview-with-silvia-federici/ (last accessed February 20, 2021).

Feeding America. (2022). "Hunger in America." www.feedingamerica.org/hunger-in-america (last accessed May 27, 2022).

Ferguson, Ann. (2018) "Socialist-Feminist Transitions and Visions." *Radical Philosophy Review*, 21(1):177–200. https://doi.org/10.5840/radphilrev 201841687.

Ferguson, Susan. (2019) *Women and Work: Feminism, Labour, and Social Reproduction*. London: Pluto Press.

Findlay, J. N. (1976 [1958]) *Hegel: A Re-examination Hb*. Oxford: Oxford University Press.

Flatow, Ira. (2018) "Maryanne Wolf's Interview with Ira Flatow." *Science Friday*. November 16. www.sciencefriday.com/person/maryanne-wolf/ (last accessed February 18, 2021).

Flores, Andrew, Gabriele Magni, and Andrew Reynolds. (2020) "Had LGBT Voters Stayed Home, Trump Might Have Won the 2020 Presidential Election."

Washington Post. December 1. www.washingtonpost.com/politics/2020/12/01/
had-lgbt-voters-stayed-home-trump-might-have-won-2020-presidential-
election/ (last accessed February 18, 2021).

Florido, Adrian, and Marisa Peñaloza. (2020) "As Nations Reckons with Race, Poll
Finds White Americans Least Engaged." *National Public Radio (NPR)*. August
27. www.npr.org/2020/08/27/906329303/as-nation-reckons-with-race-poll-
finds-white-americans-least-engaged (last accessed February 18, 2021).

Floyd, Keven. (2009) *The Reification of Desire: Toward a Queer Marxism*.
Minneapolis, MN: University of Minnesota Press.

Fonseca, Esperanza. (2021) "Don't Fully Decriminalize Sex Work." *New York
Times*. October 30. www.nytimes.com/2021/10/29/opinion/letters/sex-work.
html?searchResultPosition=1 (last accessed May 27, 2022).

Foreman, Ann. (1977) *Femininity as Alienation: Women and the family in Marxism
and Psychoanalysis*. London: Pluto Press.

Foroohar, Rana. (2012) "The Truth sbout Men, Women and Work." *Newsweek*.
May 21. http://content.time.com/time/magazine/article/0,9171,2114439,00.
html (last accessed February 14, 2021).

Fortunati, Leopoldina. (1995) *The Arcane of Reproduction: Housework, Prostitution,
Labor and Capital*, edited by Jim Fleming. New York: Autonomedia. https://
libcom.org/files/Leopoldina%20Fortunati%20-%20The%20Arcane%20of%20
Reproduction%20-%20Housework,%20Prostitution,%20Labor,%20and%20
Capital.pdf (last accessed February 20, 2021).

Foucault, Michel. (1979) *Discipline and Punish: The Birth of the Prison*. New York:
Vintage.

Fraser, Nancy. (1989) *Unruly Practices: Power, Discourse and Gender in
Contemporary Social Theory*. Minneapolis, MN: University of Minnesota Press.

——(1995a) "False Antitheses." In *Feminist Contentions: A Philosophical Exchange*,
by Seyla Benhabib, Judith Butler, Drucilla Cornell, and Nancy Fraser, pp. 59–74.
Leiden: Routledge.

——(1995b) "From Redistribution to Recognition? Dilemmas of Justice in a 'Post-
Socialist' Age." *New Left Review*, 211. https://newleftreview.org/issues/i212/
articles/nancy-fraser-from-redistribution-to-recognition-dilemmas-of-justice-
in-a-post-socialist-age (last accessed February 24, 2021).

——(2013a) *Fortunes of Feminism: From State-Managed Capitalism to Neoliberal
Crisis*. London: Verso.

——(2013b) "How Feminism Became Capitalism's Handmaiden—and How to
Reclaim It." *Guardian*. October 14. www.theguardian.com/commentisfree/2013/
oct/14/feminism-capitalist-handmaiden-neoliberal (last accessed February 14,
2021).

Freytas-Tamura, Kimiko de. (2018) "In a Landslide, Irish Voters End an Abortion
Ban." *New York Times*. May 27, p. A1. www.nytimes.com/2018/05/26/world/
europe/ireland-abortion-yes.html (last accessed February 14, 2021).

Friedman, Thomas L. (2020) "Our New Historical Divide: B.C. and A.C. —the
World before Corona and the World after." *New York Times*. March 17. www.
nytimes.com/2020/03/17/opinion/coronavirus-trends.html (last accessed
February 14, 2021).

Fuller, Sheila. (1996) "The Philosophic Meaning of Bosnia's Struggle." *News & Letters*, 41(1):5, 10. www.marxists.org/history/etol/newspape/news-and-letters/1990s/1996-01-02.pdf (last accessed February 22, 2021).

Gaither, Kecia. (2020) "Root out Systemic Racism: Equal Access to Maternal, Prenatal Care." *Ob.Gyn. News* 55(7). www.mdedge.com/obgyn/article/227664/obstetrics/rooting-out-systemic-racism-equal-access-maternal-prenatal-care (last accessed February 14, 2021).

Gant-Britton, Lisbeth. (2008) *African American History*. New York: Holt Publishing.

Garcia, Sandra E. (2017) "The Woman Who Created #MeToo Long before Hashtags." *New York Times*. October 20. www.nytimes.com/2017/10/20/us/me-too-movement-tarana-burke.html (last accessed February 14, 2021).

Garza, Alicia. (2014) "A Herstory of the #Black Lives Matter Movement." *Feminist Wire*, October 7. https://thefeministwire.com/2014/10/blacklivesmatter-2/ (last accessed July 18, 2022).

—— (2020) *The Purpose of Power: How We Come Together When We Fall Apart*. New York: One World.

Gettleman, Jeffrey, and Suhasini Raj. (2020) "Virus Closed Schools, and World's Poorest Children Went to Work." *New York Times*. September 28, p. A1. www.nytimes.com/2020/09/27/world/asia/covid-19-india-children-school-education-labor.html?searchResultPosition=3 (last accessed February 14, 2021).

Gettelman, Jeffrey, and Zia ur-Rehman. (2021) "After an Activist's Escape, Pakistan Jails Her Father." *New York Times*. February 4, p. A10. www.nytimes.com/2021/02/03/world/asia/pakistan-gulalai-ismail-father.html (last accessed February 14, 2021).

Gibson-Graham, J.K. (2003) *The End Capitalism (As We Knew It): A Feminist Critique of Political Economy*. Minneapolis, MN: University of Minnesota Press.

—— (2006) *A Postcapitalist Politics*. Minneapolis: University of Minnesota Press.

Gilmore, Ruth Wilson. (2007) *Golden Gulag: Prisons, Surplus, Crisis, and Opposition in Globalizing California*. Berkeley, CA: University of California Press.

Giménez, Martha E. (2018) *Marx, Women, and Capitalist Social Reproduction*. Boston, MA: Brill.

Girish, Devika. (2020) "'The Social Dilemma' Review: Unplug and Run." *New York Times*. September 9. www.nytimes.com/2020/09/09/movies/the-social-dilemma-review.html (last accessed February 18, 2021).

Góes, Juliana. (2020) "De Joao Pedro ate George Floyd." In *Polifonia por la vida: De la coronacrisis a la primaveral de ébano*, edited by Federico Pita et al., pp. 41–5. Buenos Aires, Argentina: CLACSO.

Goldbaum, Christina. (2021) "No Job, No Food: Virus Deepens Global Hunger." *New York Times*. August 6.

Goldberg, Emma. (2022) "Who Is the Office For?" *New York Times*. March 13.

Goldberg, Michelle. (2021) "Sex-Positive Feminism Is Falling out of Fashion." *New York Times*. September 25.

Goñi, Uki. (2020a) "Argentina President under Pressure to Keep Election Promise on Abortion." *Guardian*. September 28. www.theguardian.com/global-development/2020/sep/28/argentina-president-under-pressure-to-keep-election-promise-on-abortion (last accessed February 14, 2021).

—— (2020b) "Argentina Set to Become First Major Latin American Country to Legalise Abortion." *Guardian*. March 1. www.theguardian.com/world/2020/mar/01/argentina-set-to-become-first-major-latin-american-country-to-legalise-abortion (last accessed February 14, 2021).

Graf, Nikki. (2019) "Key Findings on Marriage and Cohabitation in the U.S." *Pew Research Center*. November 6. www.pewresearch.org/fact-tank/2019/11/06/key-findings-on-marriage-and-cohabitation-in-the-u-s/ (last accessed February 14, 2021).

Grant, Judith. (2005) "Gender and Marx's Radical Humanism in the *Economic and Philosophic Manuscripts of 1844*." *Journal of Economics, Culture & Society*, 17(1):59–77. https://doi.org/10.1080/0893569052000312908.

Grimshaw, Jean. (1986) *Philosophy and Feminist Thinking*. Minneapolis, MN: University of Minnesota Press.

Grzanka, Patrick R., ed. (2014) *Intersectionality: A Foundation and Frontiers Reader*. Boulder, CO: West View Press.

Gupta, Alisha Haridasani. (2021) "Biden Signs Executive Order to Advance Gender Equity." *New York Times*. March 8. www.nytimes.com/2021/03/08/us/gender-policy-council-biden.html (last accessed March 30, 2021).

Guy-Sheftall, Beverly, ed. (1995) *Words of Fire: An Anthology of African-American Feminist Thought*. New York: New Press.

Haar, Michel. (1985) "Nietzsche and Metaphysical Language." In *The New Nietzsche*, edited by David B. Allison, pp. 5–36. Cambridge, MA: MIT Press.

Hamouchene, Hamza, and Selma Oumari. (2020) "The Algerian Revolution: The Struggle for Decolonisation Continues." In *A Region in Revolt: Mapping the Recent Uprisings in North Africa and West Asia*, edited by Jade Saab, pp. 39–70. Ottawa, ON: Daraja Press.

Hartocolis, Anemona, and Shawn Hubler. (2020) "In America's Elite Colleges, Trump Sees a Bastion of Left-Wing Doctrine." *New York Times*. September 22, p. A14. www.nytimes.com/2020/09/21/us/trump-ivy-league-election.html (last accessed February 18, 2021).

Harvard Law School. (2014) "Does Legalized Prostitution Increase Human Trafficking?" *Harvard Law and International Development Society*. June 12. https://orgs.law.harvard.edu/lids/2014/06/12/does-legalized-prostitution-increase-human-trafficking/ (last accessed February 27, 2021).

Haug, Frigga. (2020a) "Contradictions in Marxist Feminism." In *Marxist-Feminist Theories and Struggles Today: Essentials Writings on Intersectionality, Postcolonialism and Ecofemenism*, edited by Khayaat Fakier, Diana Mulinari, and Nora Räthzel, pp. 27–39. London: Zed Books.

—— (2020b) "Thirteen Theses of Marxism-Feminism." *Transform Europe*. November 16. www.transform-network.net/en/blog/article/thirteen-theses-of-marxism-feminism/ (last accessed March 8, 2021).

Hegel, Georg Wilhelm Friedrich. (1976 [1969]) *The Science of Logic* (1812). Translated by A.V. Miller. London: George Allen & Unwin; Atlantic Highlands, NJ: Humanities Press.

—— (1978 [1975]) *Hegel's Logic: Being Part One of the Encyclopedia of the Philosophical Sciences* (1830). 3rd revised edn. Translated by William Wallace. Forward by John N. Findlay. Oxford: Clarendon Press.

—— (1978 [1971]) *Philosophy of Mind* (1830). Translated by William Wallace and A.V. Miller. Oxford: Clarendon Press.

—— (1985 [1949]) *Phenomenology of Mind* (1807). 2nd revised edn. Translated by J.B. Baillie. London: George Allen & Unwin; Atlantic Highlands: Humanities Press.

Hein, Shabnam von. (2020) "Iran's Declining Birth Rate Alarms Country's Leaders." *Deutsche Welle.* July 30. www.dw.com/en/iran-birth-rate-decline/a-54371973 (last accessed February 14, 2021).

Heller, Stanley. (2022) "Harsh Critique of Chomsky on Ukraine." *New Politics*, April 18. https://newpol.org/harsh-critique-of-chomsky-on-ukraine/ (last accessed May 26, 2022).

Hennessy, Rosemary. (2000) *Profit and Pleasure: Sexual Identities in Late Capitalism.* New York: Routledge.

Hensman, Rohini. (2018) *Indefensible: Democracy, Counterrevolution, and Rhetoric of Anti-Imperialism.* Chicago, IL: Haymarket Books.

Hernández, Javier C. (2020) "I.C.C. Declines to Investigate China's Policies for Its Muslims." *New York Times.* December 16, p. A9. www.nytimes.com/2020/12/15/world/asia/icc-china-uighur-muslim.html (last accessed February 18, 2021).

Hetherington, James. (2018) "Militarization of Police: U.S. Law Enforcement Has 1.9 Billion of Army Equipment at Its Disposal." *Newsweek.* May 31. www.newsweek.com/us-military-how-many-weapons-and-vehicles-are-given-police-951011 (last accessed February 18, 2021).

Hincks, Joseph. (2020) "In Solidarity and a Symbol of Global Injustices, a Syrian Artist Painted a Mural to George Floyd on a Bombed Idlib Building." *Time* (magazine). June 6. https://time.com/5849444/george-floyd-mural-idlib-syria/ (last accessed February 18, 2021).

Hioe, Brian. (2021) "Comments by Vijay Prashad, Richard Wolff at DSA Event, as well as David Harvey, Reveal Fanciful Idealization of China." *New Bloom: Radical Perspectives on Taiwan and the Asia Pacific.* October 11. https://newbloommag.net/2021/10/11/dsa-harvey-comments-china/ (last accessed May 27, 2022).

Holmstrom, Nancy. (1981) "'Women's Work', the Family and Capitalism." *Science & Society*, 45(2):186–211.

—— (1984) "A Marxist Theory of Women's Nature." *Ethics*, 94(3):456–73.

—— (1994) "Humankinds." *Canadian Journal of Philosophy*, 20: 69–105.

—— (2002) "A Marxist Theory of Women's Nature." In *The Socialist Feminist Project: A Contemporary Reader in Theory and Politics*, edited by Nancy Holmstrom, pp. 362–72. New York: Monthly Review Press.

—— (2013a) "Alienation, Freedom and Human Nature." Unpublished. www.academia.edu/44141727/Alienation_Freedom_and_Human_nature1_Nancy_Holmstrom (last accessed October 12, 2021).

—— (2013b) "Is Human Nature Important for Feminism?" In *Arguing about Human Nature: Contemporary Debates*, edited by Stephen M. Downes and Edouard Machery, pp. 543–56. New York: Routledge.

—— (2014) "Sex, Work and Capitalism." *Logos*, 13(3–4). http://logosjournal. com/2014/holmstrom/ (last accessed May 27, 2022).

hooks, bell. (1984) *Feminist Theory from Margin to Center*. Boston, MA: South End Press.

—— (2000) "Black Women: Shaping Feminist Theory." In *The Black Feminist Reader*, edited by Joy James and T. Denean Sharpley-Whiting, pp. 131–45. Malden, MA: Wiley-Blackwell.

Hovring, Roald (2018) "Gaza: The World's Largest Open Air Prison." *Norwegian Refugee Council*. April 26. www.nrc.no/news/2018/april/gaza-the-worlds-largest-open-air-prison/ (last accessed October 12, 2021).

Howard, Sheena C. (2014) *Black Queer Identity Matrix: Towards an Integrated Queer of Color Framework*. New York: Peter Lang.

Hua, Grace, Jess Huang, Samuel Huang, and Lareina Yee (2021) "COVID-19's Impact on Asian American Workers: Six Key Insights." *McKinsey & Company*, May 6.

Hubbard, Ben. (2021) "24 in Syria Are Executed over Series of Wildfires." *New York Times*. October 22.

Hubbard, Ben, and David D. Kirkpatrick. (2021) "A Decade after the Arab Spring, Autocrats Still Rule the Middle East." *New York Times*. February 15. www. nytimes.com/2021/02/14/world/middleeast/arab-spring-mideast-autocrats. html?searchResultPosition=2 (last accessed October 12, 2021).

Hudis, Peter. (2012) *Marx's Concept of the Alternative to Capitalism*. Leiden: Brill.

—— (2015) *Frantz Fanon: Philosopher of the Barricades*. London: Pluto Press.

Human Rights First (2017) "Human Trafficking by the Numbers." *Human Rights First*. January 7. www.humanrightsfirst.org/resource/human-trafficking-numbers (last accessed February 14, 2021).

Human Rights Watch. (2015) "Syria: Stories Behind Photos of Killed Detainees, Caesars Photos' Victims Identified." *Human Rights Watch*. December 16. www. hrw.org/news/2015/12/16/syria-stories-behind-photos-killed-detainees (last accessed February 18, 2021).

Hutchings, Kimberly. (2003) *Hegel and Feminist Philosophy*. Cambridge: Polity.

Imani, Narges. (2020) "Neoliberalism and the Conditions for the Possibility of Sexual Assault." *Naqd-e Eqtesad-e Siasi*. September 16. https://pecritique. com/2020/09/16/ (last accessed February 22, 2021).

Internationalism From Below. (2020) "Thailand, Nigeria, Belarus: Uprising, Repression, Solidarity." *YouTube*. November 18. www.youtube.com/watch?fbcl id=IwAR2BzR1vyTgBNwumLNP-K7G7xVJvG2MtR3FIYLpqvNEYVg0KGD AkrQWQkSA&v=MokmiNy2asY&feature=youtu.be (last accessed February 14, 2021).

—— (2021) "What's Happening in Myanmar? Dialogue with Debbie Stothard, Yasmin Ullah, Myra Dahgaypaw." Haymarket Books. September 20. www. youtube.com/watch?v=hyXXPJxnq6Y (last accessed October 12, 2021).

____ (2022) "How Can Feminist Solidarity Help Ukraine?" Haymarket Books. May 10. www.youtube.com/watch?v=dXMnZouKzIA (last accessed May 26, 2022).

International Labour Organization. (2017) "Statistics on Forced Labor, Modern Slavery and Human Trafficking." *International Labour Organization*. www.ilo.

org/global/topics/forced-labour/statistics/lang--en/index.htm (last accessed February 14, 2021).

Iranian Progressives in Translation. (2021a) "Conversation with Palestinian Socialist Feminist Journalist, Budour Hassan." May 22. https://iranian progressives.org/conversation-with-palestinian-socialist-feminist-journalist-budour-hassan/ (last accessed October 12, 2021).

—— (2021b) "Video of Dialogue between Myanmar, U.S., Iranian Women on Uprisings Against Police Brutality/Mass Incarceration & Pathways to Solidarity." June 7. https://iranianprogressives.org/video-of-dialogue-between-myanmar-u-s-iranian-women-on-uprisings-against-police-brutality-mass-incarceration-pathways-to-solidarity/(last accessed October 12, 2021).

Jakes, Lara. (2021) "Pandemic Lockdowns Fueled Predators Worldwide, Especially Online U.S. Says." *New York Times.* July 2.

James, Freddie [pseud. of Dunayevskaya, Raya]. (1941) "The Union of Soviet Socialist Republics as a Capitalist Society." *Workers Party International Discussion Bulletin.* February 20. https://rayadunayevskaya.org/ArchivePDFs/51. pdf (last accessed February 24, 2021).

James, Joy. (2000) "Radicalizing Feminism." In *The Black Feminist Reader*, edited by Joy James and T. Denean Sharpley-Whiting, pp. 239–60. Malden, MA: Wiley-Blackwell.

—— (2021) "The Captive Maternal and Abolitionism." *Topia: Canadian Journal of Cultural Studies*, 43(2), September.

James, Joy, and T. Denean Sharpley-Whiting, eds. (2000) *The Black Feminist Reader.* Malden, MA: Wiley-Blackwell.

James, Selma. (2012) *Sex, Race and Class—The Perspective of Winning: A Selection of Writings 1952–2011.* Foreword by Marcus Rediker. Introduction by Nina López. Oakland, CA: PM Press.

Johnston, Ian. (2016) "Scientists Smash Record for Human Embryos Grown in the Lab in Revolutionary Breakthrough." *Independent.* May 4. www.independent. co.uk/news/science/human-embryos-grown-lab-test-tube-ivf-fertility-genetic-diseases-disability-medical-ethics-a7013656.html (last accessed February 21, 2021).

Jones, Feminista. (2019) *Reclaiming Our Space: How Black Feminists Are Changing the World from the Tweets to the Streets.* Boston, MA: Beacon Press.

Kaba, Mariame. (2020) "So You're Thinking about Becoming an Abolitionist." *Level Medium.* (Online). October 30. https://level.medium.com/so-youre-thinking-about-becoming-an-abolitionist-a436f8e31894 (last accessed February 22, 2021).

—— (2021) *We Do This 'Til We Free Us.* Chicago, IL: Haymarket Books.

Kaufman, Jeff, and Marcia Ross. (2020) *Nasrin.* (Online Film). Directed by Jeff Kaufman and Marcia Ross. Newtown, PA: Virgil Films. www.nasrinfilm.com/ (last accessed February 14, 2021).

Kautsky, John. (1956) *Moscow and the Communist Party of India.* Cambridge, MA: MIT Press.

Kendi, Ibram X. (2019) *How to Be an Antiracist.* London: One World.

Khader, Jamil. (2016) "Trump's Popularity and the Rise of Authoritarian Capitalism." *Truthout.* May 23. https://truthout.org/articles/trump-s-popularity-and-the-rise-of-authoritarian-capitalism/ (last accessed February 18, 2021).

Khan, Lina M. (2017) "Amazon's Growing Monopoly Bite." *New York Times.* June 21, p. A23. www.nytimes.com/2017/06/21/opinion/amazon-whole-foods-jeff-bezos.html (last accessed February 18, 2021).

Khosravi, Kamal. (2017) "Value: Substance, Form, Magnitude." *Critique of Political Economy,* April 4. pecritique.com/2017/04/04.

Kliman, Andrew. (2011) *The Failure of Capitalist Production: Underlying Causes of the Great Recession.* London: Pluto Press.

Klotz, Marcia. (2006) "Alienation, Labor, and Sexuality in Marx's *1844 Manuscripts.*" *Journal of Economics, Culture, & Society,* 18(3):405–13. https://doi.org/10.1080/08935690600748124.

Knapp, Michael, Anja Flach, and Ercan Ayboga (2016). *Revolution in Rojava: Democratic Autonomy and Women's Liberation in Syrian Kurdistan.* Translated by Janet Biehl. London: Pluto Press.

Kojève, Alexandre. (1980) *Introduction to the Reading of Hegel: Lecture on the "Phenomenology of Spirit."* Edited by Allan Bloom. Translated by James H. Nichols Jr. Ithaca, NY: Cornell University Press.

Kolata, Gina. (2021) "Scientists Grow Mouse Embryos in a Mechanical Womb." *New York Times.* March 17.

Kolata, Gina, Sui-Lee Wee, and Pam Belluck. (2018) "Did a Gene Edit Shape 2 Babies? Experts Tremble." *New York Times.* November 27, p. A1. www.nytimes.com/2018/11/26/health/gene-editing-babies-china.html (last accessed February 21, 2021).

Kraus, Richard Curt. (2012) *The Cultural Revolution: A Very Short Introduction.* Oxford: Oxford University Press.

Kristof, Nicholas. (2020a) "A Cataclysm of Hunger, Disease and Illiteracy." *New York Times.* September 17, p. A27. www.nytimes.com/2020/09/16/opinion/coronavirus-hunger-disease.html (last accessed February 5, 2021).

—— (2020b) "We're No. 28! And Dropping!" *New York Times.* September 10, p. A22. www.nytimes.com/2020/09/09/opinion/united-states-social-progress.html (last accessed February 5, 2021).

Kurlantzick, Joshua. (2016) *State Capitalism. How the Return of Statism Is Transforming the World.* Oxford: Oxford University Press.

Kwai, Isabella, Monika Pronzuck, and Anatol Magdziarz. (2021) "Near-Total Abortion Ban Takes Effect in Poland." *New York Times.* January 28, p. A12. www.nytimes.com/2021/01/27/world/europe/poland-abortion-law.html (last accessed February 14, 2021).

Lang, Marissa J. (2019) "D.C. Effort to Decriminalize Sex Work Won't Move Forward after 14-Hour Hearing." *Washington Post.* November 17. www.washingtonpost.com/local/dc-politics/dc-effort-to-decriminalize-sex-work-wont-move-forward-after-tense-14-hour-hearing/2019/11/16/b7c77358-06ef-11ea-ac12-3325d49eacaa_story.html (last accessed February 27, 2021).

LeBlanc, Paul, and Veronica Stracqualursi. (2022) "Oklahoma Governor Signs Near-Total Ban on Abortion into Law." *CNN.* April 12.

Lee, Michelle Ye Hee. (2017) "Is the United States One of Seven Countries That "Allow Elective Abortions after 20 Weeks of Pregnancy?" *Washington Post.* October 8.

Leonard, Sarah, and Nancy Fraser. (2016) "Capitalism's Crisis of Care." Interview of Fraser, by Leonard. *Dissent Magazine.* www.dissentmagazine.org/article/nancy-fraser-interview-capitalism-crisis-of-care (last accessed February 24, 2021).

Lerer, Lisa, and Campbell Robertson. (2021) "Abortion Rights March Offers Test of Democrats' Post-Trump Enthusiasm." *New York Times.* October 2.

Lerner, Gerda. (1987) *The Creation of Patriarchy.* Oxford: Oxford University Press.

Levenson, Michael. (2021). "Near-Total Ban on Abortion in Oklahoma." *New York Times.* April 6.

Levine, Judith, and Erica R. Meiners. (2020) *The Feminist and the Sex Offender: Confronting Sexual Harm, Ending State Violence.* London: Verso.

Lewis, Helen. (2020) "The Coronavirus Is a Disaster for Feminism: Pandemics Affect Men and Women Differently." *Atlantic.* March 19. www.theatlantic.com/international/archive/2020/03/feminism-womens-rights-coronavirus-covid19/608302/ (last accessed February 5, 2021).

Lewis, Holly. (2016) *The Politics of Everybody: Feminism, Queer Theory, and Marxism at the Intersection.* London: Zed Books.

Liptak, Adam. (2021) "Conservatives Look Abroad in Abortion Case." *New York Times.* October 6.

Loong-Yu, Au. (2020) *Hong Kong in Revolt: The Protest Movement and the Future of China.* London: Pluto Press.

Lorde, Audre. (1979) "The Great American Disease." *Black Scholar*, 10(8–9):17–20. www.jstor.org/stable/41163846.

—— (1984) *Sister Outsider: Essays and Speeches.* Freedom, CA: Crossing Press.

—— (2020) *The Selected Works of Audre Lorde*, edited by Roxane Gay. New York: W.W. Norton.

Lukács, Georg. (1971) *History and Class Consciousness: Studies in Marxist Dialectics.* Translated by Rodney Livingstone. Cambridge, MA: MIT Press.

Luna, Patricia, and Joshua Goodman. (2021) "Leftist Millennial Wins Election as Chile's Next President." *AP News.* December 20.

Luxemburg, Rosa. (1913) *Die Akkumulation des Kapitals: Ein Beitrag zur ökonomischen Erklärung des Imperialismus* (*Accumulation of Capital: A Contribution to the Economic Explanation of Imperialism*). Berlin: Vorwärts-P. Singer.

Ma, Alexandra. (2019) "China Is Reportedly Sending Men to Sleep in the Same Beds as Uighur Muslim Women While Their Husbands Are in Prison Camps." *Business Insider.* November 4. www.businessinsider.com/china-uighur-monitor-home-shared-bed-report-2019-11 (last accessed February 14, 2021).

Maclean, Ruth. (2021) "In Nigeria, Women's Rights Activists Turn an Insult into a Rallying Cry." *New York Times.* March 13.

Maclean, Ruth, and Ismail Alfa. (2020) "Parents' Anguish Gives Way to Relief as Abducted Students Are Set Free." *New York Times.* December 18, p. A10. www.nytimes.com/2020/12/17/world/africa/nigeria-kidnapping-boko-haram.html (last accessed February 18, 2021).

Maclean, Ruth, and Ben Ezeamalu. (2020) "Hope Dries Up as Young Nigerians Disappear in Police Custody." *New York Times.* December 24, p. A1. www. nytimes.com/2020/12/23/world/africa/nigeria-police-SARS.html (last accessed February 18, 2021).

MacMillan, Douglas, Peter Whoriskey, and Jonathan O'Connell. (2020) "America's Biggest Companies Are Flourishing during the Pandemic and Putting Thousands of People out of Work." *Washington Post.* December 16. www. washingtonpost.com/graphics/2020/business/50-biggest-companies-coronavirus-layoffs/ (last accessed February 18, 2021).

Madgavkar, Anu, Olivia White, Mekala Krishnan, Deepa Mahajan, and Xavier Azcue. (2020) "Covid-19 and Gender Equality: Countering the Regressive Effects." *McKinsey Global Institute.* July 15. www.mckinsey.com/featured-insights/future-of-work/covid-19-and-gender-equality-countering-the-regressive-effects (last accessed February 14, 2021).

Majewska, Ewa. (2020) "Poland Is in Revolt Against Its New Abortion Ban." *Jacobin.* November. www.jacobinmag.com/2020/10/poland-abortion-law-protest-general-strike-womens-rights (last accessed February 14, 2021).

Malone, Noreen. (2022) "Seeking No Opportunities" *New York Times.* February 20.

Mandavilli, Apoorva. (2019) "F.D.A. Approves a New H.I.V.-Prevention Drug, But Not for Women." *New York Times.* October 5, p. A18. www.nytimes. com/2019/10/04/health/fda-descovy-truvada-hiv.html (last accessed February 14, 2021).

Manjoo, Farhad. (2022) "How Scary Is Apple's Power?" *New York Times.* April 1.

Mari, Francesca. (2020) "Renters Need Government Help." *New York Times.* December 3, p. A23. www.nytimes.com/2020/12/02/opinion/eviction-moratorium-ending.html (last accessed February 14, 2021).

Marquina, Cira Pascual. (2021) "Decriminalizing Abortion: The Case of Vanessa Rosales: Interview with Venus Faddoul." *Venezuelanalysis.* February 19. https:// venezuelanalysis.com/analysis/15127 (last accessed March 8, 2021).

Marx, Karl. (1845) "Theses on Feuerbach." *Marxist Internet Archives.* www. marxists.org/archive/marx/works/1845/theses/theses.htm; and www.marxists. org/archive/marx/works/1845/theses/theses.pdf (last accessed February 24, 2021).

—— (1961) *Economic and Philosophical Manuscripts of 1844.* In *Marx's Concept of Man,* by Karl Marx and Erich Fromm. New York: Frederick Ungar.

—— (1966) *Critique of the Gotha Program.* New York: International Publishers.

—— (1976) *Capital. Volume 1. A Critique of Political Economy.* Translated by Ben Fowles. New York: Vintage.

—— (1981) *Capital. Volume 3. A Critique of Political Economy.* Introduction by Ernest Mandel. Translated by David Fernbach. London: Penguin Classics.

Marx, Karl, and Friedrich Engels. (1932) *Die deutsche Ideologie (The German Ideology).* Berlin: Verlag. Edited by Roy Pascal. London: Lawrence & Wishart, 1938.

—— (1986) *Marx and Engel Collected Works.* Volume 28 of 50. New York: International Publishers. www.marxists.org/archive/marx/works/cw/index.htm (last accessed February 24, 2021).

Marx, Karl, and Erich Fromm. (1961) *Marx's Concept of Man*. New York: Frederick Ungar.

Marx, Karl, and Lawrence Krader. (1972) *The Ethnological Notebooks of Karl Marx: Studies of Morgan, Phear, Maine and Lubbock*, edited by Lawrence Krader. Assen, Netherlands: Van Gorcum.

Masri, Zeinab, Jana al-Issa, and Hussam al-Mahmoud. (2021) "Syrian Regime Burns Bodies in a Crematorium to Hide Proof of Mass Killing." *Enab Baladi*, May 9. https://english.enabbaladi.net/archives/2021/09/syrian-regime-burns-bodies-in-a-crematorium-to-hide-proof-of-mass-killing/ (last accessed October 12, 2021).

May, Tiffany. (2021) "China's Education Ministry Is Looking to Beef up Gym to Toughen 'Weak' Boys." *New York Times*. February 6, p. A9. www.nytimes.com/2021/02/05/world/asia/china-masculinity-schoolboys.html (last accessed February 14, 2021).

Mazzei, Patricia. (2022) "Florida Governor Signs Bill Fought by LGBTQ Groups, White House and Hollywood." *New York Times*. March 29.

Mbah, Fidelis. (2019) "Nigeria's Chibok Schoolgirls: Five Years on, 112 Still Missing." *Aljazeera*. April 14. www.aljazeera.com/news/2019/4/14/nigerias-chibok-schoolgirls-five-years-on-112-still-missing (last accessed February 18, 2021).

McDonnell, Patrick, and Kate Linthicum. (2021) "Abortion Restrictions Are Being Loosened across Latin America." *Los Angeles Times*. September 12. www.pressreader.com/usa/los-angeles-times-sunday/20210912/281530819145768 (last accessed October 12, 2021).

Meisner, Maurice. (1999) *Mao's China and After: A History of the People's Republic*. 3rd edn. New York: Free Press.

Metz, Cade. (2021) "A Tech-Military Reunion Away from Silicon Valley." March 3, p. B1. www.nytimes.com/2021/02/26/technology/anduril-military-palmer-luckey.html?searchResultPosition=1 (last accessed October 12, 2021).

Meyers, Steven Lee, and Olivia Mitchell Ryan. (2018) "Once Strict on Birth, China Races for a Boom." *New York Times*. August 12, p. A1. www.nytimes.com/2018/08/11/world/asia/china-one-child-policy-birthrate.html (last accessed February 14, 2021).

Middle East Monitor. (2020) "George Floyd Mural in Syria's Idlib Defaced." *Middle East Monitor*. June 10. www.middleeastmonitor.com/20200610-george-floyd-mural-in-syrias-idlib-defaced/ (last accessed February 18, 2021).

Mies, Maria. (2014 [1986]) *Patriarchy and Accumulation on a World Scale: Women in the International Division of Labour*. Foreword by Silvia Federici. London: Zed Books.

Mlambo-Ngcuka, Phumzile. (2020) "Violence Against Women and Girls: The Shadow Pandemic." *UN Women*. April 6. www.unwomen.org/en/news/stories/2020/4/statement-ed-phumzile-violence-against-women-during-pandemic (last accessed February 14, 2021).

Mock, Janet. (2014) *Redefining Realness: My Path to Womanhood, Identity, Love and So Much More*. New York: Atria.

Mohammadi, Narges. (2021) "White Torture: Why We Must Oppose Solitary Confinement." *Ms. Magazine*. November 17. https://msmagazine.com/2021/

11/17/white-torture-solitary-confinement-narges-mohammadi-arrest/ (last accessed May 27, 2022).

Mojab, Shahrzad, ed. (2015) *Marxism and Feminism*. London: Zed Books.

Moore, Mignon. (2011) *Invisible Families: Gay Identities, Relationship, and Motherhood among Black Women*. Berkeley, CA: University of California Press.

Moradi, Yahya. (2018) "Gozareshi Piramun-e 'Rahayi Zan dar Rojava" A Report on "Women's Emancipation" in Rojava). *Naghd*. October 21. https://wp.me/p9vUft-vZ (last accessed May 27, 2022).

Mukahamedov, Anton. (2021) "I don't Like Talking about Fear: Interview with Lokman Slim and Monika Borgmann." *Aljumhuriya*. February 11. www.aljumhuriya.net/en/content/%E2%80%9Ci-don%E2%80%99t-talking-about-fear%E2%80%9D (last accessed March 8, 2021).

Mustafa, Azza, and Sara Abbas. (2020) "Learning from Uprisings: Sudan's December Revolution." In *A Region in Revolt: Mapping the Recent Uprisings in North Africa and West Asia*, edited by Jade Saab, pp. 9–38. Ottawa, ON: Daraja Press.

Mvulane, Rajaram. (2020) "New Gender Based Violence Laws for South Africa." *Rajaram Mvulane* (blog). September 10. www.rajarammvulane.co.za/new-gender-based-violence-laws-for-south-africa/ (last accessed February 14, 2021).

Nash, Jennifer C. (2019) *Black Feminism Reimagined: After Intersectionality*. Durham, NC: Duke University Press Books.

Nasser, Fadi Nicholas. (2019) "Women and Women's Rights Are Central to Lebanon's Protest Movement." *Middle Eastern Information*. November 5. www.mei.edu/publications/women-and-womens-rights-are-central-lebanons-protest-movement (last accessed February 14, 2021).

Ndifon, Naomi. (2020) "Nigerian Women vs SARS: A Coalition Against Police Brutality." *Black Women Radicals* (blog). October 16. www.blackwomenradicals.com/blog-feed/nigerian-women-vs-sars-a-coalition-against-police-brutality (last accessed February 18, 2021).

Nebehay, Stephanie, and Emma Farge. (2021) "Taliban Rule Marked by Killings, Denial of Women's Rights – UN." December 14. *Reuters*. www.reuters.com/world/asia-pacific/taliban-rule-marked-by-killings-boy-soldiers-arrests-un-2021-12-14/ (last accessed May 30, 2022).

Nechepurenko, Ivan. (2020) "Women Lead Protests in Belarus, Shattering Stereotypes." *New York Times*. October 11, p. A7. www.nytimes.com/2020/10/11/world/europe/in-belarus-women-led-the-protests-and-shattered-stereotypes.html (last accessed February 18, 2021).

Nelson, Eshe. (2021) "Putting Value on Black Women's Activism." *New York Times*. February 6, p. B1. www.nytimes.com/2021/02/05/business/black-women-economists-nina-banks.html (accessed February 21, 2021).

Newburger, Emma. (2018) "A New Study Suggests Women Earn about Half What Men Earn." *NBR, CNBC*. November 28. http://nbr.com/2018/11/28/a-new-study-suggests-women-earn-about-half-what-men-earn/ (last accessed February 14, 2021).

New York Times. (2018) "Childbirth's Dangers for Black Women." *New York Times*. April 21, p. A20. www.nytimes.com/2018/04/20/opinion/childbirth-black-women-mortality.html (last accessed February 14, 2021).

—— (2019) Response to "Letter to the Editor: We Respond to the Historicans Who Critiqued The 1619 Project." *New York Times*. December 20. www.nytimes.com/2019/12/20/magazine/we-respond-to-the-historians-who-critiqued-the-1619-project.html (last accessed February 18, 2021).

—— (2020a) "Coronavirus Rages through Prisons." *New York Times*. November 22, p. SR6. www.nytimes.com/2020/11/21/opinion/sunday/coronavirus-prisons-jails.html (last accessed February 14, 2021).

—— (2020b). "The 1619 Project." *New York Times Magazine*. August 14. www.nytimes.com/interactive/2019/08/14/magazine/1619-america-slavery.html?mtrref=www.google.com&gwh=1CCF1234615EACF1E56D57F3A9C8590B&gwt=regi&assetType=REGIWALL (last accessed February 18, 2021).

—— (2021) "America's Mothers Are in Crisis. Is Anyone Listening to Them?" *New York Times*. February 7. www.nytimes.com/interactive/2021/02/04/parenting/working-moms-coronavirus.html (last accessed February 14, 2021).

Nietzsche, Friedrich Wilhelm. (1969; 2000 [1967/1995]) *On the Genealogy of Morals*. Translated and edited by Walter Kaufman. New York: Vintage.

Nossiter, Adam. (2020) "A Year after an Uprising in Algeria, an Old Repression Returns." *New York Times*. October 5, p. A10. www.nytimes.com/2020/10/04/world/africa/algeria-protests-politics.html (last accessed February 18, 2021).

Nova. (1996) "The History of Money." *PBS*. October 26. www.pbs.org/wgbh/nova/article/history-money/ (last accessed February 21, 2021).

O'Brien, Mary. (1981) *The Politics of Reproduction*. London: Routledge and Kegan Paul.

Ovide, Shira. (2021) "Big Tech Has Outgrown This Planet: The Gap Keeps Widening between the Super Rich Tech Superstars and the Merely Super." *New York Times*. July 31. www.nytimes.com/2021/07/29/technology/big-tech-profits.html (last accessed October 12, 2021).

Oxfam. (2020) "Time to Care: Unpaid and Underpaid Care Work and the Global Inequality Crisis." *Oxfam*. January 19. www.oxfamamerica.org/explore/research-publications/time-care/ (last accessed February 21, 2021).

Pal, Alasdair. 2021. "Taliban Replaces Women's Ministry with Ministry of Vice and Virtue." Reuters. September 17.

Perekhoda, Hanna. (2021) "Belarus: The People's Fight Continues." *New Politics*, 18(2):81–6. https://newpol.org/issue_post/belarus-the-peoples-fight-continues/ (last accessed May 27, 2022).

Pew Research Center. (2010) "The Decline of Marriage and Rise of New Families." *Pew Research Center*. November 18. www.pewsocialtrends.org/2010/11/18/ii-overview/ (last accessed February 14, 2021).

Phillips, Julia. (2020) "No Time to Die." *New York Times*. January 5, p. BR10. www.nytimes.com/2019/12/16/books/review/10-minutes-38-seconds-in-this-strange-world-elif-shafak.html (last accessed February 14, 2021).

Pierson, David, and Kyaw Hasan Hlaing. (2021) "Last Battle for Myanmar." *Los Angeles Times*. September 21.

Piketty, Thomas. (2017) *Capital in the Twenty-First Century*. Translated by Arthur Goldhammer. London: Belknap Press.

Pillischer, Matthew. (2012) *Broken on All Sides: Race, Mass, Incarceration and New Visions for Criminal Justice in the U.S.* Directed by Matthew Pillischer (Film). Portland, OR: Collective Eye Films.

Politi, Daniel, and Ernesto Londoño. (2020) "Argentina Legalizes Abortion in Milestone for Conservative Region." *New York Times*. December 31, p. A1.

Pollitt, Katha. (2015) *Pro: Reclaiming Abortion Rights*. London: Picador.

Plumwood, Val. (1994) *Feminism and the Mastery of Nature*. London: Routledge.

—— (2001) *Environmental Culture: The Ecological Crisis of Reason*. London: Routledge.

Postone, Moishe. (1993) *Time, Labor, and Social Domination: A Reinterpretation of Marx's Critical Theory*. Cambridge: Cambridge University Press.

Pronczuk, Monika. (2021) "In Poland, an LGBTQ Migration as Homophobia Deepns." *New York Times*. April 24.

Public Broadcasting Service (PBS). (2019) "In Syria, More Than 100,000 Have Entered Assad's Prisons—and Never Returned." *Public Broadcasting Service*. (Video). May 13. www.pbs.org/newshour/show/in-syria-more-than-100000-have-entered-assads-prisons-and-never-returned (last accessed February 18, 2021).

Pursaleh, Behzad. (2020) "Imposing Quota System to Reduce Divorce Rates." *BBC News* (Persian). January 28. www.bbc.com/persian/iran-features-51264049 (last accessed February 14, 2021).

Qin, Amy. (2019) "As China Prospers, Women Watch Futures Fade." *New York Times*. July 17, p. A1. www.nytimes.com/2019/07/16/world/asia/china-women-discrimination.html (last accessed February 14, 2021).

—— (2021) "China Is Forcing Birth Control on Muslim Women in Xinjiang", *New York Times*. May 11.

Rabin, Roni Caryn. (2022) "Maternal Deaths in the U.S. Climbed in 2020." *New York Times*. February 24.

Rahrovan, Roya. (2021) "Honor [Killing] Strengthened by Law." *Tribune Zamaneh*. November 17. www.tribunezamaneh.com/archives/54597 (last accessed May 27, 2022).

Ralston, Romarilyn. (2018) "Revisiting the Prison Industrial Complex." *Open Democracy*. (Online). April 5. www.opendemocracy.net/en/revisiting-prison-industrial-complex/ (last accessed February 22, 2021).

Ransby, Barbara. (2003) *Ella Baker and the Black Freedom Movement: A Radical Democratic Vision*. Chapel Hill, NC: University of North Carolina Press.

Räthzel, Nora, Diana Mulinari, and Aina Tollefsen. (2020) "Gender Regimes and Women's Labour: Volvo Factories in Sweden, Mexico, and South Africa." In *Marxist-Feminist Theories and Struggles Today: Essential Writings on Intersectionality, Labour, and Ecofeminism*, edited by Khayaat Fakier, Diana Mulinari, and Nora Räthzel, pp. 187–208. London: Zed Books.

Reimann, John and Cheryl Zuur et al. (2018) "Open Letter to Code Pink." *Oakland Socialist*. December 1. https://oaklandsocialist.com/2018/12/02/open-letter-to-code-pink/ (last accessed May 26, 2022).

Rich, Adrienne. (1980) "Compulsory Heterosexuality and Lesbian Existence." *Signs: Journal of Women in Culture and Society*, 5(4):631–60. https://doi.org/10.1086/493756.

—— (1986) *Of Woman Born: Motherhood as Experience and Institution*. New York: Norton.

Richie, Beth E. (2012) *Arrested Justice: Black Women, Violence, and America's Prison Nation*. New York: New York University Press.

Roberts, Michael. (2016) *The Long Depression: Marxism and the Global Crisis of Capitalism*. Chicago, IL: Haymarket Books.

Robles, Frances. (2021) "Families Often Search Alone in the Shadows." *New York Times*. October 1.

Romero, Farida Jhabvala. (2020) "Ice Detainees Go on Hunger Strike to Press for COVID-19 Protections." *Public Radio International*. September 7. www.pri.org/stories/2020-09-07/ice-detainees-go-hunger-strike-press-covid-19-protections-0 (last accessed February 14, 2021).

Roose, Kevin. (2019) "Why Napalm Is a Cautionary Tale for Tech Giants." *New York Times*. March 6, p. B1. www.nytimes.com/2019/03/04/technology/technology-military-contracts.html (last accessed February 18, 2021).

—— (2020) "What if Facebook Is the Real 'Silent Majority'?" *New York Times*. August 28, p. A20. www.nytimes.com/2020/08/27/technology/what-if-facebook-is-the-real-silent-majority.html (last accessed February 18, 2021).

Ross, Loretta, and Rickie Solinger. (2017) *Reproductive Justice: An Introduction*. Berkeley, CA: University of California Press.

Ross, Marcia, Jeff Kaufman, and Frieda Afary. (2020) "Conversation with Producers of Nasrin Documentary about Imprisoned Iranian Feminist Human Rights Attorney." *Iranian Progressives in Translation* (blog). December 15. https://iranianprogressives.org/conversation-with-producers-of-nasrin-documentary-about-imprisoned-iranian-feminist-human-rights-attorny/ (last accessed February 14, 2021).

Saad, Layla. (2020) *Me and White Supremacy: Combat Racism, Change the World, and Become a Good Ancestor*. Naperville, IL: Sourcebooks.

Saba, Michael. (2011) "Wall Street Protesters Inspired by the Arab Spring Movement." *CNN.Com*. September 17.

Saito, Kohei. (2017) "Karl Marx's Ecosocialism: Capital, Nature and the Unfinished Critique of Political Economy." *Monthly Review Press*. October. https://monthlyreview.org/product/karl_marxs_ecosocialism/ (last accessed February 27, 2021).

Salleh, Ariel. (2020) "Ecofeminism as (Marxist) Sociology." In *Marxist-Feminism Theories and Struggles Today: Essential Writing on Intersectionality, Postcolonialism and Ecofeminism*, edited by Khayaat Fakier, Diana Mulinari, and Nora Räthzel, pp. 40–50. London: Zed Books.

Samir, Huda. (2020a) "Another Attack on Women's Rights in Iraq." *Alliance of MENA Socialists*. October 12. https://allianceofmesocialists.org/another-attack-on-womens-rights-in-iraq/ (last accessed February 14, 2021).

—— (2020b) "For Iraqi Women, Silence Was Never an Option." *Alliance of Me Socialist*. September 15. https://allianceofmesocialists.org/for-iraqi-women-silence-was-never-an-option/ (last accessed February 14, 2021).

Sanger, David E. (2021a) "Defying U.S., China and Russia Set the Tone for a Cold New Era." *New York Times*. March 20. www.nytimes.com/2021/03/20/us/

politics/china-russia-biden.html?searchResultPosition=1 (last accessed October 12, 2021).

—— (2021b) "The President Calls for America to Start a New Superpower Struggle." *New York Times*. April 30.

Sanger, David E., and Zolan Kanno-Youngs. (2021) "To Counter China, U.S. Widens Its Alliance with Australia." *New York Times*. September 16.

Sanger, David E., Nicole Perlroth and Julian Barnes. (2021) "As Understanding of Russian Hacking Grows, So Does Alarm." *New York Times*. January 2.

Sartre, Jean-Paul. (1993 [1943]) *Being and Nothingness*. Translated by Hazel E. Barnes. New York: Washington Square Press.

—— (2001) *Jean-Paul Sartre: Basic Writings*, edited by Stephen Priest. London: Routledge.

Schultz, Kai, and Suhasini Raj. (2020) "In India, Work Loss Devastates Its Women." *New York Times*. June 10, p. A10. www.nytimes.com/2020/06/09/world/asia/india-coronavirus-women-economy.html (last accessed February 14, 2021).

Schwarzer, Alice. (1984) *After the Second Sex: Conversations with Simone de Beauvoir*. Translated from the French by Marianne Howarth. New York: Pantheon.

Searcey, Dionne. (2019) "Divorces Show Women's Gains in West Africa." *New York Times*. January 7, p. A1. www.nytimes.com/2019/01/06/world/africa/niger-divorce-women.html (last accessed February 14, 2021).

Sedgwick, Helen. (2017a) "Artificial Wombs Could Soon Be a Reality. What Would This Mean for Women?" *Guardian*. September 4. www.theguardian.com/lifeandstyle/2017/sep/04/artifical-womb-women-ectogenesis-baby-fertility (last accessed February 21, 2021).

—— (2017b) *The Growing Season*. London: Harvill Secker.

Sepehri Far, Tara. (2020) "Why Nasrin Sotudeh Is on Hunger Strike to Protest Iran's Dire Prison Conditions." *Human Rights Watch*. September 10. www.hrw.org/news/2020/09/10/why-nasrin-sotoudeh-hunger-strike-protest-irans-dire-prison-conditions (last accessed February 14, 2021).

Sexton, Jared Yates. (2019) *The Man They Wanted Me to Be: Toxic Masculinity and a Crisis of Our Own Making*. Berkeley, CA: Counterpoint.

Sgaier, Sema K., and Jordan Downey. (2021) "America's Mothers Are Dying." *New York Times*. November 21.

Shahabi, Siavash. (2020) "Pressure on Asylum Seekers in Greece: A Prison Like a Death Camp." *Radio Zamaneh*. www.radiozamaneh.com/549235 (last accessed February 18, 2021).

Sharpley-Whiting, T. Denean. (1997) *Frantz Fanon: Conflicts & Feminisms*. New York: Rowman & Littlefield.

Sheng-Wu-Lien. (1969) "Whither China?" *International Socialism*, 1st series, 37:24–7. www.marxists.org/history/etol/newspape/isj/1969/no037/shengwulien.htm (last accessed February 24, 2021).

Sidner, Sara, et al. (2022) "Ukraine Has Accused Russian Soldiers of Using Rape as a Tool of War." *CNN*, May 9.

Sijabat, Dera Menra, and Richard C. Paddock. (2020) "Protests Erupts across Indonesia as Workers Strike over Jobs Law." *New York Times*. October 9, p. A17.

www.nytimes.com/2020/10/08/world/asia/indonesia-protests-jobs.html (last accessed February 18, 2021).

Simons, Marlise, and Hannah Beech. (2019) "Aung San Suu Kyi Defends Myanmar Against Rohingya Genocide Accusations." *New York Times*. December 19. www. nytimes.com/2019/12/11/world/asia/aung-san-suu-kyi-rohingya-myanmar-genocide-hague.html (last accessed March 8, 2021).

Smith, Ashley, and Kevin Lin. (2020) "China and the United States: A New Cold War." *New Politics*, 18(1). https://newpol.org/issue_post/china-and-the-united-states-a-new-cold-war/ (last accessed February 27, 2021).

Smith, Barbara. (1995) "Lesbianism: An Act of Resistance." In *Words of Fire: An Anthology of African-American Feminist Thought*, edited by Beverly Guy-Sheftall, pp. 242–53. New York: New Press.

Smith, Joan. (1977) "Women and the Family: Part 1." *International Socialism*, 1st series, 100:20–6. www.marxists.org/history/etol/newspape/isj/1977/no100/smith.htm (last accessed February 21, 2021).

—— (1978) 'Women and the Family: Part 2." *International Socialism*, 1st series, 104:11–16. www.marxists.org/history/etol/newspape/isj/1977/no104/smith.html (last accessed February 21, 2021).

Smith, Molly, and Juno Mac. (2020) *Revolting Prostitutes: The Fight for Sex Workers' Rights*. London: Verso.

Snyder, Timothy. (2022) "Russia's Genocide Handbook." *Thinking About*. April 8. https://snyder.substack.com/p/russias-genocide-handbook?s=r (last accessed May 27, 2022).

Souvarine, Boris. (1930) "The Five Year Plan." *Bulletin Communiste*, 31. www. marxists.org/history/etol/writers/souvar/works/1930/02/fiveyearplan.htm (last accessed February 24, 2021).

Spector, Jessica, ed. (2006) *Prostitution and Pornography: Philosophical Debate about the Sex Industry*. Stanford, CA: Stanford University Press.

Spitz, Aaron. (2018) *The Penis Book: A Doctor's Complete Guide to the Penis—from Size to Function and Everything in Between*. Emmaus, PA: Rodale Books.

Spivak, Gayatri. (1978) "Feminism and Critical Theory." *Women's Studies International Quarterly*, 1:241–6.

Srinivasa, Amia. (2021) *The Right to Sex: Feminism in the Twenty-First Century*. New York: Farrar, Strauss and Giroux.

Stalin, J.V. (1936) "Constitution (Fundamental Law) of the Union of Soviet Socialist Republics." *Marxists*. December 5. www.marxists.org/reference/archive/stalin/works/1936/12/05.htm (last accessed February 24, 2021).

Statista Research Department. (2020) "Number of People Shot to Death by the Police in the United States from 2017 to 2020." *Statista*. www.statista.com/statistics/585152/people-shot-to-death-by-us-police-by-race/ (last accessed February 18, 2021).

Stavrou, David. (2021) "Witness after Witness, Hundreds Reveal the Atrocities of China's Concentration Camps." *Haaretz*. October 8.

Stepler, Renee. (2017) "Number of U.S. Adults Cohabiting with a Partner Continues to Rise, Especially among Those 50 and Older." *Pew Research Center*. April 6. www.pewresearch.org/fact-tank/2017/04/06/number-of-u-s-adults-cohabiting-with-a-partner-continues-to-rise-especially-among-those-50-and-older/ (last accessed February 14, 2021).

Stevenson, Alexandra, and Elsie Chen. (2019) "Where Having It All Often Means Nothing." *New York Times.* November 2, p. B1. www.nytimes.com/2019/11/01/business/china-mothers-discrimination-working-.html (last accessed February 14, 2021).

Stewart, Maria [W.] Miller. (1831/1995) "Religion and the Pure Principles of Morality, the Sure Foundation on Which We Must Build." In *Words of Fire: An Anthology of African-American Feminist Thought,* edited by Beverly Guy-Sheftall, pp. 23–4. New York: New Press.

——(1833) "An Address at the African Masonic Hall." *Black Past.* October 24, 2011. www.blackpast.org/african-american-history/1833-maria-w-stewart-address-african-masonic-hall/ (last accessed February 22, 2021).

Stewart, Nikita. (2020) "A Worrying Plunge in Child Abuse Cases." *New York Times.* June 10, p. A6. www.nytimes.com/2020/06/09/nyregion/coronavirus-nyc-child-abuse.html (last accessed February 14, 2021).

Stites, Richard. (1978) *The Women's Liberation Movement in Russia: Feminism, Nihilsm, and Bolshevism, 1860–1930.* Expanded edn. Princeton, NJ: Princeton University Press.

Strochlic, Nina. (2020) "These Schoolgirls Survived Boko Haram. Now They Face a Pandemic." *National Geographic.* April 22. www.nationalgeographic.com/history/2020/04/six-years-after-kidnapping-chibok-girls-face-coronavirus/#close (last accessed February 14, 2021).

Syrian Network for Human Rights. (2021) "The Tenth Annual Report on Torture in Syria on the International Day in Support of Victims of Torture." *Syrian Network for Human Rights.* June 26. https://sn4hr.org/wp-content/pdf/english/The_Tenth_Annual_Report_on_Torture_in_Syria_on_the_International_Day_in_Support_of_Victims_of_Torture_en.pdf (last accessed May 27, 2022).

Tankel, Stephen. (2018) With Us and Against Us. New York: Columbia University Press.

Tankersley, Jim. (2021) "President to Push a $6 Trillion Plan Aimed at Growth." *New York Times.* May 28. www.nytimes.com/2021/05/27/business/economy/biden-plan.html (last accessed October 12, 2021).

Tavernise, Sabrina. (2020) "Feeling Stuck as Shutdowns Curb Abortion." *New York Times.* April 15, p. A1. www.nytimes.com/2020/04/14/us/abortion-texas-coronavirus.html (last accessed February 5, 2021).

Taylor, Keeanga-Yamahtt. (2016) *From #BlackLivesMatter to Black Liberation.* Chicago, IL: Haymarket Books.

——, ed. (2017) *How We Get Free: Black Feminism and the Combahee River Collective.* Chicago, IL: Haymarket Books.

Tharoor, Ishaan. (2020) "The Pandemic Pushes Hundreds of Millions of People Toward Starvation and Poverty." *Washington Post.* September 25. www.washingtonpost.com/world/2020/09/25/pandemic-pushes-hundreds-millions-people-toward-starvation-poverty/ (last accessed February 14, 2021).

Tharoor, Ishaan, and Ruby Mellen. (2021) "The Pandemic May Set Women Back by a Whole Generation." *Washington Post.* April 1.

Tohidi, Nayereh. (2017) "An Interview on Feminist Ethics and Theory with Judith Butler." *Journal of Middle Eastern Women's Studies*. November 1. https://read. dukeupress.edu/jmews/article-abstract/13/3/461/132571/An-Interview-on-Feminist-Ethics-and-Theory-with (last accessed May 27, 2022).

Trotsky, Leon. (1937) *The Revolution Betrayed: What Is the Soviet Union? Where Is it Going?* Translated by Max Eastman. New York: Pioneer Publishers.

Turkewitz, Julie, and Isayen Herrera. (2020) "'Please Don't Let Me Die': The Perils of Giving Birth in Venezuela." *New York Times*. April 11, p. A1. www.nytimes. com/2020/04/10/world/americas/venezuela-pregnancy-birth-death.html (last accessed February 5, 2021).

Tyson, Alec, and Shiva Maniam. (2016) "Behind Trump's Victory: Divisions by Race, Gender, Education." *Pew Research Center*. November 9. www.pewresearch. org/fact-tank/2016/11/09/behind-trumps-victory-divisions-by-race-gender-education/ (last accessed February 18, 2021).

United Nations Office on Drugs and Crime. (2018a) "Global Study on Homicide: Gender Related Killing of Women and Girls." *UNODC Research*. November. www.unodc.org/documents/data-and-analysis/GSH2018/GSH18_Gender-related_killing_of_women_and_girls.pdf (last accessed February 14, 2021).

—— (2018b) "Global Report on Trafficking in Persons." *UNODC Research*. www. unodc.org/documents/data-and-analysis/glotip/2018/GLOTiP_2018_BOOK_ web_small.pdf (last accessed February 14, 2021).

United Nations Refugee Agency. (2021) "Figures at a Glance." *UNHCR*. June. www. unhcr.org/en-us/figures-at-a-glance.html (last accessed May 26, 2022).

United Nations Refugee Agency. (2022) "UNHCR Refugee Stastistics." *UNHCR*. www.unrefugees.org/refugee-facts/statistics/#:~:text=100%20million%20 individuals%20have%20been,violence%20or%20human%20rights%20 violations (last accessed May 26, 2022).

United Nations Women. (2020) "Facts and Figures: HIV and AIDS." *UN Women*. July. www.unwomen.org/en/what-we-do/hiv-and-aids/facts-and-figures (last accessed February 14, 2021).

Venezuelan Voices. (2021) https://venezuelanvoices.org/.

Verso Books, ed. (2018) *Where Freedom Starts: Sex, Power, Violence, #MeToo*. London: Verso.

Vitale, Alex S. (2017) *The End of Policing*. London: Verso.

Vivanco, José Miguel. (2018) "A Backward Step for Reproductive Rights in Chile." *Human Rights Watch*. April 16. www.hrw.org/news/2018/04/16/backward-step-reproductive-rights-chile (last accessed February 14, 2021).

Vogel, Lise. (1983) *Marxism and the Oppression of Women: Toward a Unitary Theory*. New Brunswick, NJ: Rutgers University Press.

—— (2014) *Marxism and the Oppression of Women: Toward a Unitary Theory*. Reprint edn. Introductions by Susan Ferguson and David McNally. Chicago, IL: Haymarket Books.

Vogelstein, Rachel, and Meighan Stone. (2021) *Awakening: #Me Too and the Global Fight for Women's Rights*. New York: Public Affairs.

Wachtell, Diane, ed. (2017) *Wolf Whistle Politics: The New Misogyny in America Today*. New York: New Press.

Walker, Chris (2021) "Six-Week Abortion Ban in Texas Goes into Effect as Supreme Court Refuses to Intervene." *Truthout*. September 1.

Walsh, Declan, Abdi Latif Dahir, and Simon Marks. (2021) "Sudan Military Crushes Hopes for Democracy." *New York Times*. October 26.

Walsh, Mary Williams, and Matt Phillips. (2020) "Poor Countries Facing an Unparalleled Debt Crisis." *New York Times*. June 2, p. B3. www.nytimes.com/2020/06/01/business/coronavirus-poor-countries-debt.html (last accessed February 14, 2021).

Wang, Vivian. (2020) "Chinese TV Drama on Virus Draws Outcry." *New York Times*. September 21, p. A10. www.nytimes.com/2020/09/20/world/asia/china-tv-women-coronavirus.html (last accessed February 14, 2021).

Wasserman, Helena. (2019) "The Most Likely Age for a Wedding (and Divorce) in South Africa—and 8 Other Surprising Facts about Marriages in SA." *Business Insider South Africa*. March 12. www.businessinsider.co.za/age-to-get-married-and-divorced-in-south-africa-2019-3 (last accessed February 14, 2021).

Weber, Max. (1978) *Economy and Society: An Outline of Interpretive Sociology*, edited by Guenther Roth & Claus Wittich. Berkeley, CA: University of California Press.

Wee, Sui-Lee. (2020a) "Beaten on Camera, She Sought Divorce. At First, China Said 'No.'" *New York Times*. September 16, p. A1. www.nytimes.com/2020/09/16/world/asia/china-domestic-abuse.html (last accessed February 14, 2021).

—— (2020c) "In China, Views on Homosexuality Evolve But Textbooks Lag Behind." *New York Times*. October 29, p. A7. www.nytimes.com/2020/10/28/business/international/china-gay-homosexuality-textbooks-lawsuit.html (last accessed February 14, 2021).

—— (2021) "China Will Let Families Have Three Children." *New York Times*. June 1.

Weeks, Kathi. (2011) *The Problem with Work: Feminism, Marxism, Antiwork Politics, and Postwork Imaginaries*. Durham, NC: Duke University Press.

Weir, Allison. (1996) *Sacrificial Logics: Feminist Theory and the Critique of Identity*. New York: Routledge.

Wezerek Gus, and Kristen R. Ghodsee. (2020) "Women's Unpaid Labor Is Worth 10.9 Trillion." *New York Times*. March 5. www.nytimes.com/interactive/2020/03/04/opinion/women-unpaid-labor.html (last accessed February 21, 2021).

Whitlock, Craig. (2021). *Pentagon Papers: A Secret History of the War*. New York: Simon and Schuster.

Wilde Botta, Emma. (2020) "Report on Socialist Feminist Dialogue between Iranian, Iraqi, Palestinian-Lebanese, Chilean Women". *Alliance of MENA Socialists*. February 8. https://allianceofmesocialists.org/report-on-socialist-feminist-dialogue-between-iranian-iraqi-palestinian-lebanese-chilean-women/ (last accessed May 27, 2022).

Williams, Casey. (2017) "Has Trump Stolen Philosophy's Critical Tools?" *New York Times*. April 17. www.nytimes.com/2017/04/17/opinion/has-trump-stolen-philosophys-critical-tools.html (last accessed February 18, 2021).

Williams, Joan C. (2020) "Real Horror Stories of Pandemic Motherhood." *New York Times*. August 8, p. A23. www.nytimes.com/2020/08/06/opinion/mothers-discrimination-coronavirus.html (last accessed February 14, 2021).

Williams, Timothy. (2019) "In Washington, a Fight to Decriminalize Prostitution Divides Allies." *New York Times.* October 17. www.nytimes.com/2019/10/17/us/washington-legal-prostitution.html (last accessed February 27, 2021).

Wilson, Christopher. (2020) "New Yahoo News/YouGov Poll Shows Profound Disagreements between Younger and Older Americans on Racial Issues, Police." *Yahoo News.* June 12. www.yahoo.com/lifestyle/yahoo-news-yougov-poll-age-gap-americans-race-police-issues-090032359.html (last accessed February 18, 2021).

Wirth, Kathleen, Eric J. Tchetgen Tchetgen, Jay G. Silverman, & Megan B. Murray. (2013) "How Does Sex Trafficking Increase the Risk of HIV Infection? An Observational Study from Southern India." *American Journal of Epidemiology,* 177(3):232–41. www.ncbi.nlm.nih.gov/pmc/articles/PMC3626049/ (accessed May 26, 2022).

Wolf, Maryanne. (2018) *Reader, Come Home: The Reading Brain in a Digital World.* New York: Harper.

World Health Organization. (2008) "Prevalence of Female Genital Cutting among Egyptian Girls." *World Health Organization.* www.who.int/bulletin/volumes/86/4/07-042093/en/ (last accessed February 14, 2021).

—— (2017) "Fact Sheet." www.who.int/news-room/fact-sheets/detail/violence-against-women (last accessed February 14, 2021).

Worldometer. (2021). www.worldometers.info/coronavirus/ (last accessed May 27, 2022).

World Prison Brief. (2021) "China: World Prison Brief Data." *WPB.* www.prisonstudies.org/country/china (last accessed February 14, 2021).

Wright, Erik Olin. (2010) *Envisioning Real Utopias.* London: Verso.

Wright, Robin. (2022) "Russia and China Unveil a Pact Against America and the West." *New Yorker.* February 7.

Wypijewski, Joann. (2020) *What We Don't Talk about When We Talk about #MeToo: Essays on Sex, Authority, and the Mess of Life.* London: Verso.

Yarrow, Andrew L. (2018) *Man Out: Men on the Sidelines of American Life.* Washington, DC: Brookings Institution.

Yassin-Kassab, Robin, and Leila Al-Shami. (2016) *Burning Country: Syrians in Revolution and War.* London: Pluto Press.

Yee, Vivian. (2021) "10 Years after Arab Spring, Tunisians Confront Failed Promises." *New York Times.* October 11.

Yeginsu, Ceylan. (2018) "Housework's U.K. Value: $1.6 Trillion." *New York Times.* October 5, p. A7. www.nytimes.com/2018/10/04/world/europe/uk-housework-value.html (last accessed February 21, 2021).

Zedong, Mao. (1937) "On Contradiction." *Marxists.* August. www.marxists.org/reference/archive/mao/selected-works/volume-1/mswv1_17.htm (last accessed February 24, 2021).

—— (1957) "On the Correct Handling of Contradictions among the People." *Marxists.* February 27. www.marxists.org/reference/archive/mao/selected-works/volume-5/mswv5_58.htm (last accessed February 24, 2021).

Zernike, Kate. (2022) "Pills Are New Target in 50-Year Abortion Battle." *New York Times.* April 6.

Index

wage system 72–3
Wages for Housework campaign 54,
    55, 69
Washington Consensus 32
Weber, Max 30, 126, 156
Weeks, Kathi 125–7, 130, 169–70
    The Problem with Work 125
Weir, Allison 160–1, 166–7
    Sacrificial Logics 101, 104–5, 156–7,
    158–9
white feminists 86, 88, 89
White Torture (film) 44
Williams, Casey 41
Winnicott, Donald 153, 154
Witke, Roxane 141
Wittig, Monique 103
Wolf, Maryanne 174
    Reader, Come Home 40–1, 146
woman
    as a category 101, 111–2
    as Other 146–7

women
    and childbearing 56
    girls 154–5, 165
    objectification of 22–3
    and protest movements 43–8
    role of 75, 77, 146–7
    sexual abuse of 14, 81–2
    trafficking of 26–7
    violence against 95–6
    for other topics relating to women
        see the topic, e.g. housework;
        prison
    see also men and women
Workers' Party (US) 135
Wren, Lottie Cunningham 172
Wright, Erik Olin *Envisioning Real
    Utopias* 120–1

X, Malcolm 97

Yarrow, Andrew *Man Out* 16–17, 21

Thanks to our Patreon subscribers:

Andrew Perry
Ciaran Kane

Who have shown generosity and
comradeship in support of our publishing.

Check out the other perks you get by subscribing
to our Patreon – visit patreon.com/plutopress.

Subscriptions start from £3 a month.

The Pluto Press Newsletter

Hello friend of Pluto!

Want to stay on top of the best radical books
we publish?

Then sign up to be the first to hear about our
new books, as well as special events,
podcasts and videos.

You'll also get 50% off your first order with us
when you sign up.

Come and join us!

Go to bit.ly/PlutoNewsletter